Ernest Davis
Courant Institute of Mathematical Sciences
New York University

Representing and Acquiring Geographic Knowledge

Pitman, London

Morgan Kaufmann Publishers, Inc., Los Altos, California

PITMAN PUBLISHING LIMITED
128 Long Acre, London WC2E 9AN

A Longman Group Company

© Ernest Davis, 1986
First published 1986

Available in the Western Hemisphere from
MORGAN KAUFMANN PUBLISHERS, INC.,
95 First Street, Los Altos, California 94022

ISSN 0268-7526

British Library Cataloguing in Publication Data

Davis, Ernest
  Representing and acquiring geographic
  knowledge.—(Research notes in artificial
  intelligence, ISSN 0268-7526)
  1. Artificial intelligence   2. Cognition
  3. Space perception
  I. Title   II. Series
  006.3   Q335

  ISBN 0-273-08769-X

Library of Congress Cataloging in Publication Data

Davis, Ernest.
  Representing and acquiring geographic knowledge.

  (Research notes in artificial intelligence,
ISSN 0268-7526)
  Bibliography: p.
  Includes index.
  1. Robot vision.   2. Geographical perception.
3. Robots—Programming.   4. Artificial intelligence.
I. Title.   II. Series.
TJ211.3.D38 1986   629.8′95   86-10673
ISBN 0-934613-22-2 (Morgan Kaufmann)

Reproduced and printed by photolithography
in Great Britain by Biddles Ltd, Guildford

Contents

List of Figures

List of Tables

List of Algorithms

Acknowledgements

First, I wish to thank my adviser, Drew McDermott, without whom this thesis would have been impossible. He led me to the topic and the approach, he drove me away from distraction, and he told me when to stop. His generosity in time, energy, and ideas, his high standards, his insight and clarity, and his wit and friendship, have all enriched the three and a half years of work with him, and will continue to be an inspiration to me.

I must thank him in two other ways as well. As a professor, he taught me most of what I know about AI and about programming. As a support programmer, he kept the NISP programming language running, never delaying in fixing bugs when I ran into them.

Chris Riesbeck and Elliot Soloway, the other readers on my committee, made invaluable comments, both stylistic and contentive, on the text of this thesis. If this document is at all readable, it is in large measure due to them. Dana Angluin and Dan Gusfield gave invaluable help with algorithm analysis.

Of my friends from Yale, I would like to single out Natalie Dehn and Larry Birnbaum with special thanks for their help, friendship, and guidance since the day I arrived there. Particular thanks are also due to Dave Miller, who help in the debugging of MERCATOR, and to Tom Dean, who helped assemble the original thesis. I also received much help and encouragement from friends outside Yale, particularly Ken Forbus and Pat Hayes.

Deepest thanks are due to all my family and friends for their support and love. In particular, I cannot express enough love and thanks to my parents, Philip and Hadassah Davis.

Finally, my thanks to my wife Bianca for her help, her patience, her trust, and her love. This book is dedicated to her.

Notes on Text

This book is a revised version of the author's Ph.D. thesis, published as Technical Report 292 by the Computer Science Department at Yale. The research described here was supported by the Advanced Research Projects Agency of the Department of Defense and monitored under the office of Naval Research under contract N00014-83-K-0281; by the National Science Foundation under contract MCS-82039804; by an NSF Graduate Fellowship; and by an IBM Graduate Fellowship. The production of camera ready copy was supported in part by NSF grant MCS-8402309.

Figures 1-1 through 1-5, 2-21, 3-4, 4-1, 4-2, 6-3, 6-8, and 8-1 through 8-8 were hand drawn by James Danella. The remaining diagrams were drawn by the author using a SUN workstation. Figure 6-8 is copied from "Representing Spatial Experiences and Solving Spatial Problems in a Simulated Robot Environment" by Dr. Peter Rowat. It is reproduced here with Dr. Rowat's permission.

One cannot easily realize what a tremendous thing it is to know every trivial detail of river and know it with absolute exactness. If you will take the longest street in New York, and travel up and down it, conning its features patiently until you know every house and window and lamppost and big and little sign by heart, and know them so accurately that you can instantly name the one you are abreast of when you are set down at random in that street in the middle of an inky black night, you will then have a tolerable notion of the amount and the exactness of a pilot's knowledge who carries the Mississippi River in his head. And then, if you will go on until you know every street-crossing, the character, size, and position of the crossing-stones, and the varying depth of mud in each of these numberless places, you will have some idea of what the pilot must know in order to keep a Mississippi steamer out of trouble. Next, if you will take half of the signs in that long street and *change their places* once a month, and still manage to know their new positions accurately on dark nights, and keep up with these repeated changes without making any mistakes, you will understand what is required of a pilot's peerless memory by the fickle Mississippi. ...

And how easily and comfortably the pilot's memory does its work; how placidly effortless is its way; how *unconsciously* it lays up its vast stores, hour by hour, day by day, and never loses or mislays a single valuable package of them all!

— *Life on the Mississippi* by Mark Twain

1 Introduction

1.1. Learning Geography: The Problem

Intelligent creatures learn the layout of their environment by wandering around it and perceiving where things are. Almost all animals do this, to some extent. Flatworms can learn a left turn, wasps can find their way home, salmon can navigate across oceans, men can learn every detail of the Mississippi river. This thesis studies how a robot which could see could do likewise.

At first, the whole problem seems to be getting the robot to see at all. Once the robot can see, the rest of the problem seems trivial; the robot sees where things are, and he records this. The problem seems to be merely one of memorization, as trivial for a computer as recording the New York telephone book. But this analysis is incorrect, since knowing the geography of an area is not a matter of tabulating objects and their places. Instead, it involves knowing a whole host of spatial relations, some precise and some imprecise. Learning an area involves taking a series of sensory impressions, each of which shows only a few objects, some only in part, and only a few inexact relations between them; relating these impressions by finding features common to them; and, finally, merging them together into a coherent whole. This is not memorization; it involves deep spatial reasoning.

Consider a typical problem facing our robot. The robot has been wandering for a while in the field illustrated in figure 1-1 and he has some idea of where things are. He gives evidence of having this knowledge in that he can perform a variety of tasks using it. For example, he may be able to plan routes: from the rock to the river, from the jungle gym to the wall. He may be able to answer questions. For example, we can ask "Which is closer to the you, the jungle gym or the hotdog stand?" and he will answer "the jungle gym"; or "Is the rock bigger than the jungle gym?" and he will answer "No". He may be able to draw a map of the area, and so on.

But the robot's knowledge is imprecise. This shows up in vague or uncertain answers to particular questions. For example, to the question "How much further is the house from the river than the jungle gym?" he answers "two or three times as far". To the question "Is the jungle gym between the rock and the rapids?" he answers that he doesn't know. A suggestive way of measuring the robot's uncertainties is in terms of the variations in maps which will conform to his vague ideas. For example, we show it the various maps in figure 1-2 and ask him which he thought was accurate; and he answers that any of them could be correct as far as he knows. On the other hand, he can be sure that none of the maps in figure 1-3 is correct; these exceed the limits of his uncertainty.

Assume now that the robot looks around, in order to fill out his partial knowledge of the area. His knowledge from seeing is like his memory in that relations are more or less precise. Figure 1-4 shows a number of maps which conform to his impression of what he sees. Some things are seen more precisely than they were before; for example, he now sees the bend in the river. Some things are seen less well than they were before; he has a less good estimate of the length and angle of the wall. Some things are seen that were not seen before at all, such as the downward turn of the river and the second jungle gym.

In order to learn, to augment his knowledge, he must combine the information in the scene with the information in his memory. He must identify the river as the one he knows about, and add the new section to his idea of the river. He must be careful to identify the seen jungle gym as different from the one in memory, and add it to its memory, together with its position. He must record his new facts about the position of the brick wall, but he must be careful not to forget his old good estimate of his own distance to point of the river due north. Once he has done this, he should know that the real world is something like the maps in figure 1-5.

This thesis centers around two of the problems raised by this example. Firstly, how can a robot deal with imprecise geographic knowledge? How can he record it, and how can he use it? Secondly, how can a robot learn the geography of an area from seeing it a bit at a time?

1.2. The Human Analogy

This kind of knowledge — the positions and shapes of specific objects — is called *geographic knowledge*. The cognitive processes that operate on it are called *geographic reasoning*. A creature's entire body of geographic knowledge is his *cognitive map*.* This thesis studies cognitive maps and geographic reasoning in terms of artificial intelligence (henceforth AI).

It is not the purpose of this thesis to explain or simulate human behavior. We make no claims for the psychological validity of any part of our theory. Still, human cognitive mapping provides the problems, the objectives, and the approach. We do not assume that a robot would have to use same methods as the human mind, but in order to do cognitive mapping he must perform the same tasks and confront the same difficulties. It is therefore worth reviewing some of the more striking features of human geographic reasoning.

Cognitive maps record information of many different kinds. There are spatial relations between objects: Pennsylvania *borders* Maryland *on the north;* Elm Street is *roughly parallel to* Whalley Avenue; my desk is *between* my terminal and my bookcase; my keys are *in* my pocket; I am *about three thousand miles from* the Golden Gate Bridge. There are relations between parts of objects, parts which are identified in terms of the object shapes: Sicily is near *the toe of* Italy; the *left end* of my desk is an inch from the *right end* of my bookcase. There is information about sets of objects and about qualities which are not discrete objects: the office building has many windows; Grove Street slopes downhill going west. There is information about the absence of objects; there are no stop signs on Main Street.

---

* The term "cognitive map" was introduced in [Tolman, 32]. I have been told that it is often used as a technical term in neurophysiology, referring to particular proposed brain structures (often located in the hippocampus). [Lieblich and Arbib, 82]. My theory, of course, is at quite a different level of description, and I use the term in the more general sense of [Downs and Stea, 73]: "Cognitive mapping is a process composed of a series of psychological transformation by which an individual acquires. codes, stores, recalls, and decodes information about the relative locations and attributes of phenomena in his everyday spatial environment. ... The product of the process at any point in time can be considered a cognitive map." My use of "geography" is not standard.

2

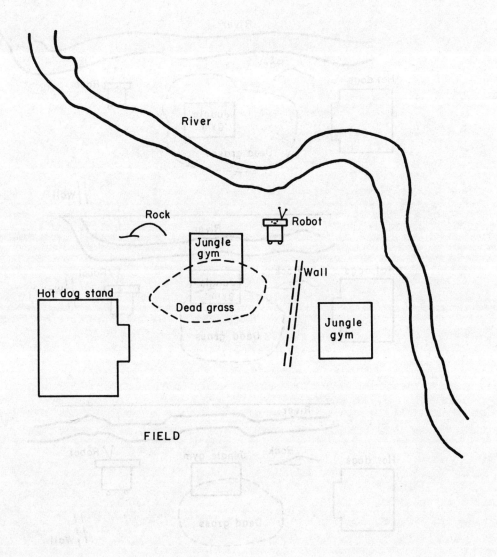

River

Rock

Robot

Jungle gym

Wall

Hot dog stand

Dead grass

Jungle gym

FIELD

Figure 1-1: A Park

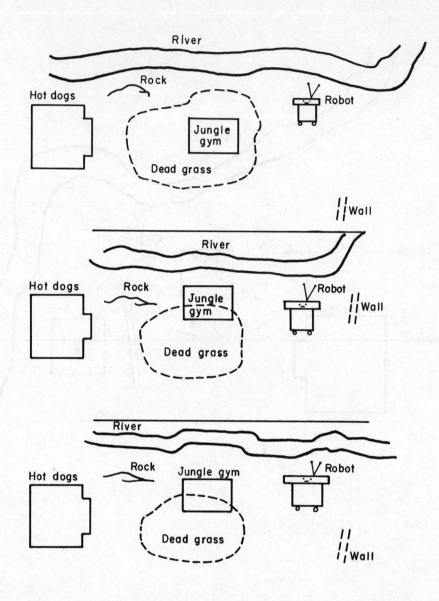

Figure 1-2: Acceptable Maps

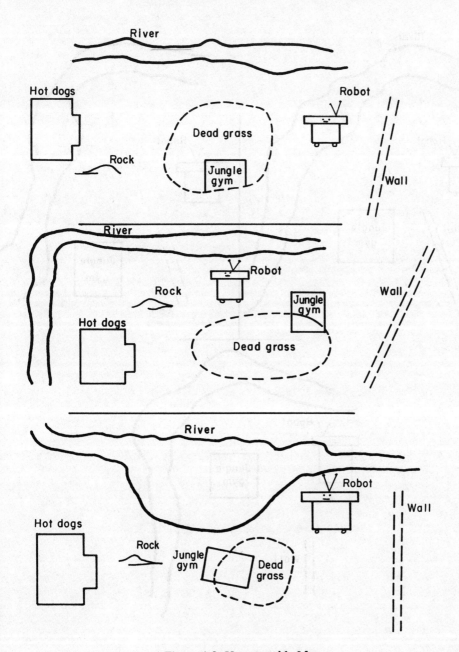

Figure 1-3: Unacceptable Maps

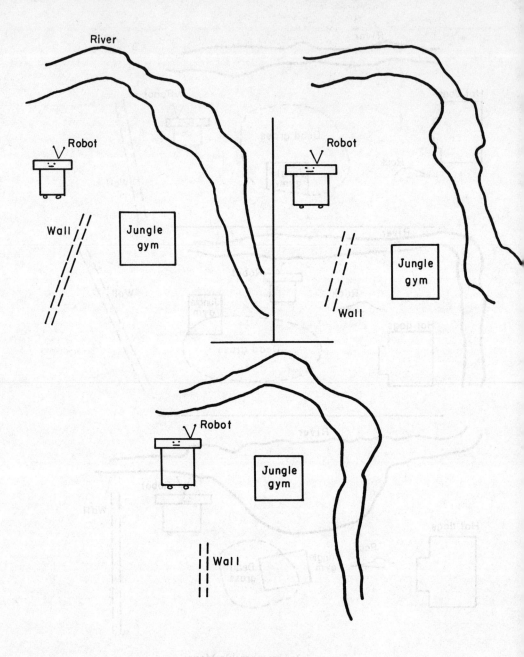

Figure 1-4: Visible Scene

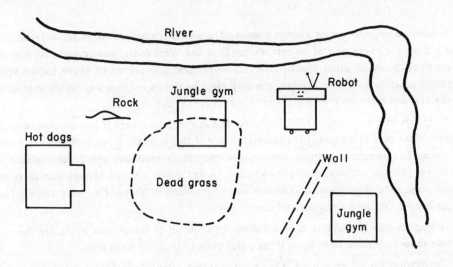

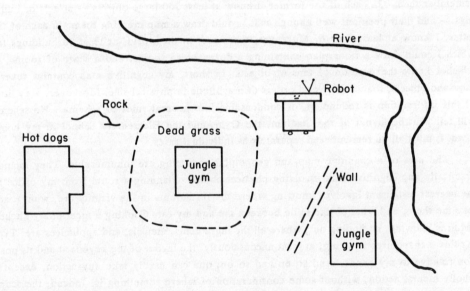

Figure 1-5: Joined Maps

Clearly, a cognitive map cannot consist of a simple enumeration of these facts. It is unlikely that, for every pair of objects on the East and West coast, you record that they are at least three thousand miles apart. It is impossible that you record of every known space everything which is not there. Rather, the map must be structured in a way which implies the information; and there must be a method of retrieving the desired facts.

Cognitive maps are necessarily imprecise and incomplete. There is imprecision of measurements. One may be unsure, for example, which of two subways stops is closer to a particular store. The cognitive map in some sense records information about the distance — enough, say, to rule out any other subway stops — but leaves it vague enough that these two distances cannot be discriminated. There is also imprecision of shape. One may know a road without knowing each of its twists and turns.

A map may be incomplete in that it does not show all of the objects which are there. It may also show only parts of objects, if the other parts have never been seen.

Cognitive maps are enormous. I have not seen any scientific studies, but it is easy to do some crude estimating. Taking myself as an available subject, I have lived over the last twenty years in four different cities, and have visited at least fifty others long enough to remember them. In each of the former, I know at least 200 large objects — streets or buildings — and their positions well enough that I could draw a map marking them. In each of the latter, I know at least 5 or 6. Moreover, there are, in the world, at least 30 buildings for which I could draw a floor plan containing a dozen or so rooms, and a score of rooms, in which I know the position of tens of objects. In short, my cognitive map contains several thousand objects, spanning several orders of magnitude in physical size. Moreover, very little of this information is redundant, or condensable into general rules or schemas. No schema will tell you the layout of the Stadium, the Gym, and the Elementary School in my home town. It must all be remembered separately as individual cases.

The uses of a cognitive map and geographic reasoning are innumerable. They include practically any cognitive task involving physical objects. Planning a route from my office to the nearest restaurant involves knowing where the restaurants in the vicinity are, what roads take me there, and what obstacles lie between me and my car. Cooking a meal in my kitchen requires knowing, or finding out, where all the ingredients, utensils, and appliances are. Typing this text requires knowing, at least unconsciously, the layout of the keyboard and its position relative to my hands. And so on and so on; one can hardly take any action, except a wholly mental action, without some consideration of where something is. Indeed, the scope of this kind of reasoning extends past dealings with the physical world. A frequent technique for dealing with abstract problems is to reformulate them in spatial terms. In doing so, you create a small cognitive map local to that particular problem.

The bulk of geographic knowledge comes from sensing the environment, from seeing and remembering where things are. But a person will augment the evidence of his eyes with knowledge derived from any number of other sources. He may be told where something is. He may look at a map. He may make inferences; for example, from the fact that it takes less than fifteen minutes to drive from downtown to the airport, one may infer that they are less than fifteen miles apart. He may use default knowledge; for example, seeing a building more than seven stories high, one may infer that there is probably an elevator in the main hall.

1.3. MERCATOR

From the point of view of AI, a cognitive map is a *knowledge base*. It is a collection of information which can be stored, accessed, and updated. The major problems in geographic reasoning are those common to knowledge bases:

Representation: A systematic method must be found to encode the cognitive map in terms of a data structure. There are many possible options; the map could be represented as a list of facts, as a bit map, as a set of drawings. The representation must be able to express many different kinds of geographic facts. It must be able to express information which is imprecise and incomplete.

Retrieval: Given a problem that requires geographic information, extract the necessary information from the representation. For example, answer questions, draw pictures, plan routes from one place to another.

Assimilation (Learning): Given an accurate representation of some geographic knowledge, and an accurate geographic fact or description, improve the representation to include the new fact or description. For example, if you see something new, add it to the map. If you read a description of an area, form a cognitive map of that area.

Error Correction: Given a representation of geography that is almost accurate, but not quite so, and given a new fact or description which is more accurate, correct the representation. For example, if you see that an object is not where you remembered it, correct your memory.

Investigation: Given a representation of geography and a query that cannot be answered from the map, devise a plan for finding new facts and improving the representation through assimilation so as to be able to answer the query. For example, if you are buying a table cloth and you do not know the length of your table in inches, then you can go home and measure your table, or search the store for tables which look about the right size.

There may be other categories, but these cover most of geographic reasoning.

We have developed a partial theory of representation, retrieval, and assimilation. The theory is implemented in a computer program called MERCATOR.*

MERCATOR studies representation, retrieval, and assimilation. It is designed so that a mobile robot equipped with a vision system, which produces scene descriptions from camera images, could use MERCATOR to build up a coherent representation of his environment as a whole. The robot begins by wandering in a new territory with a null cognitive map. He calls on his vision system for a description of the visible scene, and initializes his cognitive map with the information in this first scene. He then moves and records in his map information about his motion. He looks out again and gets a new scene description. He uses the assimilation algorithm to add the information in the new scene description into his cognitive

---

* MERCATOR is named after the geographer Gerhardus Mercator (1512-1594). The program name was chosen purely for euphony. There is no connection to the Mercator projection used in cartography.

map. This cycle — move, look, assimilate, move, look, assimilate — continues on indefinitely. After each assimilation, the cognitive map becomes more precise and more complete. Eventually, when the robot has seen his entire environment, assimilation no longer changes the cognitive map; it merely corroborates that everything is as expected. At any point, the user may ask the robot certain types of questions, and the robot will answer as well as he can based on his current map.

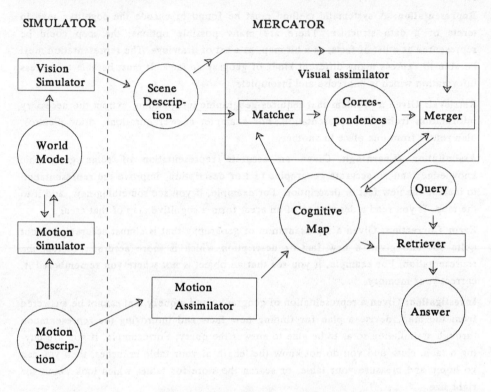

Rectangles are functions. Circles are data structures.
Arrows indicate information flow.
Figure 1-6: The Structure of MERCATOR

Figure 1-6 shows the structure of MERCATOR. In the center is the *cognitive map*, the knowledge base which MERCATOR manages. This contains all the information about geography available to the program. The representation used in the cognitive map is called a *MERCATOR map*.

To its right is the *retriever*. The retriever serves as the interface through which other modules can access the information in the cognitive map. The modules, or the user, pose a *query* of some particular form to the retriever; and the retriever generates an *answer* by consulting the information in the cognitive map.

At the top of the figure is the *scene description*, which represents the information which has been gathered from vision. Like the cognitive map, the scene description is a collection of geographic information, except that the information in the scene description covers a limited area. The scene description, like the cognitive map, uses a MERCATOR map as its representation scheme. In other words, we consider a scene description to be simply a miniature cognitive map, describing the visible world. This unification greatly simplified theory and program development: we need only one representation and one set of retrieval algorithms.

The *visual assimilator* carries out the robot's learning of geography. It adds the information in the scene description to the cognitive map. The cognitive map is changed by this process; it comes out larger and more precise. Abstractly, this process is the joining of two MERCATOR maps, one small and one large. All the information in the cognitive map comes from the assimilator at some point or another, except for the position of the robot himself, which comes from the motion assimilator.

The assimilator consists of two parts: the *matcher* and the *merger*. The matcher compares the scene to the map, and generates a set of *correspondences,* which describe the relation between objects in the scene and those in the cognitive map. The merger adds the new information in the scene into the cognitive map, using the correspondences for guidance.

The matcher attempts to use the context to identify objects which are ambiguous in themselves. The presumption is that the vision process up to this point has identified each object and its properties as well as it can considering only one object at a time. For example, I look out my front window and I see a tree. My vision processes identify it for me as a large maple tree. However, without knowing where I am or considering what is around it, I cannot distinguish it from other such maple trees. That is, if I had a picture with the tree and nothing else, I could still recognize it as a large maple, but I would not know that it was the one in front of my house. At this point, the MERCATOR matcher takes over. Using the information that I am in the house, and using other objects which are in the scene description, it identifies the tree as the one in front of my house, and, moreover, asserts that I am looking at the back of the tree. If every view of everything in the world were uniquely identifiable — if there were only one tree, one house, one horse, etc. and each part of each object were visually distinct — then the matcher would be trivial: if two objects were similar, then they would be the same. Since the world is repetitious, however, the matcher must use relative positions. My desk is distinguished from an identical desk of my office-mates by its position in the room or by the things piled on top of it — in either case, by the relation of its position to that of other things.

Once the matcher has finished, the merger tries to bring the new information in the scene into the map. The merger cannot operate without the output of the matcher, because the matcher's correspondences determine which is new information. If there is a tree in the scene, it is important to know whether this is a new tree, and should be added, or a known tree, and should not be added. If the scene gives better measurements of the distance between two known objects, it must be determined first which two objects it measures, and then the information can be added. The merger modifies and extends the relevant part of the cognitive map; the result is a new, improved cognitive map. Once the merger is complete, the scene description is thrown away.

Finally, the *motion assimilator* is responsible for maintaining the robot's beliefs about his own position, which are likewise recorded in the cognitive map. When the robot moves, the motion assimilator makes the appropriate changes to the cognitive map.

In a complete system, the scene description would come from a vision module operating on a image from an attached camera and the motion description would come from some feedback from the robot wheels. It is not practically possible to do this in the current state of the art, so both of these forms of input are provided by a simulator program. There is no real robot or real perceived objects; these are all in the mind of the Simulator. The simulator consists of a *world model,* which keeps track of the exact position of everything; a *vision simulator,* which calculates what the robot would see from his current position, and produces the scene description; and a *motion simulator,* which updates the position of the robot within the world model.

The simulator is really a completely separate program from MERCATOR. It serves only to generate testing examples; it has no theoretical content or interest. In particular, the world model is a very different type of structure than the cognitive map. The world model is a stand-in for the world. It is, by definition, complete from the beginning, and thoroughly precise. The cognitive map is MERCATOR's knowledge of the world which is built up incrementally, and is generally incomplete and imprecise. MERCATOR's objective is to get, eventually, all the information from the world model into its cognitive map, through wandering and looking around. But it would be meaningless to give MERCATOR access to the world model; it would be the equivalent of assuming that a robot has automatic access to any fact in the real world.

1.4. Scope

The MERCATOR theory addresses only some of the issues involved in cognitive maps. A MERCATOR map is a two-dimensional representation of a world consisting of immobile objects with well-defined borders. It is basically a floor plan of the world, a projection onto the horizontal plane. Retrieval algorithms have been developed for only three kinds of tasks: determining elementary positional relations between specified objects; enumerating the objects of a given kind in a given region; and sketching a given region. Thus, the user may ask the robot how far it is from the desk to the refrigerator, to enumerate all the known restaurants within a mile of home, or to draw a picture of the furniture in his kitchen. Other kinds of retrieval problems — in particular, planning and executing routes — have not been studied. The MERCATOR program does only one kind of assimilation, assimilation of a visual scene; and it does not address error correction or investigation. Moreover, the assimilation and retrieval algorithms use only geometrical information. Physical constraints and knowledge about objects, which are presumably very important in people's assimilation process, are not used at all. We will discuss in Chapter 8 how the theory could be extended to fill these gaps.

Within these limits, however, MERCATOR is quite general and robust. The representation boasts the following virtues:

1. Objects of different scales can be represented. The same map can show minnows and oceans.

2. Virtually any 2-dimensional shape can be described. Objects can be arbitrarily squiggly, they can be multiply-connected (doughnut shaped) etc. as long they are connected and bounded.

3. Any layout of objects can be described. Objects can contain one another, they can overlap, they can coincide; space can be full or empty.

4. Measurements can be stated at varying degrees of precision. Local information can be precise, despite vagueness of global information. Specifically, it is easy to state precisely the distance between the closest faces of two objects even if the overall sizes and shapes of the objects are vaguely known or unknown.

5. Multiple shape descriptions provide precise information when needed and quickly usable information when sufficient. A long thin object can be described as a one-dimensional line for coarse computations, and as a two-dimensional area for more precision.

6. Objects which are only partially known can be described.

7. The meaning of a map is defined in terms of a truth-conditional semantics.

8. The map is hierarchically organized for efficiency.

Moreover, these features of the representation are integrated and used in the algorithms. The algorithms look for the most precise information available, but they are sensitive to its imprecision. They choose the most appropriate shape description for the task at hand. They use partial object descriptions appropriately. Their actions conform to the semantics. They make use of the hierarchy for efficiency.

1.5. Problem and Goals

Spatial reasoning is a fundamental reasoning mode, crucial to any understanding of the physical world. Within spatial reasoning, the task domain of cognitive mapping, focusing on visual input, has features which are attractive for research. It is possible to find a reasonable, self-contained subset that avoids many of the hardest common knots in AI, such as time, non-monotonic reasoning, natural language, and reasoning about humans, but includes the problem of partial knowledge, which I wished to study. The task is carried out by humans, though humans use more types of information than were addressed in the MERCATOR program. Cognitive maps are large but easily structured data bases, so that the problems of combinatorial explosion can be convincingly faced and solved. The ontology of real space and the nature of geometrical calculations are well understood, simplifying the problem. Cognitive mapping is a problem of knowledge base management, and, as such, the logical problems are fairly well understood (as compared to the logical problems of explanation or generalization, for example.)

Assimilation was chosen as the focus, because it had proven to be the hardest problem in our previous study of cognitive maps (see [McDermott and Davis, 84], [Davis, 81]), and it seemed likely to be hardest in this one. Visual input was chosen as the source, because it is natural, because it can be easily formalized (as opposed to assimilation from natural language sources, say), and because it provides a lot of information in a simple structure.

Visual input has one other property, which makes it much easier to assimilate than other sources; it is comparatively regular and complete. Views of the same scene from the same viewpoint on different occasions are likely to show pretty much the same objects in the same relations. This allows us to make all kinds of assumptions about the input which are crucial in developing the program. Also, it may be assumed that any important relation between two close objects is directly visible from some point of view. This assumption justifies an important principle in the MERCATOR assimilator, the "patience" principle. This principle asserts that it is not worthwhile for the assimilator to do a lot of work to establish some particular relation. If the relation is important enough, it will eventually be perceived directly. (See section 5.1 for further discussion and an example.)

MERCATOR studies these problems from an AI perspective. It is not a psychological study, and I make no psychological claims. My guess is that the problem statements ("Put together a cognitive map from scene descriptions", etc.) and the broad characterization of the kind of knowledge in the cognitive map, though much oversimplified, probably have some psychological reality; and that the details of the data structures and the algorithms have none. I have made no attempt to explain human errors in geographic reasoning — for example, the common distortions in people's cognitive maps enumerated in [Downs and Stea, 73] — despite their probable significance for the correct psychological theory of cognitive mapping. Even if my program made the same errors as human subjects, I would hesitate to take this as evidence that it was psychologically correct, unless the errors could be explained at the knowledge level; that is, as a natural response to inadequate information. I will discuss the relation of my work to that in psychology further in chapter 6.

The significance of my work to practical robotics is somewhat less tenuous. It seems possible that the MERCATOR program, perhaps somewhat modified, could enable a robot equipped with current sensing technology, to learn a sufficiently simple world. However, there may well be no practical situations where this ability is useful. MERCATOR cannot guide a robot through a kitchen because it cannot handle either motion or three dimensions. It is unlikely to be useful in a Martian landscape, because landscapes are not objects with well defined boundaries. On the other hand, in a controlled environment, like a factory floor, there is no need to have the robot *learn* the environment; it can be programmed in.

The computational aspects of MERCATOR have been of great importance to me. These will be discussed at length in appendix A. Briefly, I may say here that the data structures and algorithms are well-defined and elegant (though some more than others); and that the algorithms are efficient in time in various asymptotic limits.

The MERCATOR program is fully running and extensively tested. Chapter 7 describes the implementation and tests in detail. In almost all respects, the data structures and algorithms implemented in the program are those described in the text of this thesis. The few exceptions are noted in section 7.2

14

1.6. Thesis Organization

This thesis is divided into two major sections. Chapters 2 to 5 present the MERCATOR theory; chapters 6 to 8 discuss it. Specifically, the representation is discussed in chapter 2, the retrieval algorithms in chapter 3, and the assimilator in chapters 4 and 5 — the matcher in chapter 4, and the merger in chapter 5. Chapter 6 reviews related work. Chapter 7 discusses the implementation and the results of the actual testing. It also contains a brief account of the simulator functions, which are important for evaluating the testing. Chapter 8 evaluates the theory in terms of AI and contains ideas for extensions. Appendix A discusses some of the mathematical issues involved.

This thesis gets quite technical and a casual reader will presumably want to skip the technical tedium. I sympathize. However, there is no way to make sense of this thesis without going into the representation in some detail. I therefore recommend to the casual reader to read all of chapter 1, if he has not already done so; work through all of chapter 2, except for sections 2.2, 2.4, and 2.7, which are very technical and not critical; skim sections 3.1, 4.1, 4.2, 5.1, and 5.2 which sketch the issues in the algorithms; and read chapter 6 and chapter 8. This will give him the most enlightenment for the least work.

2 Representation

2.1. MERCATOR maps

Figure 2-1 shows a simple scene. How can we represent its two-dimensional geography?

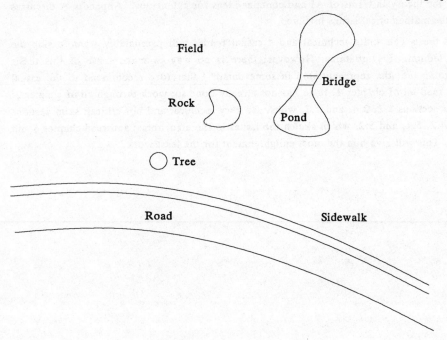

Figure 2-1: A Pastoral Scene

The basis elements of our representation are straight line segments. Other representations used pixels, generalized cones, reference frames, etc. However, note that figure 2-1 apparently captures all necessary geographic information, yet shows only the boundaries. Since the boundaries are one-dimensional, straight lines seem a natural choice. Further reasons for this choice will develop later.

Redrawing figure 2-1 with straight lines gives figure 2-2. The boundary of each object is represented by a set of *edges* connecting *vertices*. Thus, the boundary of the road is represented by the edges {edge($a-b$), edge($b-c$), edge($d-e$), edge($e-f$)}; the boundary of the sidewalk is {edge($d-e$), edge ($e-f$)}; etc; where a, b, c, ... are vertices.

This is acceptable for a drawing, but not for a representation; it does not indicate the interior of the objects. Without the pond, the field would have the same boundary as the sidewalk; how could the program distinguish them? This problem is fixed in two ways in figure 2-3. Firstly, each boundary edge of each object is labelled with the direction counter-

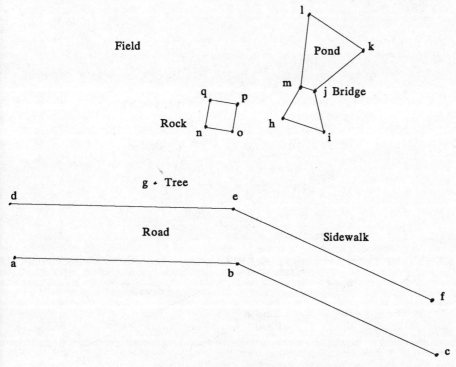

Figure 2-2: A Rectified Pastoral Scene

clockwise around the object. Such a directed edge is called a *bound*. (The diagram shows the labelling only for the edges around the road but it applies to the other boundaries as well.) Thus bound($e - d$) is on the boundary of the road, while bound($d - e$) is on the boundary of the field. The sidewalk has boundaries in both directions on each of its edges.

Secondly, we represent the interior of the object by polygons. The interior of the field is covered by the polygons {polygon($y - x - l - k$), polygon($x - d - h - m - l$), polygon($h - d - e - f - i$), polygon($f - y - k - j - i$)}; the interior of the sidewalk by the degenerate polygons {polygon($d - e$), polygon($e - f$)}; the interior of the tree by the single degenerate polygon {polygon(g)}. A complete shape description, consisting of a set of bounds and a set of polygons, is called a *region*. There are, in general, many ways to break an area up into polygons. In figure 2-3 we could have added an additional edge($e - i$) in the field, and thus has broken polygon($h - d - e - f - i$) into two polygons ($h - d - e - i$) and ($e - f - i$); but we are not obliged to. The system works better if the polygons are convex, but this is not necessary. (See sections 2.8 and 5.3.2.) Note that the field, being multiply connected, cannot be described by a single polygon. The road could be covered with a single polygon, but it is split into two convex polygons for ease of computation.

These polygons may require edges and vertices not on the object boundary. These edges fall into two classes. *Internal edges* lie inside a known object, like edge($f - i$) and edge($d - h$). *Knowledge edges* delimit the known extent of the object, like edge($a - d$) and edge($x - y$). It is unknown whether or not the road extends past edge($a - d$). The same distinction applies to

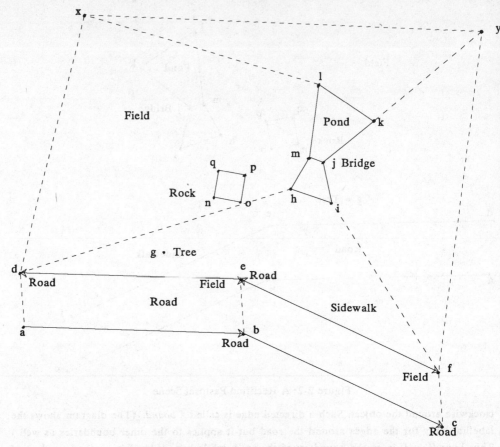

Figure 2-3: Scene with Bounds and Polygons

vertices. Vertices like vertex(*f*) are called knowledge vertices, since it is unknown whether the sidewalk extends past it. A single edge may serve different functions for different objects; it may be a boundary edge of one and a knowledge edge of another.

The next question is how to express dimensions and relative positions of objects. The easiest method would be to assign coordinates to each of the vertices. However, such precise information is usually unavailable. We might use coordinates with the understanding that they are to be taken lightly. For example, coordinates might be understood to be accurate to within five feet. This will do for a simple map, such as figure 2-3, but not for a map which extends over a wide range of scales. Generally, local information is much more precise than long distance information, but this cannot be expressed by coordinates with tolerances. If all coordinates have a five foot tolerance, then two rocks which are shown two feet apart will be interpreted as between zero and seven feet apart. On the other hand, to place both the pond and the neighboring town on the map requires that the distance between them be known to within ten feet.

The diagram itself suggests the solution: local dimensions are recorded in terms of the lengths and orientations of edges connecting the vertices. Lengths and orientations are not specified precisely. Rather, we specify ranges in which they lie: the length of edge$(a-b)$ is between 5.0 and 6.3; its orientation is between -10 and 10 degrees. We use a fixed scale and a fixed direction for measuring orientation. (See Section 2.5.)

There is no alternative to using ranges. Even if we represent these quantities as real numbers, we have to interpret them as ranges, if our system is to tolerate inaccuracy. This is particularly clear in a system which performs recognition. If I record the length of a given wall as 12.4 feet, and I see a wall which I judge to be 11.9 feet, can I say they are the same, and the discrepancy is simply the inaccuracy of the measurement? Probably. If I judge that the wall I see is 12.3 feet long, almost certainly they are the same; if I judge that it is 6 feet long, almost certainly they are different. Eventually, I must make a binary judgement as to whether they are the same, and, when I do, this will define an implicit range of seen values which are accepted. It is simpler to use ranges from the beginning; to record in memory that the wall is 12.4 +/- 1.2 and to have vision report that it is 11.9 +/- 0.7. Ranges are better than point values interpreted as ranges because true ranges allow specification of both value and tolerance. An upper and lower bound are equivalent to a value and a tolerance. Since the former is easier to compute with, we will use it henceforth. Such a range is called a *fuzz range* a quantity bounded by a fuzz range is a *fuzzy quantity*. (Fuzziness is not an attribute of the quantity, which is presumably real-valued; it is an attribute of our knowledge).

Edge lengths and orientations are less convenient than coordinates for calculations, but tolerable. The distance and direction from point a to point i in figure 2-3 is calculated from the lengths and orientations of the connecting edges $a-d$, $d-h$, $h-i$. Other quantities can likewise be calculated from the measures of connecting edges.

Note that there is no absolute frame of reference. It is meaningless to ask for the coordinates of a given point. Only relative positions are specified.

All vertices must be directly or indirectly connected by edges. In figure 2-3 the rock and the tree are not connected to the other objects, so more edges must be drawn. The rock is naturally connected to the pond by edges from vertex h to vertices o and p. Generally, edges should connect nearby vertices because their relative position is more fixed and because it simplifies search procedures.

The tree poses more problems. Suppose that the distance from the tree to the road is known fairly precisely — between 10 and 15 feet — but the position of the tree along the road is unknown. One cannot express this state of knowledge with edges which connect vertex g to the vertices of figure 2-3. The indeterminacy of g's parallel coordinate means that both the angle and the distance of the edge from d to g or from e to g are very fuzzy; but that would leave g's distance from the line $d-e$ also indeterminate.

The solution uses two edges, connected at an imaginary vertex X. Edge$(d-X)$ coincides with edge$(d-e)$ and has a fuzzy length; edge$(X-g)$ is perpendicular to edge$(d-X)$, and has a more precise length. This arrangement of two edges is common and important enough to be defined as a separate data structure. It is called a *joint* from g to d along $d-e$, and has three fuzzy quantities: perpendicular length, from g to X; parallel length, from X to d; and parallel orientation, from X to d. The parallel orientation is always either parallel or anti-parallel to the orientation of the associated edge. (See figures 2-4 and 2-5.)

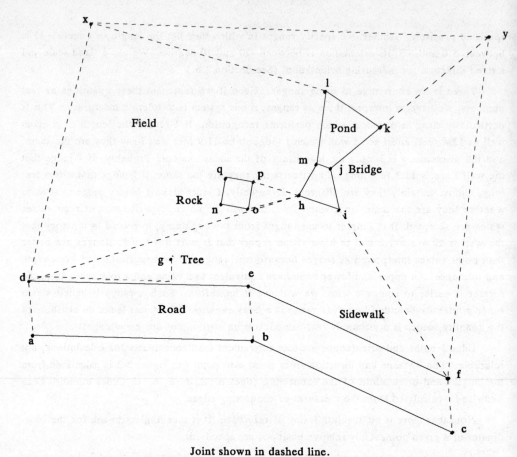

Joint shown in dashed line.

Figure 2-4: Scene with Edges and a Joint

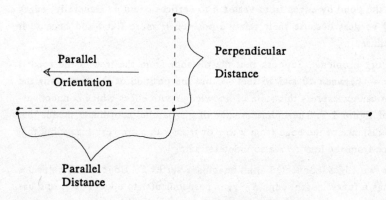

Figure 2-5: A Joint

Many objects do not have straight line borders. Therefore, these representations are only approximations. It is important to define how they are approximations, and to be able to state how inaccurate a given approximation is. The measure of the inaccuracy of a region is its *grain-size,* which is an upper bound on the distance from any point in the region to a point in the object. The smaller the grain-size, the better the approximation. Also, every bound in a region has a grain-size which, roughly speaking, is an upper bound on the distance from the bound to the corresponding part of the boundary. (See figure 2-6.) A more precise definition is given in Section 2.2.

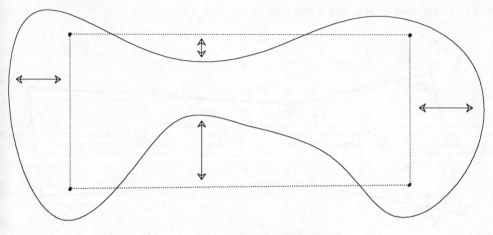

Arrows indicate grain-sizes
Figure 2-6: Grain Size

A circular object may thus be represented by a polygon with an appropriately large grain-size. Of course, the scene description and the cognitive map may represent the circle by entirely different polygons. That doesn't matter; by taking grain-sizes into account, the matcher can deduce that they may both represent the same object. Note that a polygonal representation cannot assert that an object is circular. As far as the MERCATOR representation is concerned "circularity" is an unanalyzed property of the object, like "redness" or "functionality as a chair". Although circularity is useful in some spatial reasoning, it seems to be irrelevant to the deductions of position with which we are concerned.

Sometimes it is useful to have several regions for a given object. For example, in thinking about shovelling snow, it might be useful to have a region for the sidewalk which showed it as an object with some thickness. The one-dimensional region could still be used for coarse calculations. We therefore separate the representation of the object as a whole from individual regions. The overall representation of the object is called a *clump;* it contains all the regions of the object, plus descriptions of the properties of the object, and the relations between the regions.

The description of non-geographic properties of objects is not part of our theory, and is presumably domain-dependent. Its only function in MERCATOR is determining whether two clumps can refer to the same object. Therefore, we describe objects in terms of slot-filler pairs. For example a clump described as ((IS-A BRIDGE) (MATERIAL WOOD)) can

21

match with one described ((IS-A BRIDGE) (STATE DECREPIT)) but not with ((IS-A ROAD) (MATERIAL ASPHALT)). In a more complete system, it might be possible to describe objects in terms of arbitrary predicates related by general inference mechanisms.

Some clumps are distinguished as *cliffs*. Cliffs represent opaque objects in terms of their vertical surfaces. They are characterized by a set of bounds, which go around the object, but no interior polygons, since the interior cannot be seen. For instance, in figure 2-4, the outside of the rock is a cliff. For the most part, we will ignore cliffs in this exposition; they almost always work like other clumps. They are primarily of importance to the vision simulator, since they determine what is visible and what is occluded. (See section 7.3.)

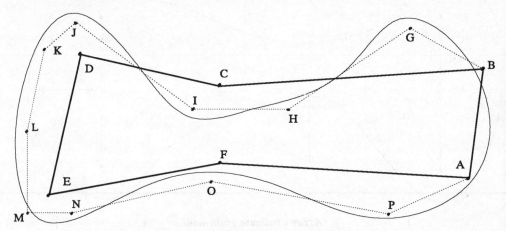

Object is curved line. Fine region is dotted line.
Coarse region is bold face line.
Connecting edges and joints not shown.
Figure 2-7: Multiple Regions

Different regions for a clump can be related to one another in three ways. Firstly, different regions may share one or more edges; in figure 2-7, the two regions share edge$(A - B)$ Secondly, vertices of different edges may be connected by edges or joints. The two regions in figure 2-7 might be connected by an edge$(H - C)$, an edge$(K - D)$, a joint from I to C along $C - D$, etc.

Thirdly, the order of the external vertices around the boundary is recorded in a *partial cyclic ordering* (PCO). This is a data structure which expresses, for any three elements, whether they are in clockwise order, counter-clockwise order, or unordered. It is analogous to a DAG which expresses, for any two elements, whether they are in increasing order, decreasing order, or unordered. A clump with a complete outer boundary and no inner boundaries will have one PCO; otherwise, it will have a PCO for each separate section of boundary.

A PCO is implemented like a DAG. The elements are placed in *nodes* which are connected by directed *arcs*. Unlike a DAG, however, certain arcs are marked as *parallel* to certain nodes. An arc $u \rightarrow v$ is parallel to node w unless the nodes are known to appear (u, v, w) in counter-clockwise order. Thus, in the PCO below, arc $D \rightarrow E$ is parallel to K, L, and M. So

(I, D, E) is known to be in counter-clockwise order but (K, D, E) is not. In general, (u, v, w) is known to be in counter-clockwise order if and only if there is a sequence of arcs from u to v to w, none of them parallel to u. (See section A.7 for a formal presentation of PCO's.)

The PCO for figure 2-7 is

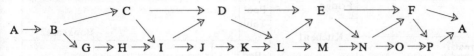

A consequence of allowing multiple regions is that the adjacency relationship becomes relative to grain-size, rather than primitive, as in many AI representations of position. At the grain-sizes of figure 2-4, for example, the road and the field share edges $d-e$ and $e-f$, and are thus adjacent. Finer regions would show that they are separated by the sidewalk. This seems plausible in our domain. For planning a walk home, my house is on Lawrence Street; for walking the last ten feet, the sidewalk is next to the street; for fixing the sidewalk, there is a stone curb between the sidewalk and the street. In other domains, such as the naive physics of building towers out of blocks, adjacency is more absolute.

Finally, a map is hierarchically arranged by containment. Clumps point to their immediate containers and contents. In our example, the rock and the tree are contained in the field. In a small map, this makes little difference. However, a map of realistic size may show furniture inside rooms inside buildings inside blocks inside ... In such a map, such organization makes calculations much more efficient. The hierarchy is a DAG, and it is assumed to be nearly a tree. (See figure 2-8.)

This representation is complex but complete. To review: We have *clumps*, representing objects; *regions* which approximate the shapes of objects at a given grain-size; *polygons*, *joints*, *edges*, *vertices*, and *PCOs*.

2.2. Formal Semantics

We now formally define the meaning of a MERCATOR map in terms of a truth conditional semantics, which gives necessary and sufficient conditions that the map be a valid description of the world. [Hayes, 77] and [McDermott, 78] argue the need for such interpretations in any system of representation. It is especially appropriate in spatial domains, where semantics are easy to define, and concepts relate in confusing ways. The informal description of the MERCATOR representation does not suffice to answer specific questions. Then it is incomplete and ambiguous. Can the same edge represent a circular arc of coarse grain-size in one object and a very straight boundary in another? If so, how? Can we leave small objects out of a map? How small must they be? Since all our descriptions have grain-size inaccuracies, why do we need fuzz ranges?

A formal semantics is particularly necessary in the matching problem, determining whether two clumps can represent the same object. There is no canonical representation of all two dimensional objects. Few useful general representation schemes for two dimensional shapes give unique representations for all shapes. If a shape has many possible descriptions, then identifying two such shape descriptions involves more than matching identical structures; it requires considering of how each description maps onto the object represented. The

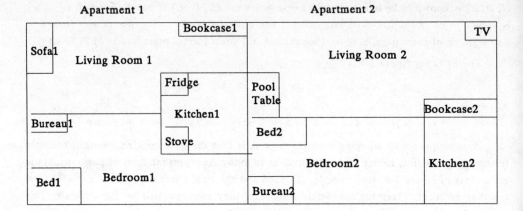

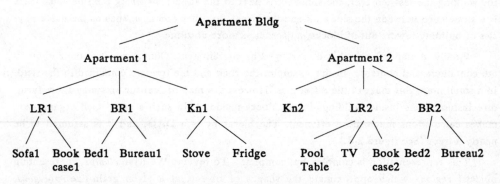

Figure 2-8: Hierarchy of Clumps

relation between description and object must therefore be defined. Two MERCATOR descriptions of a circular ring can look entirely different. One cannot write code to compare the two descriptions without rigorously specifying how they each relate to the ring.

Also, there are facts about the world which are true, and which are employed in the vision simulator, but which are not known to the MERCATOR program proper and not used, because they are not specified in the semantics. It is a fact, for example, that one cannot see past walls, and the map of the visual scene always terminates at walls, but the assimilator makes no use of the fact — it works just as well with scenes that violate this. Nor does it make any use of the fact that walls cannot intersect. Both of these facts are potentially useful in the algorithms, but they lie outside the range of the theory of MERCATOR maps.

The semantics of MERCATOR maps are rigorously defined in appendix A.2; we will briefly sketch them here. First we define the microworld that MERCATOR maps represent. An *object* is a closed, connected subset of R^2 (the real plane) with a boundary consisting of a finite number of disjoint simple closed curves; equivalently, it is a subset of R^2 homeomorphic to a disk with finitely many holes. (For example, an object cannot be a figure eight.) A *property* is a function from objects to arbitrary sets. Typical properties are "color" with image set {red, blue, white ...}; "style" with image set {Gothic, Georgian, Bauhaus ...}; "is-a" with image set {robot, pond, road, ...}. A MERCATOR map describes a set of objects with properties.

Three functions relate a MERCATOR map to the real world: REAL, COOR, and COVER. REAL maps clumps onto objects. Thus REAL(CL52) = the Empire State Building; REAL(CL101) = my coffee table, etc. REAL preserves containment — i.e., if CL1 is marked as containing CL2, then REAL (CL1) must contain REAL (CL2), (the converse need not be true) — and it takes clumps with stated properties onto objects with those properties — i.e., if CL52 is marked as ((IS-A BUILDING) (HEIGHT VERY-HIGH)) then it is OK for REAL (CL52) to be the Empire State Building, and not OK for it to be the Atlantic Ocean.

COOR and COVER relate the entities in the map to objects in the plane. This relation is somewhat involved. A MERCATOR entity can correspond to no physical phenomenon in the plane, like the internal edge$(p - h)$ in figure 2-4, or it may correspond to many physical entities in the plane, like edge$(d - e)$, which corresponds both to the lower boundary of the field, and the upper boundary of the road. In either case, it is not immediately apparent what is meant by the length and orientation of the edge. In the first case, these are not physical quantities; in the second case, these each correspond to two possibly different quantities.

We get around these difficulties by dividing the mapping into two steps. COOR is a function which maps the MERCATOR map into a abstract linear grid in the plane. The image of a MERCATOR map under COOR is a picture like figure 2-4. The image of the data structure "edge$(d - e)$" is the line $d - e$ in the figure. The length and orientation recorded for the edge in the map refer to the length and orientation of this abstract line. Pieces of this grid are then related to the real world, like figure 2-1, through a set of COVER functions. For example, there is a COVER function mapping line $d - e$ into the curve which is the lower bound of the field. There is a separate COVER function mapping it into the upper bound of the road. (See figure 2-9.) These COVER functions are ordinary functions from the plane onto itself; they map points in the line onto points on the boundary curves. They are constrained by the recorded grain-sizes. No COVER function can map any point to a image which is further away than the corresponding grain-size.

Specifically, COOR is defined as a function from vertices of the map into points in the plane. Even if the point represents an object with some extent, like vertex g in figure 2-4, COOR (g) is a single point in the plane. COOR is extended in the natural way to take edges and bounds into line segments, joints into pairs of line segments, polygons of the map into planar polygons, and regions into unions of polygons. COOR has to satisfy the following conditions:

1. For each edge e, COOR (e) has to have length and orientation within the fuzz ranges which the map specifies for e. Likewise for joints.

2. For each polygon P in the map, COOR (P) must be a legitimate, non-self-intersecting polygon in the plane.

That is, the measurements given for edges and joints are correct.

COVER is a family of functions. There is a COVER function for every bound, and for the interior of every region in the map. For each bound b in the boundary of a region, we define a continuous function $COVER_b$ from COOR (b) into the object boundary. $COVER_b$

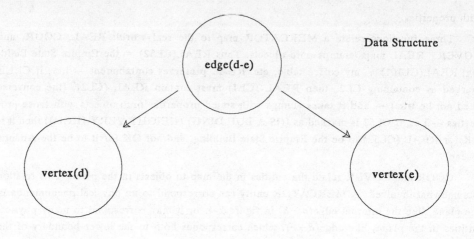

Data Structure

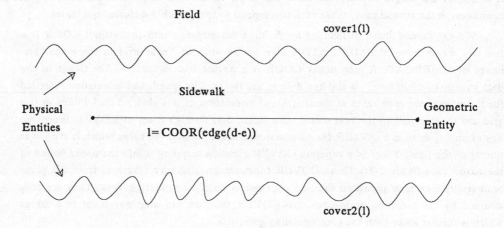

Road

Figure 2-9: COVER Function

must satisfy the following conditions:

1. For all x in COOR (b), the distance from x to $COVER_b(x)$ must be less than the grain-size of b.

2. If b and c are bounds of region REG which meet at a vertex v, and v is a real vertex of REG, then $COVER_b(\text{COOR}(v)) = COVER_c(\text{COOR}(v))$. This rules out situations like figure 2-10, which is allowed if v is a knowledge bound of REG.

3. The real vertices of a clump map into the boundary of the corresponding object so as to satisfy the PCOs of the clump.

We do a similar thing for the interior of regions. For each region R there must exist a continuous function $COVER_R$ such that $COVER_R$ (COOR (polygons of R)) is within REAL

26

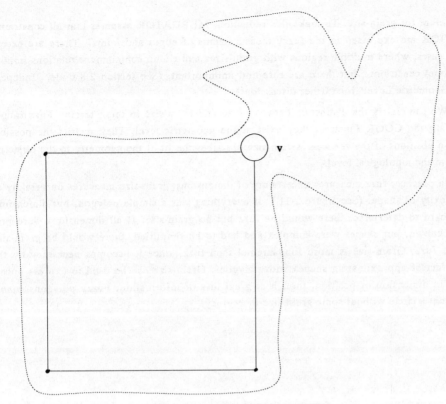

Region is square. Object is squiggly.
This situation is consistent with the semantics
if *v* is a knowledge vertex.
Figure 2-10: Semantics of Knowledge Vertex

(clump of *R*).

The MERCATOR map is valid if it is possible to define REAL, COOR, and COVER so as to satisfy all these conditions.

2.3. Levels of Representation

It is often convenient to think of a MERCATOR map as divided into *geometric* and *topological* levels. The geometric level consists of vertices, edges, joints, and polygons. These data structures represent geometric entities: point, lines, etc. Their meaning is unaffected by the existence of objects. Their semantics is completely defined by COOR. The topological level consists of bounds, regions, PCO's, and clumps. These describe objects, and relate them to the geometric level.

In general, MERCATOR algorithms work by reducing a problem involving the topological level to one involving only the geometric level. Then the problem becomes purely one of doing trigonometry on fuzzy intervals. For example, we reduce calculating the distance between two objects to calculating the distance between their boundary edges, and making an adjustment for grain-size. To make this reduction, MERCATOR assumes that all constraints on COOR are expressed in the fuzzy measurements of edges and joints. There are exceptional cases, where multiple regions with grain-sizes and clump containment relations impose additional constraints, but these are rare and unimportant. (See section 2.8 under "Independent Geometric Level" for further discussion.)

We can clarify the distinction between fuzz and grain-size in these terms. Fuzz ranges constrain the COOR function; they exist at the geometric level. They restrict the possible relative positions of the vertices. Grain-size describes the fit of the geometry to the object; it exists at the topological level.

In practice, fuzz measures uncertainty of dimensions; grain-size measures uncertainty or complexity of shape. (See figure 2-11.) If everything was a simple polygon, but dimensions were hard to determine, there would be fuzz but no grain-size. If all dimensions were precisely known, but shapes were complex and had to be simplified, there would be grain-size but no fuzz. Grain-size is more fundamental than fuzz, since it becomes necessary by the mere fact of approximating shapes with polygons. Grain-size *can* be used to express uncertainty in dimension or position, though at great loss of information. Fuzzy polygons *cannot* represent a circle without some grain-size inaccuracy.

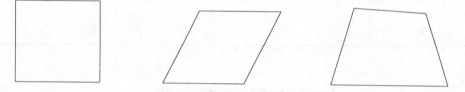

Shape variation allowed by fuzzy measurements

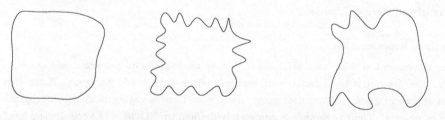

Shape variation allowed by grain-size

Figure 2-11: Fuzz Range Vs. Grain Size Imprecision

Computationally, fuzz is easier to deal with than grain-size. In comparing two regions for possible identity, for example, two regions with fuzzy edges but very fine grain-size are identical only if corresponding sets of edges have overlapping fuzzes. Two shapes whose grain-size is not much smaller than the length of sides can be wildly different, yet represent the same object. (See figure 2-12.)

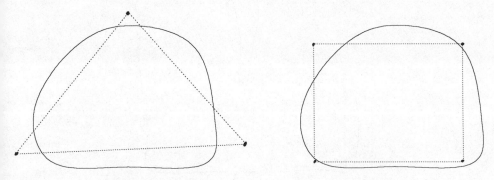

The grain-size can be as small as this:

Figure 2-12: Two Regions for the Same Object

2.4. Grain-size

The definition of grain-size is somewhat difficult and counter-intuitive. We elucidate it here.

There is a separate grain-size for each bound of each region, and for the interior of the region. For each bound b there is a continuous function $COVER_b$ from the points of COOR (b), which is a straight line, into the actual object boundary, which is a curve. The grain-size of b is an upper bound on the distance which any point is moved by $COVER_b$; that is, it is an upper bound on $DIST(x, COVER_b(x))$.

The requirement of a continuous function forces the region bounds to follow the ins and outs of the boundary curve. For example, in figure 2-13 the solid line is an accurate approximation to the boundary, but the dotted line is not. There are functions from the dotted line to the boundary which move no point by more than the grain-size, but they must "jump" from one part of the boundary to the next. A continuous function would have to traverse the large bend in the curve, and therefore would need a very large grain-size. Likewise, the dotted lines in figure 2-14 are poor approximations to their respective curves.

This may seem unnatural. Intuitively, these are good approximations; the line fits the curve if we ignore phenomena smaller than the grain-size. This is not merely an aesthetic judgement; a vision module is likely to produce these approximations. (See section 8.3) However, it is apparently difficult to formulate a definition that accepts these but does not allow some unacceptable approximations. For example, we might require only that every point on the approximating line be less than the grain-size from the boundary. Under this definition, all the dotted lines in figure 2-14 would be acceptable approximations at a small grain-size. Unfortunately, so would the dotted lines in figure 2-15. Even if we ignore our intuition and accept the latter, we will find that they are impossible to match. Given practically any two regions, we can define an object which lies within a small grain-size of both.

29

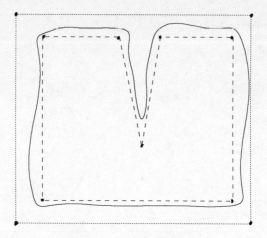

Solid curve -- actual boundary
Dashed line -- good approximation
Dotted line -- poor approximation

Figure 2-13: Good and Bad Approximations

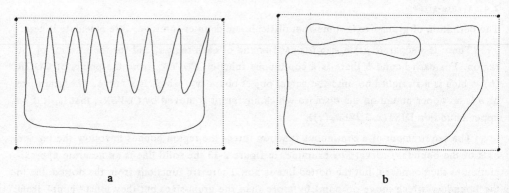

a   b

Figure 2-14: Approximations Outside the Definition

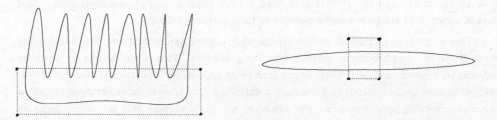

Figure 2-15: Approximations Inside a Modified Definition

Alternatively, we could replace the condition of a continuous mapping by the requirement that every boundary point be within the grain-size of a bound. This would at least allow
example (b) in figure 2-14 to be an acceptable approximation. However, the condition is

unacceptable because it requires the boundary to be wholly known and represented.

Besides the bound grain-size, we need an interior grain-size to give a meaning to the polygons associated with an object. In particular, if the region has knowledge bounds, then the bound grain-sizes do not serve to constrain the region close to the object. We use a similar definition for the grain-size of a region interior — the maximal displacement of a continuous function from the region polygons into the object. Again, this definition has mildly counter-intuitive consequences, most notably that very small holes in the object must be represented in regions of any grain-size.

2.5. Inadequacies of the representation

The most important gap in MERCATOR maps is that they only express the presence of an object, not its absence. The fact that a map does not show an object does not mean that it is not there; maps are not obliged to show everything, or anything, in a particular area. No map is inconsistent with the presence of any object anywhere, except that objects represented at one place in the map can't also be somewhere else in the map. Looking at a MERCATOR representation of your office, you can't say there are no rhinoceroses in the office, or even that there is reason to believe there aren't. (This answers the question posed previously (p. 23) how we can leave small objects out of a map. We can leave anything out of a map.)

One way to fix this gap is with *completeness* statements. These have the form "All objects with property p larger that grain-size g inside region R have a corresponding clump in the map." For example, "All buildings larger than 0.0 in the block are shown," "All solid objects with diameter greater than one foot in the room are shown," "All wild animals in the house are shown", etc. Statements of this kind allow us to deduce that if there is no rhinoceros shown in the office, there cannot be a rhinoceros in the office. Such statements can be explicit in the data base, or implicit using default inference rules. It might, for example, be part of the semantics of a region that all objects inside it larger than twice the grain-size are represented. We have not implemented this feature in any form. (The implications of this kind of information is further discussed in section 8.4.7.)

Secondly, some natural combinations of precise shape and imprecise dimensions cannot be expressed in a MERCATOR map. For example, there is no way to specify that a shape is a rectangle rather than a bizarre quadrilateral, if the lengths and orientations of all the edges are fuzzy.

The correct solution is to express lengths and orientations in relative terms. That is, length and orientation should be measured in terms like "A-B is between 2.5 and 3.0 times as long as C-D" or "The direction from A to B is between 0.5 to 0.6 counter-clockwise of the direction from C to D" rather than "A-B is between 4.0 and 5.0 units" or "The direction from A to B is between 1.0 and 1.2 in the absolute scale." Using such facts, it is easy to state that ABCD is a rectangle. It suffices to say:

31

"A-B is equal to C-D in length and orientation."
"D-A is equal to B-C in length and orientation."
"A-B is perpendicular to B-C."

In section 8.5.3 we discuss how this information can be represented effectively and incorporated into the algorithms. We have omitted this from the current version of the MERCATOR program because we felt that it would complicate the program substantially without producing much enlightenment.

MERCATOR assumes that the robot always knows his absolute orientation, which is a very strong assumption. In fact, this problem is part of the previous one. Ideally, we would express the orientation of edges in the scene description with respect to the current orientation of the robot, the orientation of edges in the cognitive map with respect to previous orientations of the robot, and the various orientations of the robot over time would be related to one another more or less fuzzily. The solution given in section 8.5.3 will apply here too. There are also a less drastic solution by which the robot keeps track of his absolute orientation within fuzz bounds, which he tightens each time he matches the scene description against the known map.

Finally, only a limited range of worlds can be represented in a MERCATOR map. MERCATOR assumes that the world is two-dimensional and that things come in well defined chunks, with perceptible boundaries. It cannot describe a hill, a Monet, or Chinatown. These simplifications are not as restrictive as it might seem. The question is not "In what kinds of environments are these assumptions true?" — obviously very few — but "How much information is lost in describing a scene in these terms?", which, for many scenes and many purposes, may not be very great. See Section 8.3 for more discussion of this point.

2.6. More Terminology

Miscellaneous technical terms and issues used in the remainder of this paper are discussed here.

The cognitive map and the scene description will often be called the "known" map and the "seen" map respectively. Likewise, their contents will be called "known" and "seen" respectively; thus, we may refer to "known object", meaning an object represented in the cognitive map, or a "seen vertex", meaning a vertex which is part of the scene description. We will assume that, in general, the cognitive map is much larger than the scene description.

If r is a real interval, then LOW (r) is its lower bound, and HIGH (r) is its upper bound. LOW $([1.0, 2.0]) = 1.0$; HIGH $([1.0, 2.0]) = 2.0$. If r is a closed arc in the unit circle, then LOW (r) is the lowest angle contained, and HIGH (r) is the highest angle. If r is the entire unit circle, then, by convention, LOW(r) is 0.0 and HIGH(r) is 2π. Interval arithmetic on angles involves many rather shallow problems and special cases — reducing modulo 2π, worrying about fuzz ranges that span 360 degrees, etc. — which we will assume solved in the paper.

We will use angle brackets to denote ordered sets and vectors. Thus, $< a, b, c >$ is a triple; $< 1.0, 2.0 >$ is a point in the plane, etc.

32

Given two points in the plane $\vec{u} = <u_x, u_y>$, $\vec{v} = <v_x, v_y>$, we define the displacement, distance, and direction functions in the usual way.

$$DX(\vec{u}, \vec{v}) = v_x - u_x$$
$$DY(\vec{u}, \vec{v}) = v_y - u_y$$
$$DIST(\vec{u}, \vec{v}) = \sqrt{[DX(\vec{u}, \vec{v})^2 + DY(\vec{u}, \vec{v})^2]}$$
$$DIR(\vec{u}, \vec{v}) = \arctan(DY(\vec{u}, \vec{v}) / DX(\vec{u}, \vec{v}))$$

The orientation of a joint is always chosen to be parallel or anti-parallel to the edge of the joint, depending on whether the head of the joint is the head or the tail of the edge. The parallel length of the joint is the directed length with respect to this orientation. The perpendicular length of the joint is the directed length with respect to an orientation $\frac{\pi}{2}$ less than the joint orientation. In this way, we can have negative lengths on the joint. Under rare circumstances, we similarly interpret edge lengths as directed lengths, and allow them too to attain negative values. (See figure 2-16.)

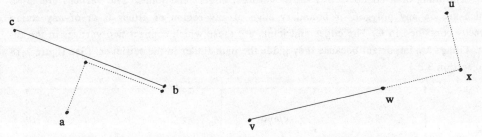

Joint (a, c) has negative perpendicular length, since the angle $<adc$ is -90°.

Joint (u, w) has negative parallel length since x lies outside edge$(v - w)$.

Figure 2-16: Joint with Negative Measurements

We will use the term *cover* loosely, to refer to the relations between entities in a MERCATOR maps and parts of objects. Thus, a bound covers part of the object boundary. A region covers part of the object interior and part of the boundary. A clump covers the part of the object which is covered by any of its regions.

A region which covers an entire object is said to be *closed*. A clump which covers an entire object is said to be *complete*.

A *chain* is a series of bounds and vertices that is known to cover a connected section of boundaries. Formally, a chain is a series of real bounds in one region such that the head of each is the tail of the next, and such that the vertex connecting two bounds is a real bounding vertex in that region.

There are two grain-sizes associated with a boundary vertex of a region: the *tight* grain-size, which is the minimum of the grain-sizes of the connecting bounds, and the *loose* grain-size, which is their maximum. We can be sure that the boundary curve comes within the tight grain-size of the vertex. On the other hand, the curve may go as far as the loose grain-size of the vertex away in the neighborhood of the vertex. (See figure 2-17.)

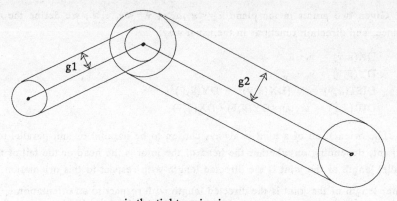

g_1 is the tight grain-size.
g_2 is the loose grain-size.
Figure 2-17: Vertex Grain Sizes

The *tiling* of a clump C is a set of vertices, edges, and joints. The vertices are those which are on any polygon or boundary edge of any region of either C or of any clump directly contained in C. The edges and joints are those which connect two vertices in the tiling. Tilings are important because they guide the path-finder in the retriever. (See figure 2-18 and section 3.3.)

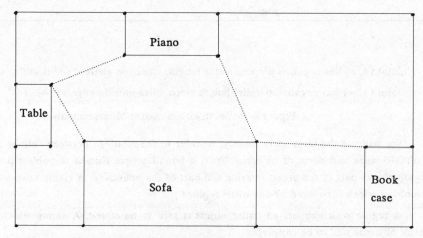

The edges shown are the tiling of the room.
Figure 2-18: A Clump Tiling

2.7. One-Dimensional Regions

The MERCATOR system allows representing long thin objects or long thin parts of objects by edges or sets of edges. (See figure 2-19.) Two particular problems arise with this representation.

The first is that, in going around the object, we may traverse edges twice and vertices more than twice, in different directions. It is important to be able to specify the order in

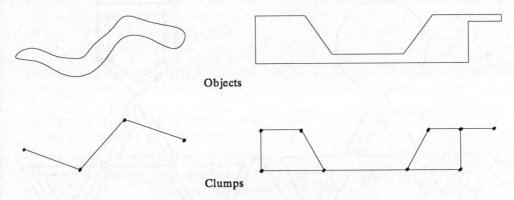

Objects

Clumps

Figure 2-19: One Dimensional Representations

which a traversal passes these by. The solution here is to specify two bounds for each such edge, and to connect bounds, not by vertices, but by *corners*. A corner is characterized by a vertex, an in bound, and an out bound. Thus in figure 2-20 we have four bounds: w from a to b, x from b to c, y from c to b, and z from b to a. We likewise have four corners: p at a, connecting z and w; q at b, connecting w and x; r at c connecting x and y; and s at b, connecting y and z. Note that different bounds on the same edge can have different grain-sizes. In fact, one can be a real bound and the other can be a knowledge bound. In this way, we can build up very complicated graphs of edges unambiguously. (See figure 2-21.)

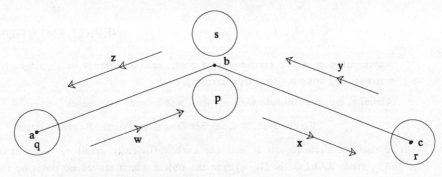

Figure 2-20: Bounds and Corners in 1-D Regions

The more difficult problem relates to the semantics of the interior of such representation. The interior in figure 2-20 is the union of the edges (degenerate polygons) $a-b$, $b-c$. Their images under COOR are two connected line segments. But, by our above definition, for this to cover the interior of the object, there must be a continuous function from the line segments onto the object, satifying the grain-size, which is impossible. We must therefore modify the semantics. Moreover, we must modify it in a way which excludes the possibility of figure 2-20 representing an object with holes, since we want to insist that all object bounds be represented explicitly.

The solution is rather ugly. For each region R and for each real number ϵ we define BALLOON (R, ϵ) as the area within ϵ of COOR (R). We then modify the semantics to

35

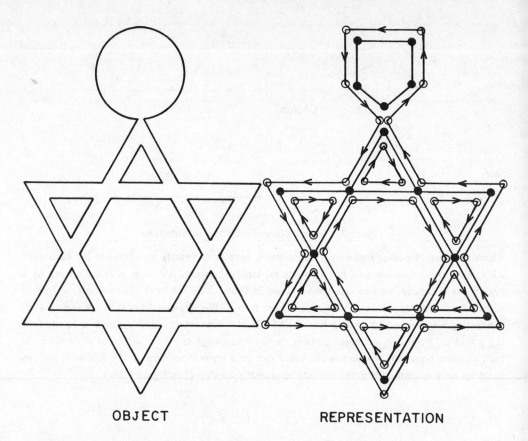

OBJECT   REPRESENTATION

Representation shows vertices (solid dots); corners (empty dots); edges (lines without arrows); and bounds (lines with arrows).

Actually, corners coincide with vertices, and bounds with edges.

Figure 2-21: A Complex One-Dimensional Representation

require that for each region R and for each sufficiently small ϵ, there exist a function $COVER_{R,\epsilon}$ from BALLOON (R, ϵ) into the object which moves no point by more than the grain-size of the interior of R. (See figure 2-22.)

One-dimensional representations are ignored in most of this thesis. In some cases, they constitute an irritating special case for the code, but they never raise any serious problems. Therefore, except in appendix A, we will forget about both corners and the modification of the semantics of interior polygons.

3. Normalcy Conditions

The semantic conditions above are necessary to the correct running of the MERCATOR functions, but they are not sufficient. They are much too loose; they allow MERCATOR maps to be almost unstructured in very confusing ways. To insure that MERCATOR maps are usable effectively, we must impose additional constraints beyond the semantic constraint

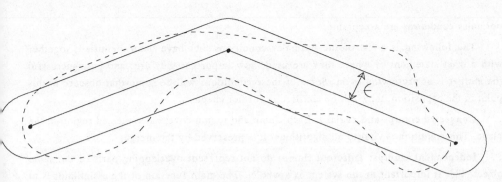

Figure 2-22: Semantics of 1-D Regions

that they be true. These additional constraints are called, for lack of a better term, *normalcy conditions*.

A normalcy condition is imposed on MERCATOR maps because some algorithm requires it either for effectiveness or for efficiency. Ideally, the vision module should always produce scene descriptions which satisfy them, and the assimilator should preserve them; that is, if two maps both satisfy the normalcy conditions then the resultant map, after they have been combined by the assimilator, should still preserve the normalcy conditions. The vision simulator has been designed so that its output always does satisfy the conditions, though it is not clear that this is a realistic model. We have worked hard to try to make the assimilator preserve the conditions — indeed, we shall see that this is the major constraint on the merger — but complete success in this is dependent on numerous outside factors. It may depend on regularities of the vision module, on regularities of the world, on the sequence in which scenes are assimilated. Some of the normalcy conditions are not maintained by the merger, even under quite benign circumstances; in such cases, we try to ensure that they are preserved in the long run,

We do not make the normalcy conditions part of the definition of a MERCATOR map or its semantics for a number of reasons. The major reason is that we want the definition to be minimal, to have the fewest possible conditions that will still allow us to assign meaning to it. Secondly, not all the normalcy conditions are capable of formal definition; they are merely broadly stated heuristics. Thirdly, it is not, in fact, possible to create the merger so as to preserve all the normalcy conditions. It is therefore important not to include them in the definition of meaning; otherwise we will end up with a merger that creates meaningless maps. Fourthly, some normalcy conditions are more important than others. Some cause algorithms to go seriously awry; others merely slow it down. Finally, it is difficult to isolate all relevant normalcy conditions. Whenever an algorithm performs an action which cannot be justified purely on the basis that the map is true, it is assuming a normalcy condition. We do not know whether all such actions and conditions have been found.

These conditions constrain not only the structure of the map but also the various states of knowledge that can be expressed in it. For example, it violates a normalcy condition if the positions of two distant objects is known much more accurately than the positions of objects of similar scale lying between them. If these constraints on knowledge are realistic, then the normalcy conditions are acceptable.

The following is a list of the normalcy conditions that have been identified, together with a brief statement of where they are used, how important they are, and how successful the merger is at preserving them. Some of these conditions will be somewhat obscure at this point in the exposition; they will be clarified in further chapters.

Connected clumps and regions: Each clump and region covers a connected region in the plane. This condition is vital to all algorithms. It is preserved by the merger.

Independent clumps: Different clumps do not represent overlapping parts of the same object. This is important to the system as a whole. The main function of the assimilator is to preserve this.

Full regions: All regions of a clump cover nearly the same area. This is important to the effective running of any algorithm.

Well structured regions: The various regions of a clump are organized so that the more complex regions express strictly more information than less complex regions. There are problems in principle in obeying both this condition and the *full regions* condition. (See section 8.5.2.) The MERCATOR merger preserves both in a trivial way by producing only one region per clump.

Polygon fitting: The polygons of a region do not overlap each other, except at common edges. This helps to preserve the *well structured tiling* condition. The merger preserves this condition in the long run. That is, after the entire object has been seen, the regions of the complete clump will satisfy this condition. (See Section 5.3.2.)

Simple Boundary: The bounds of a region do not overlap to any great extent. This is important for the correct running of the matcher. It is preserved by the merger.

Coherent Region: For each region, the edges of the bounds are edges of the polygons. This is important for the merger. It is preserved by the merger. (See section 5.3.2.)

Identifiable Knowledge Bounds: The knowledge bounds are be just those edges of polygons which are neither borders between two polygons nor real boundary edges. This is important for *identifiable closure*. It is a consequence of the *non-overlapping polygons* and the *coherent regions* conditions. It is preserved by the merger in the long run. (See section 5.3.2.)

Identifiable Closure: A region is closed if and only if it has no knowledge bounds and no knowledge vertices. This condition is important for all the algorithms, since it is vital to distinguish between complete and incomplete clumps. This condition follows from the identifiable knowledge bounds condition. It is preserved by the merger.

Meaningful bounds: Every bound in a region has a grain-size that is reasonably small compared to its length. Certainly, the grain-size should be less than half the length. (Otherwise, the bound says very little about the boundary.) This is necessary to the effective and efficient running of the matcher and merger. This is a strong constraint on the vision module, and it is not clear whether it would always be attainable in an actual system which dealt with curved objects. The merger generally preserves this, but not always.

38

Convex Polygons: Polygons should be convex if possible. The merger does not preserve this condition.

Correct Edges: Edges should connect objects which are close together in their common container. This is preserved by the merger.

Connected tilings: The tiling of any clump is connected by edges. This is vital to the fact retrieval algorithm, and therefore to the matcher and merger, which call it. It is preserved by the merger.

Edges in tilings: All edges and joints lie within the tiling of some clump. If an edge violates this rule, it does little harm, but also no good; it will almost always be ignored by the algorithms.

Universal clump: The clump containment hierarchy has a top-most element which contains all others. This insures that any two objects can be related by the fact retriever. In the MERCATOR vision simulator, we include a UNIVERSE clump in every scene description.

Independent Geometry: The MERCATOR map as a whole places no additional constraints on the COOR function beyond what is placed by the fuzzy measurements of edges and joints. This affects the effectiveness of the retrieval algorithms, by assuring that no positional information is ignored in reducing a problem to the geometric level.

There are two other types of constraints that the map could impose in principle. The positions of vertices can be constrained by multiple regions — edges of the one cannot be more than the sum of the grain-sizes from edges of the other — or by clump containments — the vertices of one clump must lie inside, or nearly inside, the other. Both of these can almost always be largely captured by joints. (See appendix A.6.)

Direct paths: Between any two vertices, there is a path of edges which stays fairly close to the straight line between them. This is somewhat important for the fact retriever, and extremely important for the object retriever. This condition is very difficult to achieve, because it requires that any two vertices that are close be known to be close. Therefore, if the robot walks around in a loop, very extensive calculation is required to achieve this. MERCATOR only preserves this under particular conditions of the robot's path and his looking habits, together with regularity in the vision module in reporting the same objects when it looks in the same area. See section 3.6 for the further discussion of this limitation.

The next several conditions limit the maximum number of entities standing in a particular relation to any individual entity. These conditions are to some extent mutually dependent. They mostly serve to ensure that the functions run efficiently.

Treelike Hierarchy: The upward branching factor in the clump containment hierarchy should be close to 1. This is necessary for efficient retrieval. (See section 3.3.)

Well Structured Hierarchy: The downward branching factor in the clump containment hierarchy should be bounded. (Say about 30.)

Preserving the last two conditions in the map depends on a property of the world and a property of the vision module. We demand that the world satisfy the constraint (i.e. that the hierarchy of visible objects be treelike and well structured). We demand that the vision module rarely produce a map which contains an objects and omits any of its containers.

Shallow Hierarchy: The clump containment hierarchy should not contain any extremely long chains of containments. This again depends on this condition being true in the world.

Clump Simplicity: A clump should not contain too many regions. This condition is imposed by our merger whether or not it is true in the input map.

Local Simplicity: The number of clumps with area greater than a which intersect a convex domain of area A should not be very much greater than $\frac{A}{a}$. In other words, there should not be many of overlapping clumps in any given size range in any given area. This again is a restriction on the world. It is important to the object retriever and the matcher.

Region Simplicity: There should be an upper bound, not very large, on the number of vertices in a region. The merger does not quite preserve this condition, but it rarely gets out of hand.

Note that if clump simplicity and region simplicity are preserved, then the size of the map as a whole is limited to be a constant times the number of clumps.

Tiling Simplicity: The tiling of any clump should not contain too many vertices. This is the key condition for efficient fact retrieval. This follows if the well structured hierarchy, clump simplicity and region simplicity conditions are observed.

Well Structured Tiling: The edges and joints in a tiling should connect nearby vertices. This is important for the retriever. The merger preserves this property.

Plenum: Each boundary edge should bound a clump on either side. A map which violates this is said to be in the *vacuum* condition. This is useful in the matcher. It is also potentially useful in other retrieval problems, such as path finding. (See section 8.4.1.) It is not preserved at all by the merger.

3 Retrieval

3.1. Introduction

The most basic operation on a knowledge base is to extract information. Often, the desired information is not explicit in the knowledge base but must be inferred. This is particularly true of MERCATOR maps, since most statements directly expressed involve geometrical entities, like edges, joints, or vertices, which have no real existence. The knowledge that edge E52 has length between 5 and 15, or that the red brick wall is approximated by edges E25, E34, and E8, is meaningless by itself. It is only meaningful in the context of other statements which relate E52 to objects. Only by combining such facts can we get useful information.

In principle, a large class of spatial queries are answerable from a MERCATOR map, up to the precision and completeness of the map. For example, "What is the diameter of the pond?" can be answered, but the answer will, in general, be a range [lower-bound, upper-bound]. If the clump for the pond is incomplete, then the upper-bound will be infinite. "Is the red brick wall between myself and the field?" can be answered "yes," "no," or "maybe." Queries which cannot be answered are mainly those which depend on absence. For example, the query "Is there a wall between me and the field?" can only be answered "yes" or "possibly not." The answer "definitely not" would require absence information

Each different kind of query requires a different retrieval algorithm. We have studied algorithms for two types of queries, namely:

1. Where is object U with respect to object V?

2. What objects are close to U?

These were chosen for study because they were needed in various parts of the assimilator.

These queries involve both the topological and geometric levels. Before analyzing them, we will consider how to do calculations simply on the geometric level. In particular, we need to be able to do the following:

1. Determine the relative position of two vertices

2. Assign consistent coordinates to the vertices. This is called "sketching" the vertices.

3.2. Calculations on Vertices

The most basic calculation on the map is to determine the position of vertex v with respect to vertex u: i.e. the value of the vector $COOR(v) - COOR(u)$, which we will write $RELPOS(v,u)$. Specifically, we are interested in particular functions of this vector, such as its length, which is the distance from u to v, or its angle, which is the direction of v from u. The map does not fix the value of the vector, or functions of the vector, to a single value;

41

rather, we retrieve the upper and lower bounds which the map places on these functions.

The general problem of finding the maximal range of such a function consistent with the map, or, for that matter, of finding a single value consistent with the map, is computationally intractable. (See appendix A.5.) Since this is so, we use a quick and easy heuristic. We calculate the relation between our two vertices using a single path of edges connecting them, and we ignore all the other edges in the net.

Formally, we define a *link* as a triple consisting of a starting vertex, an edge, and an ending vertex such that the starting vertex and the ending vertex are the head and tail of the edge, not necessarily in that order. The length of the link is the length of its edge. The orientation of the link is the orientation of the edge, if the starting vertex of the link is the tail of the edge; otherwise, it is the orientation of the edge plus π. A *path* consists of a starting vertex, an ending vertex, and a possibly null sequence of links such that

1. If the sequence of links is not null, then the starting vertex of the path is the starting vertex of the first link.

2. If the sequence of links is not null, then the ending vertex of the path is the ending vertex of the first link.

3. If the sequence of links is null, then the starting vertex and the ending vertex are the same.

4. The ending vertex of each link (except the last) is the starting vertex of the next link.

Examples of paths in figure 2-4 are

$< f, m, \{ (f, \text{edge}(f-i), i), (i, \text{edge}(i-j), j), (j, \text{edge}(j-m), m) \} >$

$< q, p, \{ (q, \text{edge}(p-q), p) \} >$

$< d, d, \varnothing >$

We write these more concisely "path (f, i, j, m)", "path (q, p)", "path (d)".

Joints are incorporated into paths by breaking them into two edges — one for the direction perpendicular to the joint edge and one for the direction parallel — and inventing an intermediate vertex. For example, we might use the joint$(g, d, \text{edge}(d-e))$ to make a path

$< g, d, \{ (g, \text{edge}(g-X), X), (X, \text{edge}(X-d), d) \} >$

where the length of the first link is the perpendicular length of the joint, its orientation is the parallel orientation of the joint minus $\frac{\pi}{2}$, the length of the second link is the parallel length of the joint, and its orientation is the parallel orientation of the joint.

Clearly, the measurements of a path p from u to v restrict the values of COOR(v) - COOR(u). To calculate this restriction, we begin with the special case where none of the link measurements are fuzzy. In this case, we can use the following formula: Let LINKS(p) be the links of path p; START-V(l) and END-V(l) be the two ends of link l; and ROT(l) and LENGTH(l) be the orientation and length of link l. Then

42

$$\text{RELPOS}(v, u) = \text{COOR}(v) - \text{COOR}(u) =$$

$$\sum_{l \in LINKS(p)} \text{COOR (END-V}(l)) - \text{COOR (START-V}(l)) =$$

$$\sum_{l \in LINKS(p)} \text{LENGTH}(l) \cdot < \cos (\text{ROT}(l)), \sin (\text{ROT}(l)) >$$

We can compute any functions of the relative position directly from the vector RELPOS(v, u).

There are two ways to generalize this to paths with fuzzy measurements. The more direct approach is reinterpret the above formula as operating on intervals. For each link l from u to v, define DX (l) = X (COOR (v)) - X (COOR (u)) and DY (l) = Y (COOR (v)) - Y (COOR (u)) and analogously for paths. Compute the ranges of cos (ROT (l)) and sin (ROT (l)); multiply each by the interval LENGTH (l) to get two new intervals, the possible DX and DY of link l; sum these to get the total possible DX and DY of path p; and apply whatever function is desired to these x- and y-intervals.

The problem with this approach is that it usually loses information, sometimes a lot of information. For example, in figure 3-1, u is clearly between 2.0 and 2.5 units from v, since the length of edge($u - v$) is bounded by [2.0, 2.5], though its orientation varies from 0 to $\frac{\pi}{2}$. Calculating the distance using this method proceeds as follows.

$$\text{ROT}(l) = [0.0, \frac{\pi}{2}] \Rightarrow$$

$$\cos (\text{ROT}(l)) = [0.0, 1.0] \text{ and } \sin (\text{ROT}(l)) = [0.0, 1.0]$$

$$\text{LENGTH}(l) = [2.0, 2.5] \Rightarrow$$

$$\text{LENGTH}(l) \cdot \cos (\text{ROT}(l)) = [0.0, 2.5] \text{ and}$$
$$\text{LENGTH}(l) \cdot \sin (\text{ROT}(l)) = [0.0, 2.5] \qquad \Rightarrow$$

$$\text{RELPOS}(v, u) \in [0.0, 2.5] \times [0.0, 2.5] \Rightarrow$$

$$\text{DIST}(u, v) \in [0.0, 2.5\sqrt{2}] = [0.0, 3.5]$$

The conclusion is not false, but it is much too weak. While it is true that the x- and y- coordinates of RELPOS (v, u) can be each separately 0.0, they cannot both be 0.0 at the same time. If one is 0.0, then the other is at least 2.0. Thus the value of 0.0 distance cannot be attained.

The one case where there is no loss of information — an important case — is in measuring the x- or y- coordinate of RELPOS (v, u). In this case, the bounds calculated are precisely those allowed by the path p. (There is also an easy, though unimportant, extension to projections of RELPOS (v, u) onto lines of fixed orientation.)

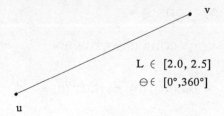

$L \in [2.0, 2.5]$

$\Theta \in [0°, 360°]$

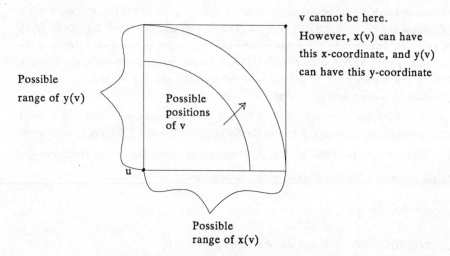

v cannot be here.
However, x(v) can have
this x-coordinate, and y(v)
can have this y-coordinate

Possible
range of y(v)

Possible
positions
of v

Possible
range of x(v)

Figure 3-1: Information Loss through Transformations

The one case where there is no loss of information — an important case — is in measuring the x- or y- coordinate of RELPOS (v, u). In this case, the bounds calculated are precisely those allowed by the path p. (There is also an easy, though unimportant, extension to projections of RELPOS (v, u) onto lines of fixed orientation.)

Instead, we use a Monte Carlo method. Note that, for fixed scalar values $d_k \in$ LENGTH(l_k) and $\theta_k \in$ ROT(l_k), the sum $\sum_k < d_k \cdot \cos(\theta_k), d_k \cdot \sin(\theta_k) >$ gives a value of RELPOS (v, u) which is consistent with the path p. Given any function of relative position such as distance, the value of the function on this sum is a value which it can actually attain on the relative position of the vertices. To get a range of consistent values, we can try a number of different sets of values of d_k and θ_k and evaluate the sum and function on these different values.

For example, to calculate the distance from u to v in figure 3-2, we might perform the computation in table 3-1. These calculations show that the distance from u to v can be as small as 2.48 and as great as 3.19.

44

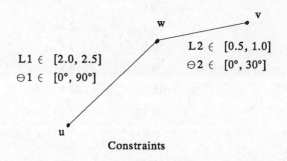

L1 ∈ [2.0, 2.5]
⊖1 ∈ [0°, 90°]

L2 ∈ [0.5, 1.0]
⊖2 ∈ [0°, 30°]

Constraints

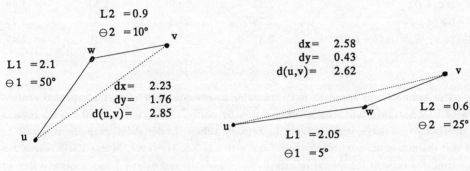

L2 = 0.9
⊖2 = 10°

L1 = 2.1
⊖1 = 50°

dx = 2.23
dy = 1.76
d(u,v) = 2.85

Position 1

dx = 2.58
dy = 0.43
d(u,v) = 2.62

L2 = 0.6
⊖2 = 25°

L1 = 2.05
⊖1 = 5°

Position 2

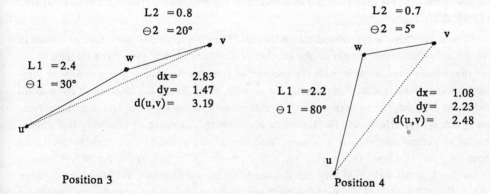

L2 = 0.8
⊖2 = 20°

L1 = 2.4
⊖1 = 30°

dx = 2.83
dy = 1.47
d(u,v) = 3.19

Position 3

L2 = 0.7
⊖2 = 5°

L1 = 2.2
⊖1 = 80°

dx = 1.08
dy = 2.23
d(u,v) = 2.48

Position 4

Calculated Range: $d(u,v) \in [2.48, 3.19]$

Figure 3-2: Monte Carlo Evaluation: Example

Term	P1	P2	P3	P4
$L_1 \in [2.0, 2.5]$	2.1	2.05	2.4	2.2
$\theta_1 \in [0.0, \frac{\pi}{2}]$	50 °	5 °	30 °	80 °
$L_2 \in [0.5, 1.0]$	0.9	0.6	0.8	0.7
$\theta_2 \in [0.0, \frac{\pi}{6}]$	10 °	25 °	20 °	5 °
$DX_1 = L_1 \cdot \cos(\theta_1)$	1.35	2.04	2.07	0.38
$DY_1 = L_1 \cdot \sin(\theta_1)$	1.61	0.18	1.20	2.17
$DX_2 = L_2 \cdot \cos(\theta_2)$	0.88	0.54	0.75	0.70
$DY_2 = L_2 \cdot \sin(\theta_2)$	0.15	0.25	0.27	0.06
$DX = DX_1 + DX_2$	2.23	2.58	2.83	1.08
$DY = DY_1 + DY_2$	1.76	0.43	1.47	2.23
$DIST(u,v) = \sqrt{(DX^2 + DY^2)}$	2.85	2.62	3.19	2.48

Table 3-1: Monte Carlo Computation

The Monte Carlo approach has two major disadvantages. Firstly, the repeated evaluation of trigonometric functions is computationally costly. More seriously, it always returns an overly narrow range; it never finds the extreme values. In the above example, it is easy to see that the maximum possible distance from u to v is 3.5. However, Monte Carlo search can only find this value if it happens to pick $L_1 = 2.5$, $L_2 = 1.0$ and $\theta_1 = \theta_2$. The minimal value of 2.06 is only attained when $L_1 = 2.0$, $L_2 = 0.5$, $\theta_1 = 90°$, and $\theta_2 = 0°$. The Monte Carlo calculation above thus cut off the upper and lower third of the true range, ([2.48, 3.19] as compared to [2.06, 3.5]).

There are three ways around this difficulty. The first is to use more sets of values in Monte Carlo evaluation. However, the number of points needed to get a fixed fraction of the true range rises exponentially with the number of links in the chain. This problem is mitigated because most paths, even among those with many links, are dominated by a small number of long edges. In such a path, all that matters is the values chosen for these dominating edges, so, effectively, the algorithm is searching in a space of relatively few dimensions. The second approach is give some direction to the search; i.e. to turn Monte Carlo search into hill climbing. Our experience with numerical hill climbers (in the SPAM system; see section 6.2) has been that they are slow and fragile; we therefore did not consider using them in the MERCATOR project. The third approach* is that, if fuzz ranges are considered to be probability distributions, then the Monte Carlo searcher will return a confidence interval of some sort, which, in a practical system, may be more valuable than the true possible upper and lower bounds.

Both of the techniques above — interval arithmetic and Monte Carlo evaluation — rely heavily on the path p that is used. Section 3.3 describes the algorithm used to find paths and discusses the adequacy of the paths which it finds. Sometimes evaluation based on paths is neccessarily inadequate; the map constrains the positions of two vertices in ways that are not

---
* Suggested to me by Dana Angluin

reflected in any single path. For example, in figure 3-3, the distance from u to v cannot be greater than 1.0 unit, though neither path $u - w - v$ nor path $u - x - v$ constrains it to be less than 10.0 units. Some of these cases, including this one, can be handled by the "sketching" module, but, in general, the problem is computationally intractable. (See appendix A.5.)

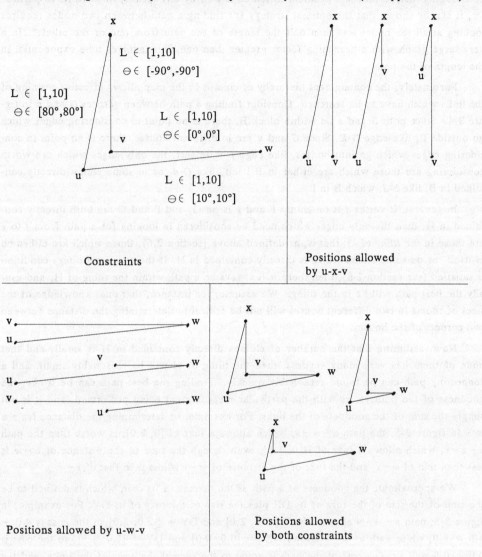

Figure 3-3: Inadequacy of Single Paths

3.3. Path Finding

Finding a path between two vertices in a map is an instance of the problem, common in AI, of finding a path between two nodes in a very large graph. This is not a particularly encouraging fact; to reduce a problem to search is not, by any means, to solve it. In particular, it can be shown that the optimal strategy for finding a path between two nodes requires looking at all the nodes less than half the length of the path from one or the other.* In a very large graph with a branching factor greater than one, this involves time exponential in the length of the path.

Fortunately, the containment hierarchy of clumps in the map allows effective pruning of the links which have to be searched. Consider finding a path between vertices G and p in figure 3-4. Since both G and p lie within block B, there is no point in considering edges which go outside B, like edge G-K. Since G and p are in different houses, there is no point in considering edges which go into houses, like edge p-r. In fact, the only edges which are worth considering are those which are either in B itself, like G-d, or in some clump directly contained in B, like b-d, which is in I.

In general, if vertex f is on clump F and g is on G, and F and G are both directly contained in H, then the only edges which need be considered in looking for a path from f to g are those in the *tiling* of H; that is, as defined above (section 2.6), those which are either on H itself or on some clump which is directly contained in H. If the *connected tilings* condition is satisfied (see section 2-8), then there will always be a path within the tiling of H, and usually the best path will be in the tiling. We assume, for instance, that ones knowledge of the sizes of rooms in two different houses will not be critical in determining the distance between two corners of the houses.

Now, assuming that the number of clumps directly contained in H is small, and that none of them has very many vertices, then the tiling of H will be reasonably small, and a connecting path can be found reasonably quickly. Finding the best path can be tricky; the goodness of the path varies with the particular measurement being performed, and it is not simply the sum of the goodness of the links. For example, in determining the distance from u to v in figure 3-5, the path $u - w - v$, which allows a fuzz of $[0, 2.0]$, is worse than the path $u - x - v$, which allows a fuzz of $[1.0, 1.5]$, even though the fuzz of the distance of $u - w$ is less than that of $u - x$, and the fuzz of the distance of $w - v$ is less than that of $x - v$.

We approximate the goodness of a path as the inverse of its *cost*, which is defined to be the sum of the size of the fuzz of its DX plus the size of the fuzz of its DY. For example, in figure 3-5, path $u - w - v$ allows DX = $[-2.0, 2.0]$ and DY = $[-2.0, 2.0]$ so the cost is $4.0 + 4.0 = 8.0$, while path $u - x - v$ allows DX = $[0.0, 0.0]$ and DY = $[1.0, 1.5]$, so the cost is $0.0 + 0.5 = 0.5$. The cost of the path is equal to the sum of the costs of the links, and the cost of a link is easily computed.

---

* Thanks to Dan Gusfield for discussions on this point.

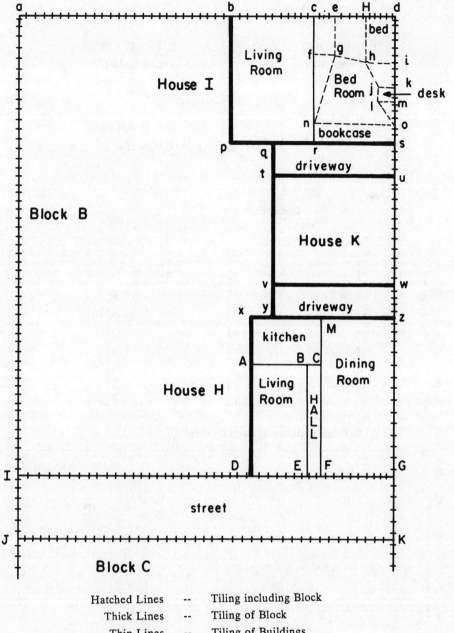

Hatched Lines	--	Tiling including Block
Thick Lines	--	Tiling of Block
Thin Lines	--	Tiling of Buildings
Dotted Lines	--	Tiling of Rooms
Fine dots	--	Internal edges

Figure 3-4: Path Finding: Example

49

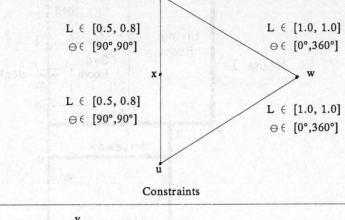

Constraints

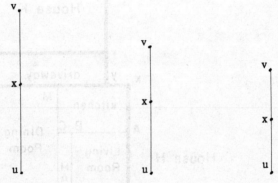

Possible positions allowed by u-x-v

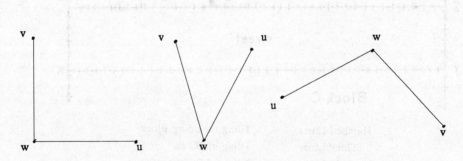

Possible positions allowed by u-w-v

Figure 3-5: Failure of Summing Link Measures

50

We have thus reduced the problem to finding the minimum cost path between two vertices in a graph of moderate size, with no negative costs. This problem is well understood. There is a well known algorithm which finds the shortest path between all pairs of vertices in the graph in time n^3, where n is the number of vertices in the graph, and another algorithm, due to Dijkstra, which finds the shortest path from a fixed vertex v to all other vertices in time n^2. [Aho, Hopcroft, and Ullman, 74]. In our context, it might well be worthwhile to use the first algorithm to determine the shortest paths in each clump once and for all (that is, until the merger changes the tiling), and to keep the results in a table. However, in the interests of saving space, we have not implemented this. Rather, we perform a bidirectional search spreading out from each vertex in turn. Each vertex points to the preceding vertex on the minimum cost path found thus far. The process terminates either when some vertex has been reached from both starting points; or some fixed number of iterations later; or when all outstanding paths have cost greater than the cost of the cheapest path found.

A frequent subtask in retrieval algorithms is, given two sets of vertices, U and V, lying in a single clump tiling, to find a set of good, short paths from some elements of U to some elements of V. (See the paragraphs immediately following, and section 3.5 for examples of use.) The very same algorithm can be used to accomplish this, merely starting from all the points in the two sets simultaneously.

We now address the problem of finding a path between vertices which are not in a single tiling. Consider, for example, the problem of finding a path from B to g in figure 3-4. In this case, we reason as follows. The major component of the relative position of B and g is the relative position of the two houses H and I. Correspondingly, the most important part of the path from B to g will lie in the tiling of the block B. We therefore begin by finding paths P from the outer vertices of H, $\{x, z, D, G\}$, to the outer vertices of I, $\{b, d, p, s\}$. We find paths P = {path (z, w, u, s), path (x, y, v, t, q, p)} using the above algorithm. We define the sets W and X to be the beginning and ending endpoints of P — $\{z, x\}$ and $\{s, p\}$ — respectively.

There are two ways to extend the paths P to extend from B to g. The first approach relies on the fact that the distance from B to any vertex in W is no greater than the diameter of H. Therefore, we can extend any path p in P by adding a link from B to the beginning of p with distance between 0 and HIGH (DIAMETER (H)) and direction between 0 and 2π and a link from the end of p to g with distance between 0 and HIGH (DIAMETER (I)) and direction between 0 and 2π.

The second approach is simply to iterate the path-finding method in smaller tilings. We find paths P_2 = {path (B, C, M, z), path (B, A, x)} from a to W in the tiling of I and splice these onto the paths P to get P = {path (B, C, M, z, w, u, s), path (B, A, x, y, v, t, q, p)} We then connect X to the vertices of the bedroom, $\{c, d, r, s\}$ using P_3 = {path (s)} (the null path of s); splice P_3 onto P to get P = {path (B, C, M, z, w, u, s)}; connect the ends of P, $\{s\}$, to g using paths P_4 = {path (s, r, n, g), path (s, d, H, e, g)}; and splice P_4 onto P, giving P = {path $(B, C, M, z, w, u, s, r, n, g)$, path $(B, C, M, z, w, u, s, d, H, e, g)$}.

The second technique costs more time, but gives more accurate results than the first. I would guess that the best solution is to use paths spanning two or three levels in the clump hierarchy, but to approximate any levels below that.

Either technique requires finding two chains of clumps, each starting with a clump on which the source vertex lies, proceding upward to a direct container, and ending in a common container of the two vertices. Finding these two chains is another graph searching problem. The solution is analogous; start with all the clumps of u and all the clumps of v, and move up containment links until reaching a common container. Since the upward branching factor in the containment hierarchy is small, this is very efficient.

In practice, since the number of links between source vertices tends to be extremely small, we begin the entire path-finding algorithm by a completely undirected search across edges with few (2 or 3) iterations. If the size of tilings is bounded, as suggested above, then the entire algorithm takes time proportional to the number of clump containments traversed and produces a path of proportional length. In a well structured map, this should be logarithmic in the size of the map.

One difficulty remains. If a clump has a region of great accuracy and complexity, then the tiling of the container of the clump will be large, and the search in the tiling will be slow. Section 8.5.1 presents a possible solution to this problem.

3.4. The Sketcher

Path based methods serve to compare the positions of two vertices. This pairwise information is often inadequate in problems involving numerous vertices. For example, we wish to determine whether vertex v lies inside polygon P. It is difficult to solve this problem using interval arithmetic on the relative positions of the polygon vertices with respect to each other and to v; and such a solution would probably work only if the fuzzes involved were quite precise. On the other hand, given coordinates for all the vertices involved, the calculation is easy. If we had an algorithm which computed a random set of consistent coordinates, and these coordinates placed the vertex inside the polygon, then we would conclude that it is at least consistent with the map (or as much of it as we are considering in our calculation) that the vertex is actually inside. If we iterated the algorithm and produced many different consistent sets of coordinates, all of which placed the vertex inside the polygon, then we would conclude that probably the map requires the vertex to be inside the polygon.

The sketcher is an algorithm which produces a random consistent set of coordinates for a given set V of vertices. The coordinates are not necessarily consistent with the map as a whole, but only with the joints and edges which connect two vertices in V. It works strictly on the geometrical level, and only if V is connected by edges and joints.

The sketcher treats joints and edges in exactly the same way, as independent constraints on vertices. This is adequate for most purposes, though it leads to one particular problem, to be discussed at the end of this section. Therefore, to simplify the exposition, I will henceforth write "edges" to mean "joints or edges".

We first consider an easy class of examples: where the edges used form the arcs of a tree. In this case, an acceptable set of coordinates can be found easily, using algorithm 3-1.

For each fuzzy edge parameter, pick an arbitrary value within the fuzz range.

Place an arbitrary vertex at the origin.

Calculate the other vertex positions by propagating out along tree edges.

Algorithm 3-1: Easy Sketcher

It can easily be shown that any such assignment of parameters is internally consistent and leads to a permissible assignment of coordinates. Choosing sets of random values for the parameters gives a random distribution of points. This is a generalization of the method presented above of calculating the relative position of two points using Monte Carlo evaluation on a single path.

Generally, the edges do not form a tree. We can, however, simply extract a tree of edges, and perform the above operation on that tree. We wish to pick the best possible such tree; that is, the tree which minimizes some function of the link costs (sum of link costs, sum of path costs, maximum path fuzz cost, etc.) Depending which function is chosen, either an optimal, or a close to optimal tree can be found reasonably quickly. For example, in figure 3-6 using the tree of marked edges would give reasonable estimates for most different measurements — the distance between two vertices, the angle formed by three, etc.

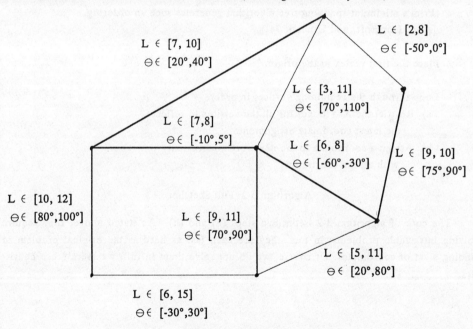

Thick Lines indicate Tree
Figure 3-6: Optimal Tree for Sketcher

Often, however, the graph constrains the vertices in ways which no single tree comes even close to capturing. Figure 3-7 is an example. { $a-b$, $a-d$, $b-c$ } is a minimal cost tree. Algorithm 3-1 might well pick length $a-b$ = 4, length $b-c$ = 7, length $a-d$ = 3. This would force $d-c$ to have length 5.6 and angle 45°, which is well outside the range. Though the cost of the tree path is only three times that of the edge $d-c$, which under some circumstance might be an acceptable factor, the edge constrains the relation much more than the path. Cost is not a very good measure here.

We have adopted the following expedient to get around this problem in some cases. We modify the algorithm to pick the random parameter values sequentially, rather than simultaneously, and we record bounds on vertex positions to constrain the choice of parameter values. We fix one vertex at the origin, and then associate an X-Y box with each vertex, representing the possible range in each dimension of the vertex, given the constraints on the edges and the chosen parameters of the edges. The result is algorithm 3-2.

Find the minimal cost tree.

Order the vertices so that
   i) each vertex after the first is connected to some preceding vertex
        by an edge in the tree; and
   ii) edges of low cost are traversed early.
(Prim's minimum spanning tree algorithm generates such an ordering.
[Aho, Hopcroft, and Ullman, 74])

Place the first vertex at the origin.

Loop through the remaining vertices in order:
   a) Restrict the X-Y boxes for all the vertices to reflect
        the latest coordinate assignment.
   b) Assign a coordinate to the next vertex consistent
        with all the constraints.

Algorithm 3-2: Full Sketcher

The core of algorithm 3-2 is the two steps (a) and (b). As stated above, they require solving intractable problems; in fact, they are each just as hard as the original problem of finding a set of coordinates. Of course, we do not solve them in full, we merely use heuristics.

54

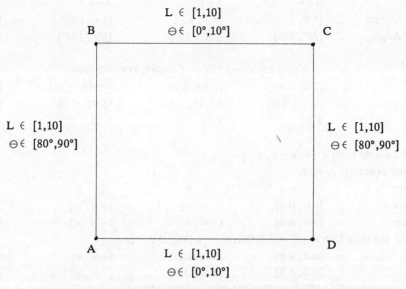

Figure 3-7: Constraints not Expressible in a Tree

The heuristic we use in (a) is to consider only one edge at a time, independently of their interactions. Each edge has certain fuzz ranges of DX and DY which are easily calculated from its length(s) and orientation. (The sketcher calculates them once and for all at the beginning of the process, rather than repeating the calculation with each iteration). If an edge E goes from vertex u to vertex v then

$$X (COOR (v)) = DX (E) + X (COOR (u));$$
$$Y (COOR (v)) = DY (E) + Y (COOR (u)).$$

Equation 1

We can use these equations, applied to intervals, either to tighten the fuzz range of COOR (v), given a new fuzz range for COOR (u), or vice versa.

The heuristic is executed as follows. After we assign a coordinate to a vertex, we calculate new fuzz ranges for all the connecting vertices using the above equation. If any of these are changed, we calculate new ranges for all the vertices connecting to it. We iterate until quiescent. This algorithm is basically the Waltz algorithm for finding a consistent labelling, using intervals rather than discrete disjunctions. (See [Waltz, 75], [Davis, 85].) It can be shown that this procedure always terminates, since the equations used have only coefficients 1 and -1. Table 3-2 shows the progress of this step after a has been assigned to the origin, in Figure 3-8.

Edge	$a-b$	$b-c$	$d-c$	$a-d$
L = Length	[1.0, 5.0]	[4.0, 9.0]	[4.0, 9.0]	[1.0, 5.0]
θ = Angle	[80°, 90°]	[-10°, 10°]	[80°, 100°]	[0°, 10°]

Apply equations $DX = L\cos(\theta)$, $DY = L\sin(\theta)$.

	$a-b$	$b-c$	$d-c$	$a-d$
DX	[0.0, 0.87]	[3.93, 9.0]	[-1.56, 1.56]	[0.93, 5.0]
DY	[0.93, 5.0]	[-1.56, 1.56]	[3.93, 9.0]	[0.0, 0.87]
Cost	4.94	9.19	9.19	4.94

Minimal cost tree: $a-b$, $a-d$, $d-c$
Vertex ordering: a, b, d, c.

Vertex	a	b	c	d
X Box	[0.0, 0.0]	$[-\infty, \infty]$	$[-\infty, \infty]$	$[-\infty, \infty]$
Y Box	[0.0, 0.0]	$[-\infty, \infty]$	$[-\infty, \infty]$	$[-\infty, \infty]$

Apply equation $COOR(b) = COOR(a) + <DX, DY>$ $(a-b)$

	[0.0, 0.0]	[0.0, 0.87]	$[-\infty, \infty]$	$[-\infty, \infty]$
	[0.0, 0.0]	[0.93, 5.0]	$[-\infty, \infty]$	$[-\infty, \infty]$

Apply equation $COOR(d) = COOR(a) + <DX, DY>$ $(a-d)$

	[0.0, 0.0]	[0.0, 0.87]	$[-\infty, \infty]$	[0.93, 5.0]
	[0.0, 0.0]	[0.93, 5.0]	$[-\infty, \infty]$	[0.0, 0.87]

Apply equation $COOR(c) = COOR(b) + <DX, DY>$ $(b-c)$

	[0.0, 0.0]	[0.0, 0.87]	[3.93, 9.87]	[0.93, 5.0]
	[0.0, 0.0]	[0.93, 5.0]	[-0.63, 6.56]	[0.0, 0.87]

Apply equation $COOR(c) = COOR(d) + <DX, DY>$ $(d-c)$

	[0.0, 0.0]	[0.0, 0.87]	[3.93, 6.56]	[0.93, 5.0]
	[0.0, 0.0]	[0.93, 5.0]	[3.93, 6.56]	[0.0, 0.87]

Apply equation $COOR(b) = COOR(c) - <DX, DY>$ $(b-c)$

	[0.0, 0.0]	[0.0, 0.87]	[3.93, 6.56]	[0.93, 5.0]
	[0.0, 0.0]	[1.37, 5.0]	[3.93, 6.56]	[0.0, 0.87]

Apply equation $COOR(d) = COOR(c) - <DX, DY>$ $(d-c)$

	[0.0, 0.0]	[0.0, 0.87]	[3.93, 6.56]	[1.37, 5.0]
	[0.0, 0.0]	[1.37, 5.0]	[3.93, 6.56]	[0.0, 0.87]

Quiescent

Table 3-2: X-Y Box Assignments

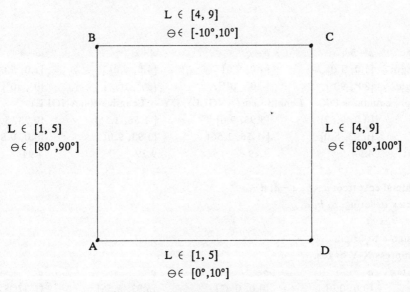

L ∈ [4, 9]
Θ∈ [-10°,10°]

L ∈ [1, 5]
Θ∈ [80°,90°]

L ∈ [4, 9]
Θ∈ [80°,100°]

L ∈ [1, 5]
Θ∈ [0°,10°]

Figure 3-8: Sketcher: Example

Sometimes it happens that one of the above equations has no solution, given the current X-Y ranges. This can happen either because the map is inconsistent, or, more commonly, because coordinates have been misassigned. In this case, we return all the non-fixed X-Y fuzzes involved to what they were before the current iteration, and we do not propagate.

Step (b), in which vertex coordinates are assigned is conceptually simple, though computationally recalcitrant. There are three types of constraints on the vertex coordinates: the X-Y box of the coordinate, edges which connect the vertex to fixed vertices, and edges which connect the vertex to vertices within X-Y boxes. In figure 3-8, for example, after a has been assigned to the origin, vertex b is constrained by the X-Y box ([0.0, 0.87], [1.37, 5.0]); it is constrained to be within distance [1.0, 5.0] and direction [80°, 90°] of vertex a, which is in the origin, and it is constrained to be within distance [4.0, 9.0] and direction [170°, 190°] of vertex c which is in the box ([3.93, 6.56], [3.93, 6.56]). (In this case, the last constraint is superfluous given the first, but this is not generally true.) The object is to find a point satisfying all these constraints, as well as may be.

The approach we use to find this satisfying point uses Monte Carlo methods. First, we pick out the tightest of these constraints on the vertex. Then we pick random values of the parameters of this tight constraint, and evaluate how well the other constraints are satisfied.* If we find a value which satisfies all the other constraints, we stop; otherwise, after a fixed number of iterations, we return the best answer found thus far. Since we are searching in a space of only two dimensions, it might well be worth while to use a hill climber here, but we have not implemented it.

---

* Determining whether a given coordinate satisfies a given constraint can be difficult. In particular, I do not have a closed form solution if the constraint is a joint. The program uses an approximation.

Table 3-3 shows one complete run of the sketching algorithm on figure 3-8.

Edge	$a - b$	$b - c$	$d - c$	$a - d$
Length	[1.0, 5.0]	[4.0, 9.0]	[4.0, 9.0]	[1.0, 5.0]
Angle	[80°, 90°],	[-10°, 10°],	[80°, 100°]	[0°, 10°]

Apply equations DX = Length · cos(ANGLE), DY = Length · sin(ANGLE).

DX	[0.0, 0.87]	[3.93, 9.0]	[-1.56, 1.56]	[0.93, 5.0]
DY	[0.93, 5.0]	[-1.56, 1.56]	[3.93, 9.0]	[0.0, 0.87]
Cost	4.94	9.19	9.19	4.94

Minimal cost tree: $a - b$, $a - d$, $d - c$
Vertex ordering: a, b, d, c.

Assign a to origin
Compress X-Y boxes.

Vertex	a	b	c	d
	[0.0, 0.0]	[0.0, 0.87]	[3.93, 6.56]	[1.37, 5.0]
	[0.0, 0.0]	[1.37, 5.0]	[3.93, 6.56]	[0.0, 0.87]

Strongest constraint on b are bounds on $a - b$.
Pick length 4.12 and orientation 87° for $a - b$, satisfying other constraints.
Find coordinates (0.21, 4.12) for b.
Compress X-Y boxes.

	[0.0, 0.0]	[0.21, 0.21]	[4.14, 6.56]	[2.58, 5.0]
	[0.0, 0.0]	[4.12, 4.12]	[3.93, 5.68]	[0.0, 0.87]

Strongest constraint on d are bounds on $a - d$.
Pick length 3.51 and orientation 3° for $a - d$, satisfying other constraints.
Find coordinates (3.50, 0.18) for d.
Compress X-Y boxes.

	[0.0, 0.0]	[0.21, 0.21]	[4.14, 5.06]	[3.50, 3.50]
	[0.0, 0.0]	[4.12, 4.12]	[4.21, 5.68]	[0.18, 0.18]

Strongest constraint on c is the X-Y box.
Pick coordinates (4.34, 5.05) for c from X-Y box, satisfying other constraints.

Final solution: a = (0.0, 0.0), b = (0.21, 4.12), c = (4.34, 5.05), d = (3.05, 0.18)

Table 3-3: Trace of Sketching Algorithm

At each step where coordinates have to be found, it will take, on average, not more than two or three tries to find coordinates that satisfy all the constraints. By contrast, it would require on average almost 100 tries of algorithm 3-1 to find values which satisfy all the constraints. However, in algorithm 3-2 there is the danger of choosing an impossible value somewhere near the beginning, which is consistent with the local constraints as far as may be calculated, but not with the map as a whole. Therefore, this algorithm should ideally incorporate a method for testing when it is off to a bad start, and either correcting itself or restarting from scratch. I do not know how this can be done.

There is a large class of graphs like figure 3-8 in which this revised algorithm gives good results. Algorithm 3-2 is more general than algorithm 3-1; it always works at least as well. There are, however, many graphs in which it does not work. It is very sensitive to angle. If figure 3-8 is rotated by 45 degrees (figure 3-9), the X-Y boxes do not carry much information, and hence do not constrain search much. Figure 3-10 is more difficult yet. Here the geometry constrains the direction $a - b$ to be 0 degrees, but this can only be determined through a complex geometrical argument, or a general method for solving quadratic inequalities.

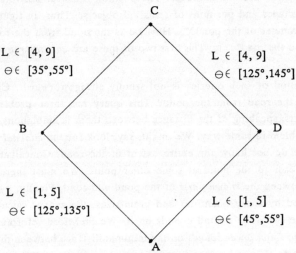

Figure 3-9: Orientation Dependence of Sketcher

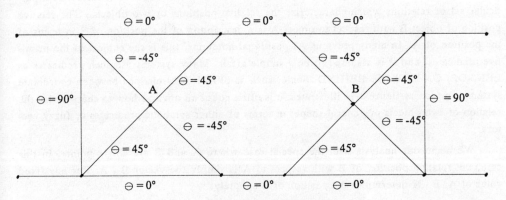

All lengths variable from 0 to ∞.

Difficult Sketcher Example

This theory handles joints inadequately. The parallel angle of the joint is treated as independent of the angle of its edge; they are simply two different parameters. Thus, the final solution may end up assigning them different values, and thus leaving the tail of the joint further from the edge than it ought to be. The problem is that constraining the two to be collinear causes each of the involved vertices (the two ends of the edge and the tail of the joint) to be dependent on the coordinates of the other two through the combination of joint and edge in a complicated way. Not only that, if there were more than one joint involving the same edge, the coordinates of any one vertex would be dependent on the coordinates of any other two. We would have to replace equation 1 by something much more complicated, and almost certainly the algorithm to compute X-Y boxes would cease to converge.

3.5. Relative Position

We can now develop the position retriever. The position retriever answers a class of problems involving the shapes and positions of specified objects. Thus, in figure 2-4, we might ask "What is the diameter of the pond?", "How far is the pond from the road", "Is the rock between the tree and the road", etc. The first two of these are *quantity retrievals*; the last is a *fact verification*

The interpretation of such queries is not wholly straightforward. Consider a typical query: How far is the road from the pond? This query has three problems. Firstly, the objects are not points: speaking of the distance between them is ambiguous. We must therefore specify the problem in some way. We might, say, look for the *minimal* distance between them. Secondly, we do not know the entire extent of the road. Conceivably, it could curl round and come closer to the pond at some other point. We must therefore ask for the minimal distance between the *known parts* of the pond and road. Finally, owing to imprecise knowledge expressed by fuzzy quantities and grain-sizes, we cannot calculate this distance exactly; the most we can do is to find bounds on it. We therefore reformulate the problem once more: *Find upper* and *lower bounds* on the minimal distance between the known parts of the pond and the road.

We illustrate the workings of the position retriever by showing how it calculates a particular set of relations which characterize the relative positions of two objects. The relative position of object B with respect to object A is a description of the position of B in terms of the position of A. In many previous AI positional notations, this is the subject of the primitive predicates, and it is assumed to be a simple affair. Many systems use such predicates as LEFT-OF, ON-TOP-OF, BEHIND. Some, such as SPAM, use relations between coordinate systems. In fact, as figure 3-11 illustrates, it is often not at all obvious how to characterize the relation of two objects of general shape, in terms of either symbolic predicates or fuzzy vectors.

We begin our analysis with the special case where A and B are single points. In this case, the relative position of B with respect to A is simply the vector B - A. For any fixed value of A, B - A determines the position of B uniquely.

We generalize this to extended objects A and B as directly as possible. The relative position of B with respect to A is defined as $B - A = \{ (b - a) \mid b \in B \land a \in A \}$. Now, it is not true that A and B - A uniquely determine B. However, if B is already determined up to translation — that is, the shape and orientation of B are determined — then A and B - A do determine the position of B. This suffices for our purposes.

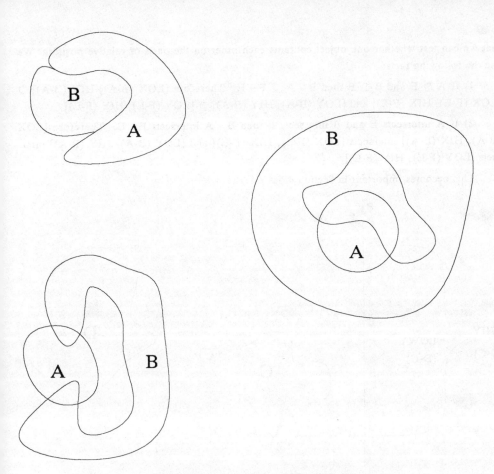

Characterize the position of B relative to A

Figure 3-11: Difficult to Characterize Relative Position

Moreover, we do not need the whole shape description of B - A, which can be complicated. Any two parameters which will distinguish translations of B - A will suffice: for example, the coordinates of the center of mass of B - A, or the two coordinates of the point in B -
A with minimal X - coordinate, or the angles of the lines through the origin tangent to B - A.
None of these, as it happens, are very good measures. The center of mass is very hard to calculate. The y-coordinate of the point with minimal x-coordinate is unstable with respect to
small variations in A and B, so if there is any fuzz or grain-size, then the y-coordinate is
unknown. The two tangent lines are undefined if B - A contains the origin.

Our solution actually involves four quantities: the lowest and highest x- and y-
coordinates of B - A, written LOWX (B-A), HIX (B-A), LOWY (B-A), and HIY (B-A).
Note that LOWX (B-A) = LOWX (B) - HIX (A), HIX (B-A) = HIX (B) - LOWX (A),
LOWY (B-A) = LOWY (B) - HIY (A), and HIY (B-A) = HIY (B) - LOWY (A). (See figure 3-12.) These are, as we shall see, reasonably easy to calculate; they are stable with
respect to variation in A and B; and they are always defined. Two of these quantities would
suffice to test whether two pairs of objects have identical relative position. We use four so

61

that we can test whether one object contains each other on the basis of relative position. We use the following facts:

1) If A $\supseteq$ E and B $\supseteq$ F then B - A $\supseteq$ F - E. Therefore [LOX (B-A), HIX (B-A)] $\supseteq$ [LOX (F-E), HIX (F-E)] and [LOY (B-A), HIY (B-A)] $\supseteq$ [LOY (F-E), HIY (F-E)].

2) If A intersects E and B intersects F then B - A intersects F - E. Therefore [LOX (B-A), HIX (B-A)] intersects [LOX (F-E), HIX (F-E)] and [LOY (B-A), HIY (B-A)] intersects [LOY (F-E), HIY (F-E)].

This becomes important in Section 4.5.

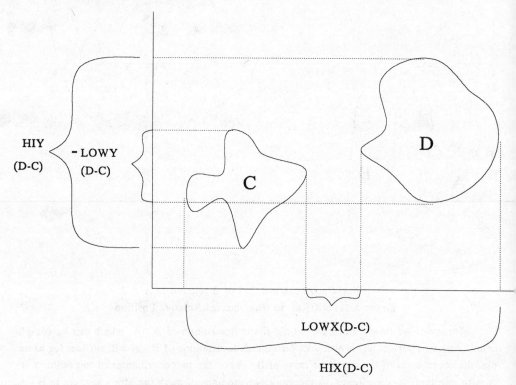

Figure 3-12: Useful Definition of Relative Position

We cannot get exact values of the quantities LOWX, HIX, LOY, HIY from a map; we can only get fuzz ranges for them. Moreover, if one or both of the clumps is incomplete, then we cannot calculate fuzz ranges for the quantities evaluated on the entire objects, but only on that part of the object covered by the clump. In short, for two clumps C and D, we are looking for a quadruple of fuzzes:

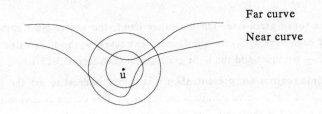

Far curve
Near curve

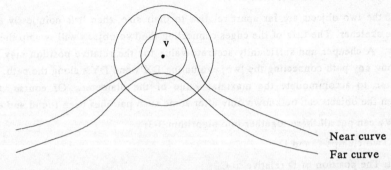

Near curve
Far curve

u and *v* are two extreme vertices of two regions. Their tight and loose grain-sizes are shown by the dotted circles around them. The minimum value of LOWY is attained by the two near curves whose distance at the nearest point is the distance from *u* to *v* minus the sum of the two loose grain-sizes. The maximum value of LOWY is attained by the two far curves, whose distance at the nearest point is the distance from *u* to *v*, plus the sum of the two tight grain-sizes.

Figure 3-13: Accommodating Grain-Size in Relative Position

rel-pos (C,D) = < LX (C,D), HX (C,D), LY (C,D), HY (C,D) > such that
LOWX (COVER (C), COVER (D)) ∈ LX (C,D),
HIX (COVER (C), COVER (D)) ∈ HX (C,D),
LOWY (COVER (C), COVER (D)) ∈ LY (C,D), and
HIY (COVER (C), COVER (D)) ∈ HY (C,D).

and such that each of the fuzz ranges is minimal, given the information.

We begin with the case where C and D have only one region each, R and S respectively. We note that, for any fixed value of COOR, the maximal x-coordinate of R is attained at a vertex of R; and likewise for all the other extreme coordinates of R and S. Therefore LOWX (COOR (R), COOR (S)) = COOR (*s*) - COOR (*r*) for some vertices *s* and *r* of S and R. We can use the sketcher to determine which are the extreme vertices, and the vertex retriever to calculate COOR (*s*) - COOR (*r*).

The grain-sizes of the vertices must of course be taken into account. The object may stretch out beyond each vertex by the "loose" grain-size of the vertex in any direction. So for the "outer" extremes — the low values of LX, LY and the high values of HX, HY — we must add the loose grain-size. On the other hand, the object must come within the "tight" grain-size of each vertex. So for the "inner" extremes — the high value of LX and the low value of HX — we must add the tight grain-sizes. (See figure 3-13.)

If multiple regions are present, then it is in our interest to use the most precise region, as long as it does not involve pointless complexity. If a vertex is covered by the boundary of another region, and if the grain-size of all the covering vertices are smaller than the grain-size of the starting vertex, then it can be ignored. The PCO determines which are the covering vertices. (Note that here we require neither the *full regions* nor the *well-ordered regions* normalcy conditions. See section 2.8.)

If the two objects are far apart relative to their size, then it is pointlessly expensive to call the sketcher. The fuzz of the edges connecting the two objects will swamp the sizes of the objects. A cheaper and sufficiently accurate value for the relative position may be obtained by taking any path connecting the two, evaluating DX's and DY's along the path, and stretching these to accommodate the maximal value of the diameter. Of course, the distance between the objects can be known only after some such path has been found and evaluated.

We can put all these together into algorithm 3-3:

Input: Two clumps C and D

Output: The position of D relative to C.

Find a path between arbitrary vertices *c* and *d* of C and D.

Calculate the distance from *c* to *d*.

If the distance from *c* to *d* is much greater than the sizes of C and D,

> then calculate the relative positions of C and D using the path (*c*, *d*) correcting for the diameters of C and D

> else begin

>> Determine the regions of C and D which are worth using;

>>> Determine which boundary vertices are not covered by more accurate vertices from other regions

>>> Calculate coordinates for each chosen boundary vertex using the sketcher.

>>> Find the extreme vertices. Pair off opposite extremes.

>>> Connect opposite vertices by edge paths. Evaluate coordinate difference. Add appropriate grain-sizes.

> end.

Algorithm 3-3: Finding Relative Position

Table 3-4 shows the workings of the complex branch of algorithm 3-3 to find the relative positions of the pond and the road in figure 2-4. Table 3-5 shows the workings of the easy branch in calculating the relative positions of the two clumps C and D in figure 3-14.

64

1) Pick random vertices a from Road, m from Pond

2) Find path, path (a, d, h, m)

3) Evaluate DIST $(a, m) \in [\ 2.96, 4.04\ ]$

4) Compare to diameters of clumps. Since DIAM (Road) $\in [4.6, 5.1]$ and DIAM (Pond) $\in$ [1.7, 1.9], this distance is not large compared to the diameters.

5) Sketch the points of each clump separately.

$a = (0.0, 0.0)$, $b = (2.0, -0.5)$, $c = (4.5, -1.5)$, $d = (.02, 0.6)$, $e = (2.3, 0.25)$, $f = (4.8, -0.9)$

$h = (0.0, 0.0)$, $i = (1.62, -0.25)$, $j = (1.25, 0.62)$, $k = (2.2, 1.55)$, $l = (0.3, 1.8)$, $m = (0.5, 0.75)$

6) Find the extreme pairs of vertices

LOWX: (f, h); HIX: (a, k); LOY: (d, i); HIY: (c, l)

7) Find the values of displacements

DX $(f, h) \in (-3.4, -2.7)$; DX $(a, k) \in (3.1, 4.6)$; DY (d, i) $(0.8, 1.3)$; DX $(c, l) \in (4.4, 5.5)$;

8) Correct for grain-sizes:

Let LG (x) be the loose grain-size and TG (x) the tight grain-size

LX $=$ DX $(f, h) + (- (LG (f) + LG (h)), (TG (f) + TG (h)))$
$= (-3.4, -2.7) + (- (0.2 + 0.4), (0.2 + 0.3)) = (-4.0, -2.2)$

HX $=$ DX $(a, k) + (- (TG (a) + TG (k)), (LG (a) + LG (k)))$
$= (3.1, 4.6) + (- (0.1 + 0.5), (0.1 + 0.5)) = (2.5, 5.2)$

LY $=$ DY $(d, i) + (- (LG (d) + LG (i)), (TG (d) + TG (i)))$
$= (0.8, 1.3) + (- (0.2 + 0.4), (0.2 + 0.3)) = (0.2, 2.0)$

HY $=$ DY $(c, l) + (- (TG (c) + TG (l)), (LG (c) + LG (l)))$
$= (4.4, 5.5) + (- (0.3 + 0.2), (0.3 + 0.5)) = (3.9, 5.3)$

Answer: $< (-4.0, -2.2), (2.5, 5.2), (0.2, 2.0), (3.9, 5.3) >$

Table 3-4: Calculation of Relative Position

Choose *u* and *v* from C and D.

Path *p* connects *u* to *v*.

DX (*p*) ∈ [10.0, 12.0]; DY (*p*) ∈ [-9.0, -6.0]

DIAM (C) ∈ [1.5, 2.0]

DIAM (D) ∈ [0.6, 1.0]

LX (C,D) ∈ [10.0 - (2.0 + 1.0), 12.0] = [7.0, 12.0]

HX (C,D) ∈ [10.0, 12.0 + 2.0 + 1.0] = [10.0, 15.0]

LY (C,D) ∈ [-9.0 - (2.0 + 1.0), -6.0] = [-12.0, -6.0]

HY (C,D) ∈ [-9.0, -6.0 + 2.0 + 1.0] = [-9.0, -3.0]

Table 3-5: Easy Calculation of Relative Position

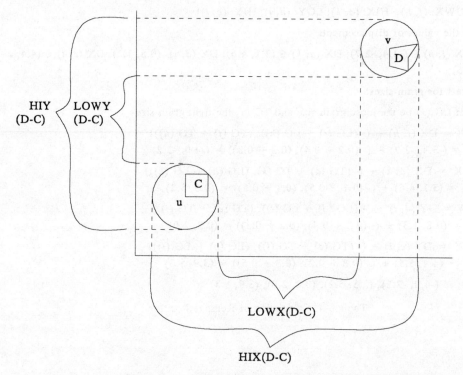

Figure 3-14: Easy Calculation of Relative Position

3.6. Object Retrieval

The second major retrieval task is to enumerate all the important objects in an area. The specific form of the query is "Given a *center clump*, a *minimal diameter*, and a *target distance*, enumerate all the clumps larger than the minimal diameter within the target distance of the center clump." For example, in figure 3-15 we might ask for all clumps larger than 1 foot within 30 feet of the refrigerator.

66

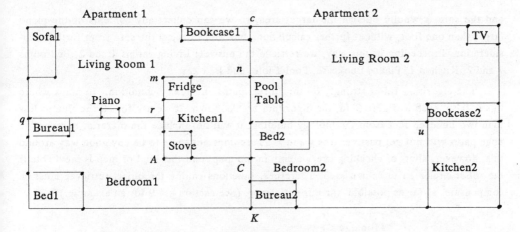

Figure 3-15: Object Retrieval: Example

We use a simple algorithm. Starting with the center clump, move up clump containments until reaching a container whose size is the same order of magnitude as the target distance. Then move out in all directions along edges in the tiling of this clump and parallel clumps, exploring out each path until the distance of the vertices reached is definitely greater than the target distance. Identify all clumps containing the marked vertices. All their containers are retrieved. Move down containment links, gathering clumps until reaching clumps smaller than the target size. Divide the retrieved clumps into two classes: those wholly within the target distance, and those partially within it. After moving down each containment link from a clump partially within the target distance, test whether the contained clump is wholly in the target area, partially within it, or not at all within it. If the last, reject it.

The distance of marked vertices is calculated by keeping a running tally of DX and DY displacement from the center as we explore out edges. The distance between clumps is estimated from their relative positions. Clumps and vertices are ruled out as too distant only if they are definitely too distant. Similarly, a clump is considered to be wholly within the target area unless it is definitely partially outside the target area.

For example, to answer the query "Enumerate all clumps larger than 1 foot within 30 feet of the refrigerator" on figure 3-15, we first move up from the refrigerator to the kitchen. Since the dimensions of kitchen are about ten by ten, we do not explore any higher up. Instead, we explore out the tiling of the two apartments, starting at vertices m, n, A and C, and traversing edges $A - r$, $r - q$, $n - c$, $n - s$, $s - u$, $C - K$. We stop because vertices q, c, u, and K are more than 30 feet from the refrigerator. We then note than vertices m, n, A, C, s, and r are contained in the two living rooms, the two bedrooms, and kitchen 1. The kitchen is wholly within the target area, the others are partially within it. Moving up clump containments, we retrieve the building, the block, the city, and all other significant containers. Moving down clump containment links from the kitchen, we retrieve the refrigerator and the stove. We do not proceed down from the refrigerator to the tomatoes, or from the stove to the burners, because these are too small. Moving down from living room 1, we note that the piano is wholly within the target distance, the bookcase is partially within the target distance, and the sofa is wholly outside the target area, so we can collect any contents of the piano larger than one foot, without further calculation, and we can reject the sofa from further consideration. Proceeding in this way, we retrieve the answer: Living rooms 1 and 2, Bedrooms 1 and 2, Kitchen 1, Piano, Bookcase, Pool Table, and Bed 2.

The algorithm relies strongly on the "direct paths" normalcy condition. In maps where this is false, such as figure 3-16, the algorithm breaks down. If we ask for all the clumps less than two hundred feet from the biology building, it will not include the pizzaria, because the edge paths will not get past vertices y and z. There does not seem to be any good way around this, however, short of checking every clump in the map; and this kind of map is inevitable if the robot circles an unknown area. Therefore, functions calling the object retriever must be compensate, as far as possible, for this deficiency. (See section 8.4.9 for an example.)

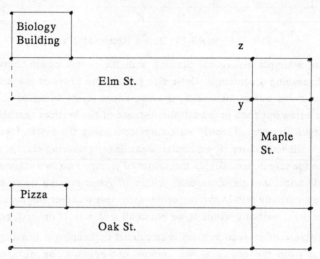

Figure 3-16: Hard Example for Object Retriever

This algorithm could easily be modified to return all clumps with a specified position relative to a center clump by going to the appropriate level of the clump hierarchy and moving out on edges in the correct direction(s). It could also be modified into a spiral search algorithm, which would return a stream of objects roughly in order of distance, by having it report on clumps as it passes them in an outward search of edges. (See [McDermott, 81] for a detailed discussion of how this is done in a similar data structure.) Neither modification has been implemented.

4 Matching

4.1. Introduction

MERCATOR is primarily a study of how a cognitive map may be learned through vision. In our model, the robot is presented with a sequence of scene descriptions, each of which includes himself, and with rough descriptions of his motions between them. He takes each successive scene description and *assimilates* it into his cognitive map. This process of assimilation is broken into two parts. Firstly, he *matches* the two maps together to determine how they relate: which of the objects seen are already known, and which are new; which parts of seen objects correspond to which parts of known objects; where vertices and edges in the seen map lie with respect to vertices and edges in the known map. Secondly, the scene description is merged into the cognitive map. New objects in the seen map, new parts of objects, and more precise information about known objects, including the position of the robot himself, are added to the cognitive map from the scene description. This chapter will deal with matching; the next will deal with merging.

Matching uses object properties and object relations to relate the scene description to the cognitive map. It is analogous to resolving anaphoric reference in natural language understanding; the object of the new reference must be identified with some object explicitly or implicitly referred to in the previous text. Like anaphora resolution, it must precede adding the new information into the knowledge base so that we can know where to attach the new information. A matching of MERCATOR maps is not a simple isomorphism. On the contrary, as figures 4-1 and 4-2 illustrate, two MERCATOR maps of the same area may look quite different. They may show different objects; MAP-K shows BOOK-K, MAP-S does not. They may use different polygonal approximations; compare CHAIR-K1 with CHAIR-S1. They may show different parts of the same object; compare WALL-K with WALL-S. They may show objects in slightly different relations. In MAP-K, CHAIR-K1 is shown next to TABLE-K2; more accurately, MAP-S shows them slightly separated. The matcher must see past these surface differences to the underlying identity.

The following real identities are available to the MERCATOR matcher:

- The robot is the same in the two maps.
- Object properties do not change.
- Object shapes do not change.
- Relative positions of objects do not change.

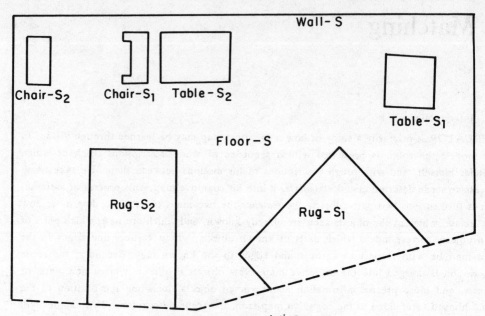

Figure 4-1: Scene Description

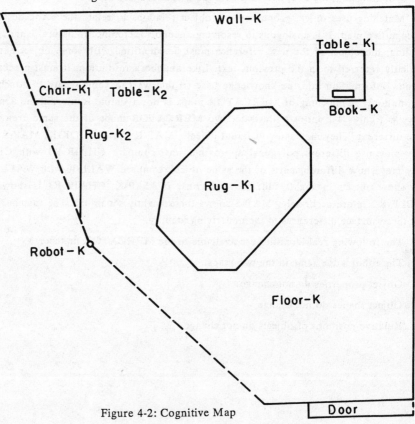

Figure 4-2: Cognitive Map

MERCATOR uses all of these. Our major interest is the use of relative position, and the integration of relative position with matching of shape. Our treatment of matching properties and shapes is adequate to our representation, but many additional subtleties would enter into a system which did actual vision recognition.

The matcher tries to match as much as possible. It looks for the set of correspondences which matches as many clumps as possible while being consistent. This is in accordance with Occam's razor; the more objects in the scene description correspond to known objects, the fewer objects there must be in the world. On these bases, consistency and number of matches, it resolves ambiguities. For example, in figure 4-3, the tree can match either tree, the hydrant can match either hydrant. From the geometrical constraints, we can reduce the possible sets of matches to four:

1. HYDRANT-S <=> HYDRANT-K1 and TREE-S <=> TREE-K1;

2. HYDRANT-S <=> HYDRANT-K2;

3. TREE-S <=> TREE-K2;

4. no matches at all.

The match HYDRANT-S <=> HYDRANT-K2 is geometrically inconsistent with the match TREE-S <=> TREE-K2, because TREE-S and HYDRANT-S are known to be close together, while TREE-K2 and HYDRANT-K2 are known to be far apart. Using the criterion of matching as much as possible, we arrive at the matches HYDRANT-S <=> HYDRANT-K1 and TREE-S <=> TREE-K1 as the best possible pair.

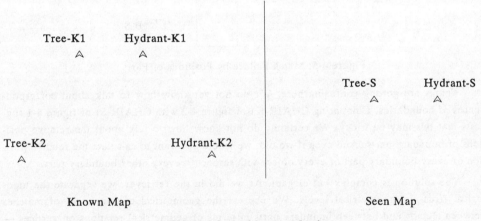

Figure 4-3: Ambiguous Match

4.2. Correspondences

It is therefore important to test a set of matches for consistency. What does a proof of consistency entail? Obviously the properties of the two clumps must correspond. Their boundary descriptions must correspond. For example, in figure 4-4, we can rule out the match between BUILDING-S and BUILDING-K because they are demonstrably different shapes. Also, as figure 4-3 illustrates, given two matches, the relative positions of the two objects in the two maps must correspond. Moreover, corresponding boundary parts must have the same relative position. For example, in figure 4-5, it is inconsistent that both A-S matches A-K and that B-S matches B-K, because the position of A-S with respect to the horizontal edge of B-S differs from the position of A-K with respect to the horizontal edge of B-K.

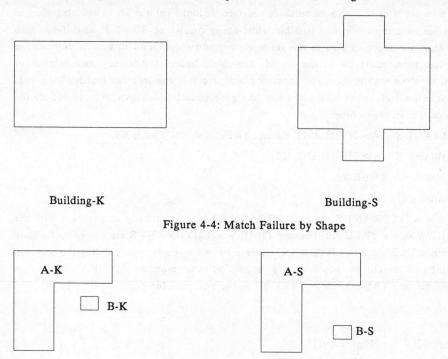

Building-K   Building-S

Figure 4-4: Match Failure by Shape

Figure 4-5: Match Failure by Positions of Parts

Things are getting confusing here. We do not yet know how to talk about correspondences of boundaries. Comparing CHAIR-K1 of figure 4-2 with CHAIR-S1 of figure 4-1 suggests that this may be tricky. We certainly do not know how to talk about the relative positions of boundary parts. And even if we did, we would not want to calculate the relative position of every boundary part of every object with respect to every other boundary part.

The solution is complex but elegant. As we did in the retriever, we separate the topological from the geometrical levels. We express the geometrical consequences of matches between clumps and between boundary parts in terms of geometrical relations on vertices — joints, to be specific. We then test for consistency of the joints, and thus determine geometrical consistency of the matches. We reduce combinatorial explosion by comparing only joints relating closely connected vertices.

We are thus led to the following four types of data structure, collectively called *correspondences*. A *clump match* "cl-match (A, B)", where A is a seen clump and B is a known clump, asserts that A represents the same object as B. An *edge match* relates a seen boundary edge to a known boundary edge. A *chain match*, which is simply a set of edge matches, relates two chains of boundary edges. A *joint*, as we have seen, relates the position of vertex to that of an edge. The joints used in the matcher relate the position of a vertex in one map to an edge in the other.

By a fortunate coincidence, these correspondences also carry the information needed to run the merger. They are therefore the output of the matcher as well as its internal data structures.

Clump matches and joints are quite straightforward. The former are statements of identity; the latter are geometrical relations. Edge matches are trickier. As we have remarked above as regards the match of CHAIR-K1 with CHAIR-S1, the relation between boundary edges is somewhat subtle. It is certainly not a one-to-one correspondence. Rather, we use an assymetric relation, "e matches into f", also written "edge-match (e, f)" or "$e => f$". Such a matching asserts, more or less, that the boundaries corresponding to e are mostly contained within the boundaries corresponding to f. (See figure 4-6.) e is called the "source" edge; f is called the "image" edge. We will expand on this cryptic definition in section 4.6.

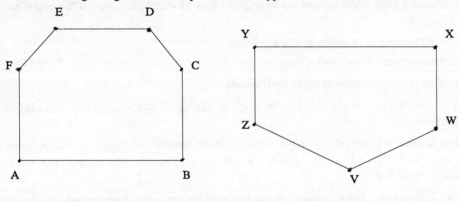

Known Region   Seen Region

Edge matches: $z - v \Rightarrow A - B$, $v - w \Rightarrow A - B$, $w - x \Rightarrow B - C$,
$B - C \Rightarrow w - x$, $C - D \Rightarrow x - y$, $D - E \Rightarrow x - y$,
$E - F \Rightarrow x - y$, $F - A \Rightarrow y - a$, $y - a \Rightarrow F - A$

Figure 4-6: Edge Matches

The correspondences have definite logical relations. If one or more correspondences imply one or more others, we say that the former *support* the latter. For example, a chain match, being merely a conjunction of edge matches, supports each of its conjuncts. (This does not mean that the edge matches are created from the chain match. By "implication" here, I refer to the logical relation that if the chain match is true, the edge matches are true, not to an action of inferring the edge matches from the chain match.) An edge match, as we shall see, implies that the vertices of the source edge are not far from the image edge. We express this constraint as a pair of joints and say that the edge match supports the joints. Finally we will find that a pair of joints often imply new joints; again, we say that the former support the latter.

It is also the case that a chain match will imply the corresponding clump match, barring a monstrous coincidence. The converse is not the case. If a clump match is true then the boundaries of the two clumps must correspond in some way, and there will be a chain match which expresses this correspondence. However, there will often be many possible chain matches, and it will be difficult to determine which is correct at an early stage of processing. We therefore think of the clump match as implying the disjunction of all the candidate chain matches. We say that the clump match *suggests* the chain match. We also say that the clump match suggests each edge match in the chain match.

4.3. The Algorithm

The matching algorithm is as follows:

1. Restrict the known map to objects possibly within the range of vision.

2. Propose clump matches between all pairs of clumps which are compatible in properties and position with respect to the robot.

3. Propose edge matches between boundary edges of matched clumps with compatible orientations.

4. Find topologically coherent chain matches.

5. Deduce joints from edge matches.

6. Find the best consistent set of correspondences.

We will illustrate this algorithm on the maps in figures 4-1 and 4-2; we will then explain it in detail.

Step 1 excludes everything in the cognitive map outside the range of vision; other rooms, other buildings, other cities. In other words, we confine attention to objects of MAP-K shown in figure 4-2.

Step 2 proposes clump matches which are possible on cursory inspection. Thus we match FLOOR-S with FLOOR-K, WALL-S with WALL-K, RUG-S1 with RUG-K1 ... Ultimately every true match is proposed, plus one mismatch: CHAIR-S2 is matched with CHAIR-K1. For purposes of this example, we assume that the position of CHAIR-S2 relative to the robot cannot be distinguished from that of CHAIR-K1, because of the fuzzy measurements. The other potential mismatches can be ruled out because the positions relative to the robot are incompatible. That is, TABLE-K1 is not the same as TABLE-S2 because the former is right of the robot and the latter is left of him; and we can rule out matching TABLE-K2 with TABLE-S1, RUG-K1 with RUG-S2, or RUG-K2 with RUG-S1 on similar grounds.

Step 3 constructs edge matches between the boundary edges of matched clumps by comparing their orientations. If e matches into f, then e and f must have very close orientations. How different the orientations can be is an increasing function of the grain-sizes of the two edges, and a decreasing function of their lengths. This step proposes matches between all pairs of edges from matched clumps with orientations which may be close enough to satisfy this constraint.

Step 4 groups these edge matches into chain matches, and thereby prunes some as impossible. For example, in figure 4-7 the true match of $e-f$ into $z-w$ will be proposed, but so will all other matches of $e-f$: into $w-x$, $x-y$, and $y-z$. Edge $e-f$ is so short

74

relative to the grain-sizes of all the edges of CHAIR-K1 that no constraint can be placed on its orientation. Likewise, $g-h$ can be matched into any edge of CHAIR-K1. However, if we may assume that $d-e$, $f-g$, and $h-a$ are long enough that they match unambiguously into $z-w$, and all other matches can be excluded, then, by connectedness, $e-f$ and $g-h$ must likewise match into $z-w$. So the program finds a unique topologically coherent set: $\{a-b <=> w-x, b-c <=> x-y, c-d <=> y-z, d-e => z-w, e-f => z-w, f-g => z-w, g-h => z-w, h-a => z-w\}$.

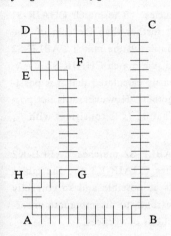
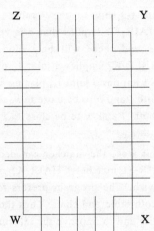

Chair-S1   Chair-K1

Hatch marks show grain-size
Figure 4-7: Forming a Chain Match

Each edge match constrains the relative position of the two edges. If e matches into f, then neither vertex of e can be very far from f. However, e can "slide" to any position along f. The edge match thus gives tight bounds on the perpendicular distance from the vertices of f to e and weak bounds for their position parallel to e; as described above, a joint expresses this kind of information. Step 5 of the algorithm creates the joints implied by each edge match.

Finally, we use the joints to determine the "best" "consistent" set of matches. We rule out inconsistent matches by geometric calculations on the joints that they imply. "Best" and "consistent" are in scare quotes above, "consistent" because the consistency check is only partial, "best" because the measure of goodness is debatable, and because, even if the measure is accepted, the algorithm may not find the best solution.

The algorithm operates by forming pairwise comparison of closely related joints. This pairwise comparison has three possible outcomes. The two joints may be inconsistent. They may be consistent, but only for restricted ranges of the fuzzy quantities. Or they may be consistent for all ranges of the fuzzy quantities.

For example, in figure 4-8 the edge match $a-b => w-x$ implies a joint asserting that b is not far from $w-x$. The edge match $b-c => x-y$ implies a joint asserting that b is not far from $x-y$. Each of these joints has a small perpendicular fuzz and a large parallel fuzz. These statements are consistent, but only if the actual parallel distance of each joint is small, since the parallel distance of one joint more or less corresponds to the perpendicular distance of the other. Thus, by considering the two joints together, we can infer a new joint which is better — that is, less fuzzy — than either of the original joints.

Figure 4-9 shows the value of finding inconsistencies. The match CHAIR-S1 $<=>$ CHAIR-K1 implies that b is very close to x (not much further than the sum of the grain-sizes) and there will be a joint j_{bx} which asserts this. Similarly, the match TABLE-S2 $<=>$ TABLE-K2 implies a joint j_{ix} placing i close to x, and the match CHAIR-S2 $<=>$ CHAIR-K1 implies a joint j_{nx} placing n close to x. Now, it is easily calculated that it is possible for both i and b to be close to x, since i and b are close together. However, it is not possible for both i and n to be close to x since i is far from n. That is, j_{ix} is consistent with j_{bx} but not with j_{nx}.

In this way, the matcher can deduce that either both TABLE-S2 matches TABLE-K2 and CHAIR-S1 matches CHAIR-K1 or that CHAIR-S2 matches CHAIR-K1 and the tables do not match. The program prefers to match as many objects as possible and so correctly matches both table and chair. Thus the consistency check serves both to disambiguate uncertain matches and to improve the information about relative positions of vertices.

4.4. Restricting the known map

Using what is known about the the robot position, we can exclude large portions of the known map as irrelevant, and concentrate exclusively on those clumps known to be nearby. If seen clump A matches known clump B and the diameter of the seen map is r, then one need look for matches only among clumps possibly within r of B. To restrict the map in this way, we use the object retriever described in Section 3-6. We start at any of the robot and retrieve all clumps within the diameter of the seen map and which are larger than the smallest seen clump. Throughout the rest of the matching, these are the only known clumps considered. Therefore, in the remainder of this chapter, we will use the phrase "known clump" to mean one of these.

In maps of realistic size, this restriction of the known map is the most important step in making assimilation efficient. If the seen map is always small and simple, the known map is locally simple (see section 2.8) and the position of the robot is well known, then the known map retrieved will be of manageable size. If not, then the matcher must compare the seen clumps against tremendous numbers of known clumps, and the problem becomes almost hopeless.

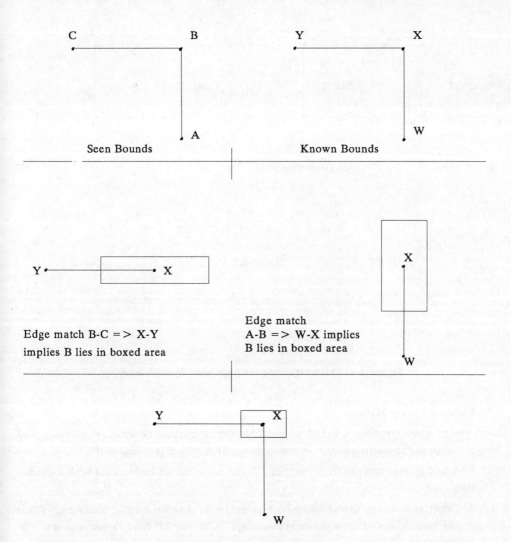

Seen Bounds | Known Bounds

Edge match B-C => X-Y
implies B lies in boxed area

Edge match
A-B => W-X implies
B lies in boxed area

Together they imply that B is somewhere in the intersection

Figure 4-8: Inferring a Joint

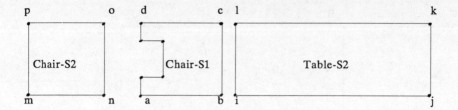

Scene Description

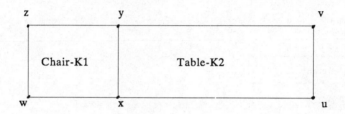

Cognitive Map

Figure 4-9: Disambiguating through Joint Inconsistency

4.5. Building Clump Matches

Next, the program compiles a list of all plausible clump matches between seen clumps and known clumps in the restricted map. A clump match of A with B is plausible if

1. A and B have compatible properties. A red truck cannot be matched with a dalmation.

2. Either at least one of the clumps is incomplete or they have equal diameters. (That is, the fuzz ranges of their diameters overlap). A 20′ by 30′ field cannot match a 100′ by 200′ field.

3. A and B have the same position with respect to the robot. A brick wall known to be behind the robot cannot be matched with a brick wall seen in front of the robot.

We can therefore use algorithm 4-1:

> Loop for each known clump A
>> Loop for each seen clump B
>>> If the properties of A match those of B
>>> and the diameters match
>>> and the positions with respect to the robot match are compatible
>>> then propose cl-match (A, B) as plausible.

Algorithm 4-1: Proposing clump matches

A more precise statement of the last condition is that if F and G are the clumps representing the current position of the robot in the known and seen maps, then the position of A with respect to F must be compatible with the position of B relative to G.

In section 3.5 we defined the relative position of clump A with respect to clump F to consist of four fuzz ranges:

$$\text{rel-pos } (A,F) = <\text{LX }(A,F), \text{HX }(A,F), \text{LY }(A,F), \text{HY }(A,F)>.$$

These satisfy the relations

$$\text{LOWX }(V\text{-}U) \in \text{LX }(A,F); \text{HIX }(V\text{-}U) \in \text{HX }(A,F);$$
$$\text{LOWY }(V\text{-}U) \in \text{LY }(A,F); \text{ and HIY }(V\text{-}U) \in \text{HY }(A,F);$$

where V = COVER (A) and U = COVER (F). We also noted the following relations:

If $A \supseteq E$ and $B \supseteq F$ then
$$[\text{LOX }(B\text{-}A), \text{HIX }(B\text{-}A)] \supseteq [\text{LOX }(F\text{-}E), \text{HIX }(F\text{-}E)] \text{ and}$$
$$[\text{LOY }(B\text{-}A), \text{HIY }(B\text{-}A)] \supseteq [\text{LOY }(F\text{-}E), \text{HIY }(F\text{-}E)].$$

If A intersects E and B intersects F then
$$[\text{LOX }(B\text{-}A), \text{HIX }(B\text{-}A)] \text{ intersects } [\text{LOX }(F\text{-}E), \text{HIX }(F\text{-}E)] \text{ and}$$
$$[\text{LOY }(B\text{-}A), \text{HIY }(B\text{-}A)] \text{ intersects } [\text{LOY }(F\text{-}E), \text{HIY }(F\text{-}E)].$$

We can therefore state the following compatibility relations:

rel-pos $(A,F) = <$ LX (A,F), HX (A,F), LY (A,F), HY $(A,F) >$

   is compatible with

rel-pos $(B,G) = <$ LX (B,G), HX (B,G), LY (B,G), HY $(B,G) >$

   iff

1) A, B, F, and G are complete and
   LX (A,F) intersects LX (B,G); HX (A,F) intersects HX (B,G);
   LY (A,F) intersects LY (B,G); HY (A,F) intersects HY (B,G);

2) A and F are complete; B or G is incomplete; and
   FULL-SPANX (A,F) intersects LX (B,G);
   FULL-SPANX (A,F) intersects HX (B,G);
   FULL-SPANY (A,F) intersects LY (B,G); and
   FULL-SPANY (A,F) intersects HY (B,G)
where FULL-SPANX $(A,F) = [$ LOW (LX (A,F)), HIGH (HX (A,F)) $]$
   FULL-SPANY $(A,F) = [$ LOW (LY (A,F)), HIGH (HY (A,F)) $]$

3) A or F is incomplete; B and G are complete; and
   FULL-SPANX (B,G) intersects LX (A,F);
   FULL-SPANX (B,G) intersects HX (A,F);
   FULL-SPANY (B,G) intersects LY (A,F); and
   FULL-SPANY (B,G) intersects HY (A,F)
where FULL-SPANX and FULL-SPANY are defined as above.

4) A or F and B or G are incomplete and
   FULL-SPANX (A,F) intersects FULL-SPANX (B,G) and
   FULL-SPANY (A,F) intersects FULL-SPANY (B,G)

It may seem overly restrictive to demand that two clumps overlap before they can be matched. After all, in real life, we often assume that separated views correspond to the same object. However, this relies on world knowledge which is entirely beyond the scope of the MERCATOR model. Using the type of knowledge available in the model, there are really only two choices; either always to match two incomplete clumps, irrespective of their relative position, since they could be the same object, or never to match two clumps, unless they overlap. The former is clearly the worse. It generates enormous numbers of false matches *which cannot be disproved* until a new view is taken. Moreover, the restriction step would have to be eliminated; seen clumps could perfectly well match clumps outside the range of vision. Finally, note two disjoint parts of an objects recorded as separate clumps will presumably be connected when the connecting part of the object is seen. In accordance with our principle of waiting for explicit information, we can afford to wait until then. (See section 5.1.)

80

4.6. Building Edge Matches

We now wish to relate the boundaries of the matched clumps, and we do so via edge matches. We have chosen edge matches as a relating structure, because of a number of properties outlined below. It turns out, however, that edge matches are, in effect, useful conglomerations of a different relation called a *bound match*. We will therefore begin with the latter.

A *bound match* is an asymmetric two place relation on two bounds, b and c.

Definition 4-1: bound-match (b,c) iff

1. b and c describe the boundaries of the same object.

2. There exist points $p_1, p_2 \in$ COOR (b) such that

    a. DIST $(p_1, p_2) \geq$ LENGTH $(b) / 2$;

    b. $COVER_b(p_1) \in COVER_c$ (COOR (c))

    c. $COVER_b(p_2) \in COVER_c$ (COOR (c))

(See figure 4-10.) Informally, *b matches into c* if at least half of b corresponds to the same part of the boundary as c. We say that *b matches with c* if either c matches into b or b matches into c.

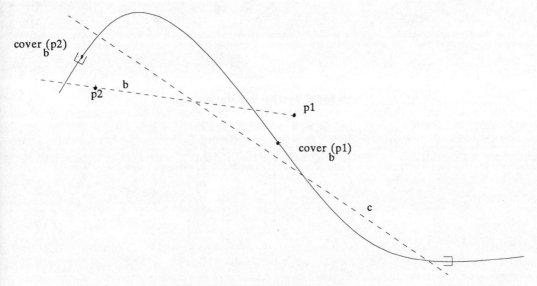

Figure 4-10: Edge Match: Definition

The reason for choosing this definition is that it is guaranteed to produce enough bound matches to fix each bound, but not too many bound matches. Specifically we can prove the four theorems below. Assume that the functions COOR, and COVER have fixed values. Let R and S be two regions for the same object.

Theorem 4-1: If the real bounds of S do not overlap, then, for any real bound b of R, there can be at most two real bounds c of S such that bound-match (b,c). If the weak inequality of Definition 4-1 (2.a) is changed to a strict inequality, then there can only be one such value of c.

Theorem 4-2: Let $B = \{ b_1 \cdots b_k \}$ be a connected chain of bounds of R and let c be a real bound of S. If COVER (COOR (c)) $\subset$ COVER (COOR (B)) then for some $b_j \in$ B, either bound-match (b_j, c) or bound-match (c, b_j).

That is, if two chains represent the same section of boundary, then each edge either maps into one edge of the other chain (the cases where it maps into two edges can be ignored) or is mapped into by edges of the other chain.

Theorem 4-3: Let B and C be incomplete chains of real bounds of R and S respectively. Let M be the set of all bounds in B which can be matched with some bound in C.

$M = \{ b \in B \mid \exists c \in C \mid$ bound-match $(b, c) \vee$ bound-match $(c, b) \}$ Then M forms one or two connected chains of bounds. If M forms a single connected chain, then the first element of M is either is the first element of B or is matched into the first element of C; and the last element of M either is the last element of B or is matched into the last element of C. If M forms two chains then the above statements are true of both of the connected components of M. (See figure 4-11.)

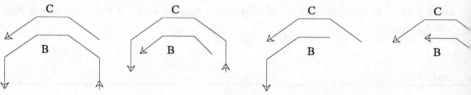

B and C overlap in a single chain

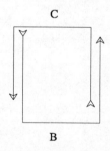

B and C overlap in two chains

Figure 4-11: Possible Overlaps of Bound Chains

Theorem 4-4: If S is complete, then, for each real bound b of R, there exists a real bound c of S such that either bound-match (b, c) or bound-match (c, b).

The actual structure implemented in the MERCATOR program is not a bound match but an edge match. An edge match consists (conceptually) of a source edge and an image edge. An edge match asserts all the bound-matches which would identify the two edges. Formally, we may define the semantics of an edge match as follows:

Definition 4-2: edge-match (e, f) iff for all bounds b and c such that e is the edge of b, f is the edge of c, and the clump of b matches the clump of c, it is the case that bound-match (b, c)

The advantage of using edge matches over using bound matches is that edge matches are more compact; each edge match incorporates two or three bound matches. The disadvantage is that information may be lost; but this is relatively rare. Information can be lost in any of three ways. Firstly, it may be that some, but not all, of the bound matches implied by an edge match are valid. In this case, the edge match is not created, and the valid bound matches are lost. Secondly, it may be that the bound matches implied are true with very different inaccuracies. (See below). These cases occur only if the geometry of one of the two maps is anomalous, and they make a difference only if it is very anomalous.

We associate two distances with an edge match. If you consider the matched half of e and ask "how far is the farthest point of this half from f?" then the *inaccuracy* is the upper bound of this value, and the *simple score* is the lower bound. (See figure 4-12.) That is, it is certain that no point in the matched half of e is more than the inaccuracy from f; it is possible that no point is more than the simple score from f.

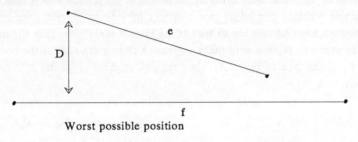

Worst possible position

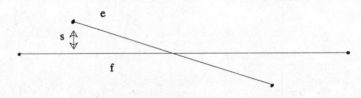

Best possible position

d is the *inaccuracy* of edge-match (e, f)

s is the *simple score* of edge-match (e, f)

Figure 4-12: Inaccuracy and Score of Edge Match

Finally, edge matches have a flag indicating whether the source and image edges correspond head-head/tail-tail or head-tail/tail-head. (Bounds in bound matches always correspond head-head/tail-tail, but one edge or both may be antiparallel to the bound).

How do we find edge matches? Firstly, all edge match are suggested by clump matches. (An edge match which was not would satisfy definition 4-2 vacuously, but would not be very interesting.) So we can get all possible edge matches from matching up all boundary edges in the two clumps of the proposed clump matches.

Secondly, the source edge has to look like part of the image. The source cannot be much more than twice as long as the image, and must be roughly parallel. In particular, let i_1 = GRAIN-SIZE(b_1); i_2 = GRAIN-SIZE(b_2); L_1 = LENGTH(b_1); L_2 = LENGTH(b_2). If bound-match (b_1, b_2) then

1. $L_2 \geq \dfrac{L_1}{2} - 2(i_1 + i_2)$

2. If $L_1 > 4i_1$ then $|\ \mathrm{ROT}(b_2) - \mathrm{ROT}(b_1)\ | \leq \sin^{-1}(\dfrac{4i_1}{L_1}) + \sin^{-1}(\dfrac{4i_2}{L_2})$

Any pair of edges whose fuzz ranges in orientation and length make this impossible can be ruled out.

Thirdly, although Theorems 4-1 through 4-4 apply to any two regions, if the grain-size of the bounds of R_2 of the same order as the length of the bounds of R_1, then there is no way of determining whether two edges match simply by looking at them; the orientation of an edge of R_1 need have no relation to that of the edge it maps into. (See Figure 4-13.) Therefore, we try to match regions with other regions of close grain-size. If the clumps have sensible sets of regions (see section 2.8), then regions of close grain-size will have comparable descriptions.

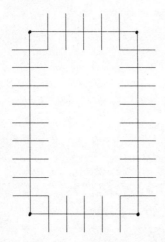

Region-K

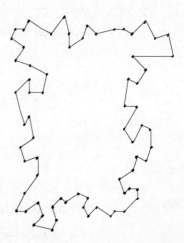

Region-S

Region grain-sizes shown by hatch marks.
Each edge of Region-S could, by itself, match into any edge of Region-K.
Figure 4-13: Difficult Edge Matches

We therefore use algorithm 4-2 to construct plausible edge matches.

Loop for each proposed clump-match (C, D)
  begin
    find the two regions R and S of C and D which are closest in grain-size;
    Loop for each real boundary edge *e* of R
      Loop for each real boundary edge *f* of S
        If edge-match (*e*, *f*) has not been marked impossible
          then if *e* and *f* satisfy the geometric constraints (1) and (2)
            then propose edge-match (*e*, *f*)
            else mark edge-match (*e*, *f*) as impossible
  end.

Algorithm 4-2: Proposing edge matches

4.7. Building Joints

Each edge-match supports two joints. They connect an endpoint of the source edge to the corresponding endpoint of the image edge through the image edge. The fuzz on the perpendicular length is from minus three times the inaccuracy of the edge match to plus three times the inaccuracy of the edge match. The fuzz on the parallel length is much greater: the parallel length can range from a low value of [-1/2 ((length of source edge) + (inaccuracy of edge match))] to a high value of [(length of image edge) + (inaccuracy of edge match) - (1/2)(length of source edge)] (See figure 4-14.)

Also, if a clump has a region whose interior is a single polygon consisting of a single vertex, then any clump match involving that clump generates joints. We take the region of maximal inaccuracy from the other clump, and connect each of the real vertices of the latter to the single vertex of the former with a joint. The joint has a perpendicular length of 0.0, and a parallel length of the sum of the inaccuracies of the two regions. The orientation of the joint can vary from 0.0 to 2π. There is no associated edge. An edge would suffice to express the information here, but we use a joint for uniformity in the data structures. (See figure 4-15.)

4.8. Building Chain Matches

We now organize the edge matches into chain matches. Each chain match is a set of edge matches which satisfies Theorems 4-3 and 4-4. The chain matches need not be disjoint; the same edge match can appear in more than one chain match.

We begin with a proposed clump match between clumps A and B. Let E be a connected chain of A and F be a connected chain of B. We will try to match E with F. Let us assume that neither E nor F is a cycle; cases with cycles are not very different.

We can turn Theorem 4-3 around to get a step by step rule for constructing plausible chains. Let S be the correct chain of edge-matches. To start, we note that the first edge-match in S must involve either the first bound of E or the first bound of F. This gives us a number of startings for S. We then proceed edge by edge on each region. If we have a

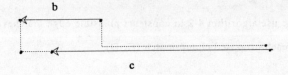

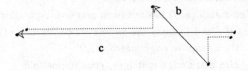

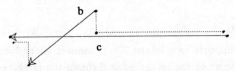

b matches into c. The relation between corresponding vertices is fairly tight in the direction perpendicular to c and much looser in the direction parallel to c.

Figure 4-14: Joints implied by edge match

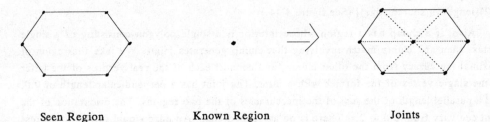

Seen Region　　　　　　Known Region　　　　　　Joints

Figure 4-15: Joints Implied by Matches of Point Clump

matching of e and f (either edge-match (e, f) or edge-match (f, e)), and neither e nor f is the last bound of E or F, then we proceed to matchings involving e' and f', the edges following e and f in their respective regions. Specifically, S must contain either a matching between e' and f, or a matching between e and f' or a matching between e' and f'. This gives us a number of continuations. We can terminate only when e' or f' does not exist.

We thus construct a number of chains of matchings satisfying the two theorems. In cases where edge-matches in both directions have been proposed, we still have to resolve whether both are true, or only one; and, if only one, which one. The topological theorems do not help us here. Rather, we find a maximal set which is geometrically consistent. We will discuss how to check for geometrical consistency in Section 4.9. Also, we will find cases where one set of matches will properly include another. The latter are discarded as uninteresting.

86

Consider, for example, matching chain E with chain F in figure 4-16. The matches proposed are: all matches between full length horizontal sides, in either direction; all matches between down-going sides, in either direction; all matches between up-going sides, in either direction; and matches from E3-E4 and E4-E5 into the horizontal sides of F; thirty-two matches in all.

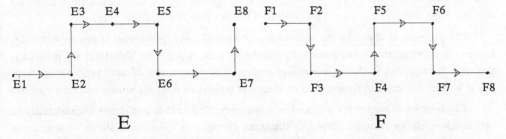

Figure 4-16: Chain Match: Another Example

The first match in S must involve either E1-E2 or F1-F2. So it must be either E1-E2 <=> F1-F2; E1-E2 <=> F3-F4; E1-E2 <=> F5-F6; E1-E2 <=> F7-F8; E3-E4 => F1-F2; E4-E5 => F1-F2; or E6-E7 <=> F1-F2.

Extending each of these to the next edge, we find that if E1-E2 <=> F1-F2 is in S then S must also contain either E1-E2 <=> F2-F3; E2-E3 <=> F1-F2; or E2-E3 <=> F2-F3. Since none of these are possible edge matches, we can rule out E1-E2 <=> F1-F2. Similarly, we can rule out E1-E2 <=> F5-F6 and E6-E7 <=> F1-F2. At this stage, we have the following possibilities left:

{ E1-E2 <=> F3-F4, E2-E3 <=> F4-F5, ...};

{ E1-E2 <=> F7-F8 }; (complete)

{ E3-E4 => F1-F2, E4-E5 => F1-F2, ...}

{ E4-E5 => F1-F2, E5-E6 <=> F2-F3, ...}

Each of these can be extended to a complete set of matchings. When this is done, it will be found that the fourth is contained in the third, and so is unnecessary. In the end, the following three chain matches are returned:

{ E1-E2 <=> F3-F4, E2-E3 <=> F4-F5, E3-E4 => F5-F6,
E4-E5 => F5-F6, E5-E6 <=> F6-F7, E6-E7 <=> F7-F8 }

{ E1-E2 <=> F7-F8 }

{ E3-E4 => F1-F2, E4-E5 => F1-F2, E5-E6 <=> F2-F3,
E6-E7 <=> F3-F4, E7-E8 <=> F4-F5 }

4.9. Choosing the Best Matches

The final and most difficult section of the matcher is to extract the correct correspondences out of all the clump matches, chain matches, edge matches, and joints proposed. Of course, the program has no access to correctness. All it can do is to return a set of correspondences which is possibly correct — i.e. consistent — and, preferably, the best consistent set, the set with the most correspondences. This section of the matcher is called the *selector*.

The problem of checking the consistency of a set of correspondences seems bewildering. In fact, it is intractable computationally (see Appendix A.5.) The algorithm we present is therefore incomplete, in that it sometimes returns inconsistent sets of matchers, though usually it is quite effective in finding sets of matchers which are not only consistent but also true.

The selector detects three kinds of inconsistency. The first is qualitative inconsistency of two or more clump matches involving the same clump. As mentioned above, it sometimes happens that two incomplete clumps in the same map represent different parts of the same object. If the connecting part of this object is seen, then the seen clump will be matched with both of the known clumps. In fact, it is possible for arbitrarily many seen clumps to be matched with arbitrarily many known clumps. (See figure 4-17.) However, two conditions must be satisfied. Firstly, the properties must all be compatible. Secondly, it is not possible in this set of matched clumps to have a complete clump and another clump from the same map. (This relies on the normalcy condition of not having redundant complete clumps, rather than on the strict semantics.)

The second kind of inconsistency is inconsistency of chain matches. Chain match A is inconsistent with chain match B if they are both suggested by the same clump match, and there is some edge *e* such that A and B match *e* into different edges.

The third is geometrical inconsistency of a set of joints. This is discussed in the next section.

Recall the logical structures of correspondences. Chain matches support edge matches which support joints, and chain matches support clump matches. Therefore, all three of these tests can be applied to a set of chain matches; a set of chain matches is consistent only if the chain matches pass the second test above, the clump matches supported by the chain matches pass the first test, and the joints supported (indirectly) by the chain matches pass the third test. The converse is not true. There are inconsistent sets of chain matches which pass all three tests. However, these are all the tests we have.

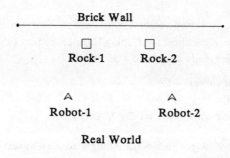

Real World

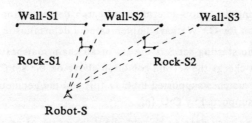

First Scene

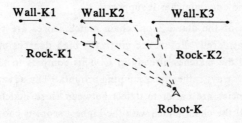

Second Scene

Clump matches:

WALL-K1 <=> WALL-S1, WALL-K2 <=> WALL-S1,

WALL-K2 <=> WALL-S2, WALL-K3 <=> WALL-S2,

WALL-K3 <=> WALL-S3

Figure 4-17: Multiple Clump Matches

89

The problem, then, is to find the best consistent set of chain matches. Generally speaking, there are two simple algorithms for finding large consistent subsets of a set S. They start out the same way, as the greedy algorithm 4-3:

C (the consistent subset) ← ∅
Loop for (p in S)
    If C ∪ {p} is self-consistent, set C ← C ∪ {p}.

Algorithm 4-3: Finding a consistent set

After the loop is finished, one can either terminate (a deterministic search) or backtrack to look for a bigger set (a non-deterministic search). A deterministic search demands a good order for enumerating S. A non-deterministic search demands good pruning methods and a good scoring function for C. We have implemented a deterministic search.

In our case, the starting set S is the set of all chain matches that have been proposed. The consistency test checks the second condition above on the set C ∪ {p}; the first condition on the set of clump matches supported by C ∪ {p}; and the geometric joint consistency check on the set of joints supported by C ∪ {p}.

There is nothing very deep to be said about the order of search. We use a number of rather obvious criteria, combined in a largely arbitrary manner. The justification is empirical; our method has given good results.

We begin by assigning scores to the edge matches. An edge match get points for length, for a low simple score, and for being suggested by many different clump matches. A edge match loses points if there are other edge matches which match its source edge into a different image edge. We next assign starting scores to the chain matches, depending on the sum of the scores of the edge matches it supports.

At each iteration of the above loop, chain match scores are recomputed for the chain matches still to be considered. Points are given for high degrees of interaction between the given chain match and the matches already in C. This compels to the search to move out in the map in a connected way, rather than jumping around. (The advantage of moving connectedly is that inconsistencies are easier to detect between close matches than far ones). After scores are recalculated, the chain match with the highest score is chosen for the next test.

One of the defects of the matcher is that it is quite sensitive to the details of this scoring scheme, which is without any good theoretical foundations. However, the scheme we have now seems to be generally effective.

Once we have found a good, consistent set of chain matches, then we can collect the clump matches, edge matches, and joints which they support and assume that these are true. This step is fully justified logically; if the chain matches are true, then what they support is true. The converse is false; there may be true clump matches or joints which are not supported by any true chain match. In the case of joints, this does not matter; they may be true by chance, but there is no reason to believe them true. However, there are two kinds of clump matches which do not suggest any true chain matches, but are nonetheless likely. These require special treatment.

Firstly, there are clump matches where one of the clumps has only a single region, and the graph of that region is a single vertex. These clump matches suggest joints (section 4.7), but no edge matches. To handle these, we must extend the definition of chain matches to include a structure which implies a clump match of this kind and the single joint the clump match suggests. The joint is included in the set of joints to be tested for geometrical consistency.

Secondly, there are clump matches between clumps which overlap in their interior and not in their boundaries, and which can be shown to overlap. In principle, there could be many ways to show that two clumps overlap. One might, for example, show geometrically that polygons of the one overlap those of the other. However, in fact we consider only one kind of proof that two clumps overlap in their interior; if they contain matching clumps. If cl-match (A,B) is true, then presumably A overlaps with B. If C contains A and D contains B, then we can deduce that C and D overlap. If, finally, C and D are incomplete and the match cl-match (C,D) has been proposed — i.e. C and D are compatible in properties and position — then we assume that C matches D.

4.10. Joint Consistency

The third type of correspondence inconsistency used by the selector in algorithm 4-3 is geometrical inconsistency of a set of joints. On account of its complexity, we deferred discussion of how to detect such inconsistency to this section.

The joint checker is a forward inference engine. A forward inference engine starts with a bunch of facts and a number of inference rules, which are presumably logically deductive. Each rule takes a number of facts and either reports that they are contradictory, or that they are consistent. If they are consistent, the rule may deduce some new facts. The inference engine starts with the input facts and keeps applying relevant rules. When a rule deduces new facts, these are added to the pile of facts, and subjected to new rules. The inference engine keeps grinding away until one of three things happens:

1. A rule reports contradiction. In this case, the inference engine concludes that the original set of facts was inconsistent.

2. The engine runs out of steam; i.e., no rule applications report contradiction or generate any new facts.

3. Something else happens. For example, the engine might exhaust its alloted resources of time or space; or it might succeed in proving a desired result. What events besides contradiction and exhaustion are allowed to stop the engine depends on its particular function and domain.

Unless the engine finds a contradiction, it returns all the facts which it has deduced as true.

The "facts" on which the joint checker operates are joints. The "rules" are procedures which take two joint j and k, together with the two maps, and calculate whether the two joints are consistent, and, if so, whether they together imply tighter bounds on their fuzzy quantities. If the latter, then the procedure builds new joints j' and k' with the tighter bounds. These are marked as supported by the pair (j, k); j' and k' are true if j and k are true. The procedure does not modify the old quantities in j and k, because we may later wish to reject k and return to the old value of j, or vice versa.

Consider, for example, Figure 4-8. Edge $a-b$ is matched into edge $w-x$. The joint builder (Section 4.7) has therefore constructed a joint j from b to v through $w-x$ whose perpendicular length has a very small fuzz (the sum of the two inaccuracies) and whose parallel length is quite large (about the length of $w-x$). Similarly edge $b-c$ has been matched into $x-y$, and this creates a joint k from b to x through $x-y$ with tight perpendicular length and fuzzy parallel length. However, if both these edge-matches are true, then the actual parallel displacement in each edge-match is the same as the perpendicular displacement in the other. Therefore, we can create two new joints $j\prime$ and $k\prime$ with very much smaller parallel displacements

The constructive aspect of the rules is important, not only because it gives a better chance of finding a contradiction, but also because it gives better information for the merger. The conclusion that b is very close to v can be important for relating the two maps, as we shall see in chapter 5.

Figure 4-18 illustrates a case where the joint checker finds a contradiction. The plausible edge-match $a-b$ into $u-v$ implies a joint from b and v, and the plausible edge-match $c-d$ into $w-x$ implies a joint from c to w. However, if both of these joints are true, then the path $[\ c \rightarrow$ joint $(c, w) \rightarrow w \rightarrow$ edge $(w-v) \rightarrow v \rightarrow$ joint $(v, b) \rightarrow b \rightarrow$ edge $(b-f) \rightarrow f \rightarrow$ edge $(f-c) \rightarrow c\ ]$ forms a closed cycle. However, the measures of the various links show that this cannot be a closed cycle; so the two edge-matches cannot both be true.

Figures 4-8 and 4-18 illustrate two of the different geometries which are examined by the joint checker. There are six such geometries in all (see figure 4-19):

1. Aligned joints - joints with the same tail, head, and edge.

2. Cojoining joints - joints with the same endpoints.

3. Double bound joints - joints with the same tail and same edge.

4. Bridge joints - joints whose edge is the same, and whose tails are connected by an edge.

5. End Sharing joints - joints which share one endpoint.

6. Internally connected joints - joints which have one endpoint connected by an edge not involved in any active edge-matches. (We place this restriction, so that this procedure will not be invoked too often when it is redundant.)

Some of these are obviously special cases of others. They are included separately, because their procedures are either faster or more powerful than the general procedure.

I will not describe these procedures in detail; they are exercises in interval trigonometry, a field which has been accorded a well merited neglect. Aligned joints are almost trivial; corresponding measurements are intersected. A special procedure was written to handle the case of cojoining joints. The other cases are handled by a general procedure which take the measurement of joints and edges presumed to form a cycle, and either reports that there is a contradiction or returns tightened values for the quantities.

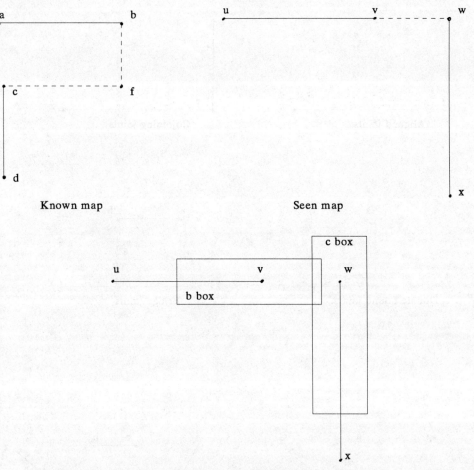

The relative positions of b and c, as fixed by comparisons to v and w, are inconsistent with the measurements of edges $b-f$ and $f-c$.

Figure 4-18: Joints Joined by Internal Edge

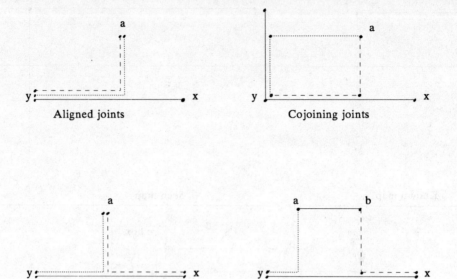

Aligned joints

Cojoining joints

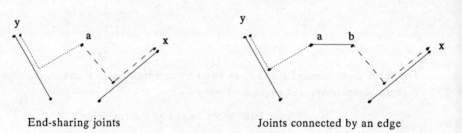

Double bound joints

Bridge joints

End-sharing joints

Joints connected by an edge

Figure 4-19: Joint Comparisons

94

We can use dependency information to cut down on the number of rule applications which have to be tried. If j and k imply j' and k', then j' has the same structure as j, but with tighter fuzz ranges. Therefore, as long as j' is active, we never again apply any rule to j; applying it to j gives results which are as good or better.

The major problem with the above scheme is termination. It is perfectly possible for the checker, as described above, to go into an infinite loop by continually generating more joints with tighter and tighter bounds. There are cases where this actually will happen. Moreover, this does not reflect merely inadequacies in the rules or their implementations; it is, rather, a problem inherent to the entire approach [Davis, 85]. We use the following cheap trick to avoid this: in checking joint j for consistency with joints $k_1 \cdots k_n$, once we have checked one of the k's, we never go back to it. That is, if j and k_1 generate j' and k_1', then we compare both of these against k_2. However, if j and k_2 generate j' and k_2', we do not compare these against k_1. Any modification to the forward inferencer which forces termination will have to be arbitrary. The justification for this particular modification is partly laziness — this is particularly easy to implement, in fact, easier than a correct inferencer — and partly empirical — it seems to work well enough.

4.11. Omissions and Flaws

The matcher uses most of the information which is readily available in a MERCATOR map to prune the matchings. However, there are a few important types of inference which are omitted or inefficiently implemented. We will discuss three of these.

The matcher will occasionally propose edge matches which force a boundary to cross itself. It takes no precautions against this. For example, in figure 4-20, it will freely propose the match edge-match $(a-b, x-y)$, which would force $w-z$ to cross $c-b$. The polygon splicer will notice the contradiction, and object; but by that time, it will be too late. (See section 5.3.2.) This kind of contradiction is difficult to detect without the sketcher, which is computationally expensive. Figure 4-21 shows an even harder form of the same problem. Matching $a-b$ into $x-y$ forces $w-z$, supposedly the boundary of the grass, to lie inside polygon (a, b, c), the interior of the grass. Note that there are the same kind of geometric difficulties in detecting and considering this kind of contradictions as in the contradictions raised by completeness information. For a very good reason; this information used here — that an object does not extend past its bounds — is basically a form of completeness information on a single object.

There is a major omission in the joint consistency checker. Frequently, comparison of joints can tighten fuzzy measurements of edges as well as joints. For example, in figure 4-22, we can deduce that the length of edge $a-b$ is in [4.8, 6.2], an improvement over [3.0, 7.0]. In this way, matching would allow us to carry over measurements from one map to another. This new information would be very useful in the merger. (See section 5.3.3.) Also, it would be available in future inferences in the joint consistency checker to give tighter estimates, and, sometimes, to find contraditions which are either ignored under the current system, or detected at a later stage. Moreover, the new measurements would come for free; they are effectively calculated anyway with the new joint measurements. The only reason I did not implement this feature is that I did not wish to tackle the bookkeeping that would be involved

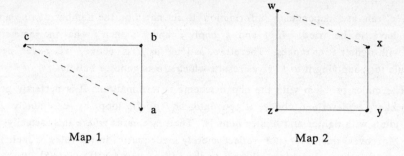

Map 1   Map 2

$x - y$ will match $a - b$, leading to the region below:

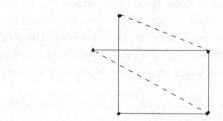

Figure 4-20: An Undetected Illegal Match

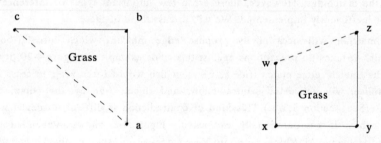

Figure 4-21: A Harder Undetected Illegal Match

in recording tentative fuzzy measurements on edges. However, there are no theoretical obstacles to doing so.

The final major gap in the MERCATOR matcher is that it does not exploit the clump hierarchy. If scene descriptions include several levels of the hierarchy, then it will be more efficient to match first on the uppermost level, and then work downward, using higher levels to guide lower levels. I have not developed a theory to do this.

There are also two serious flaws in the way that the algorithm forms chain matches. As specified in section 4.8, after edge matches are formed, they are organized into internally consistent chain matches. However, we consider only maximal chain matches, on the theory

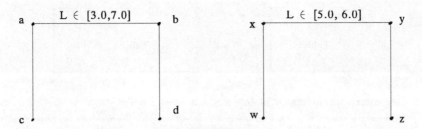

Grain-size of each bound is 0.05.

Joints place x and y within 0.1 of a and b.

Hence, LENGTH (edge a, b) $\in$ [4.8, 5.2]

Figure 4-22: Fuzz Constriction in Joint Checking

that the more edge matches the better, and to avoid a particularly pointless type of combina-torial explosion. Given two chains of n edges each, if every edge can match with exactly one edge from the other chain, there are 3^n possible chain matches. For each matching pair e and f, the chain match can contain either edge-match (e, f) or edge-match (f, e) or both, and it can make independent choices for each pair. Most of the time, the correct match will be the maximal match which has every pair. (See figure 4-23.)

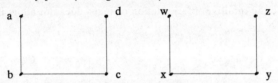

There are 27 chain matches which are consistent with theorem 4-4:

$$\{a-b \Rightarrow w-x, w-x \Rightarrow a-b, a-b \Leftrightarrow w-x\} \times$$
$$\{b-c \Rightarrow x-y, x-y \Rightarrow b-c, b-c \Leftrightarrow x-y\} \times$$
$$\{c-d \Rightarrow y-z, y-z \Rightarrow c-d, c-d \Leftrightarrow y-z\}$$

Not all these are, in fact, topologically possible; a stronger theorem
could exclude some of these.

Figure 4-23: Many submaximal chain matches

These two rules taken together produce both slowness and error. On the one hand, there are often many possible maximal chain matches. Generating them all and testing them for consistency is very expensive. On the other hand, the presumption that the correct chain match is maximal is often mistaken, as in figure 4-24. In such a case the program will over-look the correct chain match, and reject the maximal chain match because of geometrical inconsistency. It turns out, in fact, that these two flaws are responsible for most of the prob-lems with the current version of the MERCATOR program. (See section 7.6.) It may be possible to solve or alleviate these problems by a preliminary pruning using consistency of joints with position relative to the robot.

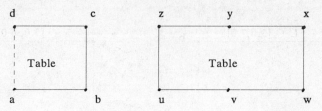

The correct chain match is $\{a-b <=> v-w, b-c <=> w-x, c-d <=> x-y\}$. However $u-v => a-b$ and $y-z => c-d$ are, by themselves, geometrically possible. Therefore, the maximal chain match allowed topologically is $\{u-v => a-b, a-b <=> v-w, b-c <=> w-x, c-d <=> x-y, y-z => c-d\}$.

Figure 4-24: Submaximal chain match is correct

Another problem arises in constructing chain matches, because there is very little interaction between the different chain matches chosen for different clump matches. Figure 4-25 illustrates the problem. In constructing chain matches for A1 $<=>$ A2 and B1 $<=>$ B2, we correctly propose the matches $a-b$ with $u-v$ and $b-c$ with $v-w$ However, in constructing the match C1 $<=>$ C2, we prefer the chain match $\{ a-b => u-v, b-c => u-v,$ and $c-d => v-w \}$. If the fuzzes are large enough that this is geometrically consistent, then it will be acccepted. This is not technically a flaw — there are geometries consistent with these maps in which these are the correct chain matches — but it is certainly an anomaly, because the intuitive interpretation of maps does not allow it.

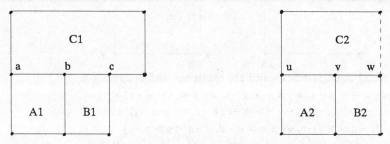

Figure 4-25: Chain matches should interact

5 Merging

5.1. Introduction

The merger is the second stage of the assimilator. The merger uses the correspondences created by the matcher to add new information from the scene description into the cognitive map.

Viewing MERCATOR as an AI data base manager, the merger is a fact adder. Fact adders take input information and modify the data base to reflect the information. Two operations are involved: *incorporation*, placing the fact into the data base while maintaining the structure of the data base; and *forward inference*, generating new facts deductively and incorporating them into the data base. (Often, both operations are subsumed in a single process, but conceptually they are separable.) (See [Charniak, Riesbeck, and McDermott, 80].)

Fact adders are much harder to evaluate theoretically than retrievers. A retriever is looking for a specific answer, and it is adequate to the extent that it gives the best possible answer given the data base. Thus, we can define the target behavior in purely logical terms. There is a logical component to the fact adder, in that the output data base should ideally be exactly equivalent to the input data base conjoined with the new fact. However, an adder can be logically correct in this sense, and still not adequate. An adder must also leave the data base in a state where it can be interpreted by the retriever and by subsequent calls to the adder itself. Thus, adequacy of the adder depends on details of the input demands of the retriever and of the adder itself. (If the retrievers are perfect, then logical correctness of the adder will suffice). For this reason, we have carefully collected the normalcy conditions, under which the algorithms will work correctly. The adder must preserve these conditions or try to.

For a propositional data base, incorporation is almost trivial, involving no more than adding the new proposition to a list or tree. The hard problem is controlling forward inference. In MERCATOR, the situation is exactly the reverse. Incorporation, as we shall see, can be quite difficult. However, we do not use forward inference. We exploit the patience assumption: any fact which should be expressed directly in the data base will, sooner or later, be directly perceived, and we can simply wait until it is. We lose some potential accuracy in the retriever in the meantime; however, we are willing to sacrifice it to simplify assimilation. The adequacy of the merger is not measured mainly in terms of the cognitive map which it produces at each step; rather, it is measured in terms of the map which it ultimately produces.

For example, in figure 5-1, the robot first sees the white wall, then turns and sees the red wall. It *could* go ahead and calculate the edges connecting their endpoints, but it doesn't. The rationale is that, if these walls are closely enough related that it is worth having edges connecting them directly, then eventually these edges will be seen. Some scene description will contain both walls and construct the connecting edges. When this happens, the edges can be spliced into the map. Until it happens, the program can make do with using paths going through vertex *v*.

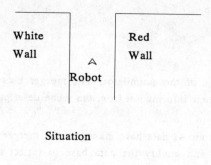

Situation

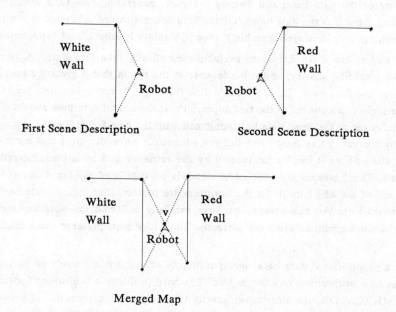

First Scene Description   Second Scene Description

Merged Map

Figure 5-1: Two Facing Walls

Assimilation from sources other than vision does not permit this evasion of forward inference. We cannot assume that we will have a second chance at any given inference. This is, in fact, one of the major advantages of visual assimilation over other forms.

Since the merger does only incorporation without forward inference, it ought to be simple, and in some ways it is. In areas which are covered by the old map but not the new map, we use the old map unaltered, and *vice versa*. In areas where the two maps overlap, we use whichever is better. At the borderline, we fit the two maps together.

Figure 5-2 illustrates this kind of unproblematic merging. The combining of A and B into C can be done directly by eye. We identify corresponding vertices and object, eliminate edges and regions which are redundant after this identification, and that is practically all that has to be done. The only complication is that since there may be slight differences in position between vertices *a* and *w* and between *b* and *x*, all edges such as edge($w-y$) and edge($x-z$) must have their measurement fuzzes slightly increased. The merger can perform this merge without hesitation.

Unfortunately, the two MERCATOR maps do not always fit together so neatly. Consider, for example, figure 5-3. It is hard even to decide what the merger *should* do, quite aside from the problems of getting it to do it. How do we make a single region for the different parts of the rock and pond? How do we fit the path between the pond and the parking lot? Do we throw out the old boundary between the pond and parking lot? If so, what happens to the connection between the playground and the old corner? Similarly with old upper right hand vertex of the pond. If we replace it by the new, more accurate representation, how do we locate the tree?

Cases like figure 5-3 are hard because each possible solution has trade-offs, and, at this point, we have no principled way of choosing between them. Therefore in analyzing the merger, we first enumerate the various goals of the merger; next, we study the ways in which they conflict and the possible choices for resolving the conflict; finally, we present the solutions that we have chosen, with justifications.

5.2. Desiderata

There are five goals common to fact-adding modules of knowledge base systems. The adder should not add unwarranted information. It should not lose information. The output data base should be usable effectively by all modules of the system, including the adder. The output data base should be usable efficiently. Finally, the adder should run efficiently.

Deduction: The merger is supposed to be deductive; any model which satisfies the two input maps and the correspondence should satisfy the output map. It is not disastrous if this is violated — after all, the assimilator as a whole is not and cannot be deductive — but clearly, unwarranted tightening of constraints should be avoided when possible. This is the only way to keep the map true and thus avoid the need for error correction routines. If the actions of the merger cannot be deductive in all cases, the next best thing is to have some well defined set of cases in which they are deductive.

Preservation of Information: A MERCATOR map expresses six types of information. A merging algorithm must preserve this information in the cognitive map, and bring new information of this kind from the scene to the cognitive map.

1. Objects. For example, in merging figure 4-1 into figure 4-2, we have to add CHAIR-2 to figure 4-2.

2. Object properties: If the scene description records that CHAIR-1 is (MATERIAL WOOD), then this information must be added to the clump for CHAIR-1.

3. Object containments: If the scene description records that RUG-2 is in FLOOR, and the cognitive map does not, then this must be added to the containment hierarchy.

4. Relative positions: The more precise measurement given in the scene description for the distance from CHAIR-1 to TABLE-2 should be recorded in the cognitive map.

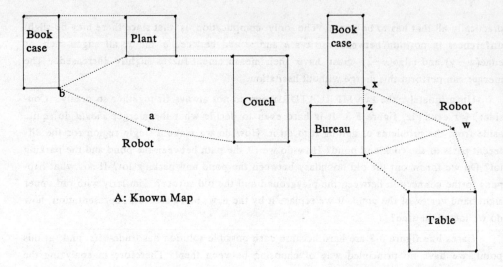

A: Known Map

B: Scene Description

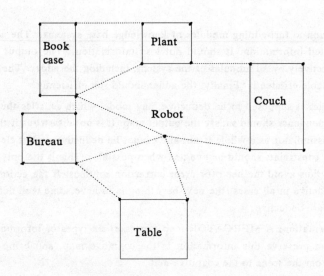

C: Merged Map

Figure 5-2: A Trivial Merging Problem

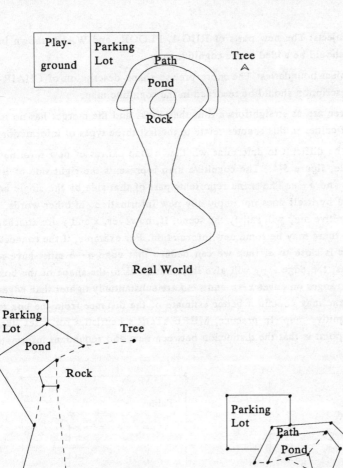

Real World

Known Map

Seen Map

Figure 5-3: A Hard Merging Problem

5. Extent of objects: The new parts of RUG-1, FLOOR, and WALL shown in the scene description should be added to the cognitive map.

6. Shape of object boundaries: The more precise shape description of CHAIR-1 given in the scene description should be recorded in the cognitive map.

The first three are as straightforward as they look, and the merger has no trouble with them. All the difficulties in this chapter relate to the last three types of information.

It can even be difficult to determine whether a map expresses new information. Consider, for example, figure 5-4. The cognitive map represents the right side of BOX by the two bounds $a-b$ and $b-c$. The scene represents part of that side by the single bound $x-y$. That single bound by itself does not imply any new information. In other words, any model satisfying the cognitive map will satisfy the scene. If, however, x and y are attached by edges to the table, then there may be some new information. For example, if the connections to the table imply that x is close to a, then we can deduce that edge $a-b$ must have angle quite close to $\pi/2$. Thus, the edge $x-y$ will give information as to the shape of the box. Alternatively, if the fuzz ranges on edges $x-p$ and $y-q$ are substantially tighter than edges $a-e$ and $b-f$, then the scene may contain a better estimate of the distance from the box to the table than does the cognitive map. In practice, MERCATOR's heuristics for cases like these are quite crude. The point is that the distinction between new and redundant information can be subtle.

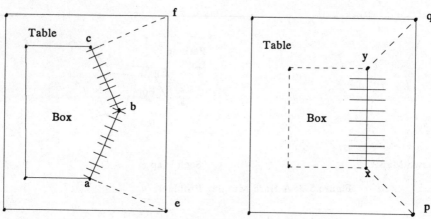

Hatch marks show grain-size.

Figure 5-4: Does This Express New Information?

Effectiveness of the output map: The normalcy conditions (see section 2.8) must be preserved as far as possible, so that the algorithms will run correctly. The most significant conditions here are the *full region* condition (each region covers all that is known of the object), the *well structured regions* condition (regions are in a definite order of increasing complexity and precision), the *polygon fitting* condition (the edges of polygons in a region either are shared with another polygon or bound the region), the *simple boundary* condition (bounds from one region should represent disjoint parts of the actual object boundary), and the *correct edges* condition (edges connect objects which are close together). If the merger cannot be written to guarantee these, then at least it should be the case that these conditions should be true after the object or area has been seen in its entirety and the cognitive map representation of the object or area has stabilized.

There are particular problems associated with the *plenum* condition that every edge of real bound have an object on either side. We will discuss these in section 5.3.4.

Efficiency of the output map: The major concerns here are preventing redundancy, preserving simple shape descriptions and topologies, and preserving the clump containment hierarchy.

The merger combines two maps which contain much of the same information. Therefore, there is great potential for redundancy, the more so since, as mentioned above, redundant information is often difficult to identify.

The relevant redundancy here is practical redundancy, which is related to, but different from, logical redundancy. A MERCATOR entity can be logically redundant, but practically useful, if it causes algorithms to run faster. For example, a edge whose fuzz ranges can be deduced from other edges, but connects two close points, might be practically useful though logically redundant. Likewise, a crude but simple region for an object might be logically redundant, because it is implied by a finer region, but practically useful, because it can be used faster or more effectively. Conversely, an entity may be logically necessary but practically superfluous, if it constrains the world in ways too subtle for the ordinary retrieval functions to detect.

Responsibility for identifying corresponding clumps and bounds lies with the matcher. If the matcher operates correctly, the merger will ensure that the output map has no redundant clumps or bounds. A region is judged to be redundant if there is some other region that is as simple and as accurate. This test, though not logically correct, generally suffices for practical purposes. (Note that this test bypasses subtleties to declare the box region in figure 5-4 redundant.) A polygon is redundant if it is wholly contained in other polygons of the same region, a straightforward though time consuming test. The hardest entities to characterize are vertices and edges. The solution that we have adopted is that a vertex is useful only if it lies on a bound or polygon of a region and that an edge is useful only if it connects two useful vertices. This last criterion necessarily includes all edges of bounds and polygons. Again, this solution seems to be practically sufficient, though without logical basis.

The effects of redundancy range from slight to disastrous. At the very least, redundancy fills memory unnecessarily. Redundant information will frequently slow down algorithms by a linear factor. For example, a redundant region will cause the matching algorithm to spend a little longer looking for the best region to match, and a redundant polygon will cause the merger to spend considerably longer to determine whether the entire object has been seen. Widespread redundancy can cause an exponential increase of time. If each vertex has twice as many edges as it needs, then the bidirectional search used by the retriever may require the square of the time otherwise required. In the worst case, redundancy may cause severe degradation of the results produced by the various algorithms by making poor information much more accessible than good information.

The second efficiency problem is that of preserving simple shape descriptions. We wish to record crude shape representations for quick calculations. We also wish to record simple topologies. For example, we might wish to save the four sided CHAIR-1K#, both because it is inherently simpler than the eight-sided CHAIR-1S#, and because it has a simple relation to the table.

The last efficiency problem is that of organizing the clump containment hierarchy to ensure efficiency. The only action which can be taken here is creating new intermediate clumps when the downward branching factor of some node becomes too large. For example, in figure 5-5, we might wish to break the clump HOUSE into the three clumps LEFT-WING, RIGHT-WING, and CENTER, and thus cut down searching time from one room vertex to another. However, adding such clumps for convenience would require minor changes in the semantics, and create major problems for the merger; so we have not pursued this approach.

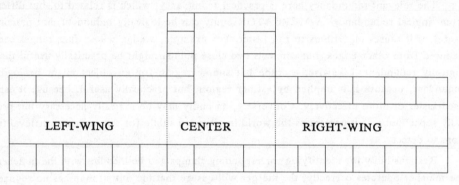

MOTEL FLOOR PLAN

Figure 5-5: Splitting a Clump

5.3. Incompatibilities and Tradeoffs

It is easy to construct a logically perfect merger, which produces a map logically equivalent to the two input maps plus correspondences. Algorithm 5-1 accomplishes this by saving everything from the two maps, except redundant copies of matched clumps, and encoding the joints and edge-matches in the combined map.

Place everything that is in the new map into the old map
except clumps which have been matched.

Merge matched clumps as follows:
  a) Add the properties of the seen clump to the known clump.
  b) Add the regions of the seen clump to the known clump.

Add all the matcher joints to the old map.

Encode all edge matches in the PCO's of the relevant clump
(see section 5.3.1.)

Fix the clump containments (see algorithm 5-6.)

Algorithm 5-1: Logically Perfect Merger

Algorithm 5-1 never adds any information without justification, and it never loses any information, except, occasionally, an edge match. However, it creates maps of awesome redundancy, with one region for each time it has seen an object. The information does not combine in any way. For example, it can never deduce that it knows an entire object unless it sees it all at once. Thus, the purely logical approach, which refuses to worry about any issues but logical adequacy, is inappropriate here; it leads to a trivial and uninteresting merger.

A useful merger must consider all the objectives listed above. Its form is determined by the way in which it resolves clashes between objectives. The most important clashes to be resolved are between the need to preserve information about the extent of objects and the normalcy conditions; between the need to preserve relative position measurements and the problem of redundancy; and between the need to save crude estimates for quick calculations and the problem of redundancy.

5.3.1. Bound Splicing

The most important difficult problem for the merger is to splice together two regions representing overlapping parts of the same object. In the example of figures 4-1 and 4-2, we have regions such as FLOOR-K# and FLOOR-S#, or WALL-K# and WALL-S#. On the one hand, the clump in our output map should cover the entire extent of both regions put together. On the other hand, the normalcy conditions require that this full extent be covered in its entirety by each region of the clump; that each bounds of each region form well ordered chains; and the polygons of each region fit together without holes or overlapping, like a jigsaw puzzle. And we have to accomplish this while respecting the ignorance which our maps express in grain-sizes and fuzzy measurements in the maps and in the correspondences relating the maps.

We will first consider bounds, which are both simpler and more important than polygons. The bound splicer takes as input a number of chains of bounds in seen regions and known regions, and edge-matches and joints relating them. It must derive the bounds for a number of new regions. Each new region requires a *complete* set of chains of bounds, spanning the entire boundaries of all of the input regions.

There are many possible criteria for the new bounds. One region will generally be chosen to be the finest possible region, with bounds of the smallest possible grain-size. We may also wish to create cruder, simpler regions for fast computation. We may wish to ensure that a particular vertex or edge is recorded as a boundary part of the object; if so, we will have to build a region containing that vertex or edge. We may wish to have two clumps recorded as adjacent at some grain-size; this requires interaction in choosing the bounds for the two clumps.

Whatever criterion we use, we will wish to have a chain of bounds which traverses the entire known boundary. Moreover, as we will discuss in section 5.3.3, there are good reasons to use only existing vertices, and not ever to create vertices in the merger. If we accept this restriction, the problem becomes one of chaining together the known vertices into boundaries satisfying the given criterion.

Any such chain must traverse the vertices *in order* and it must start from the beginning of the chains and go to the end (or go all around, if the chains form a cycle). In figure 5-6 the bounds must go from a to z. The sequence $a-b-c-x-y-z$ cannot be a valid chain, because c comes after x on the boundary. Nor can the chain $a-b-x-y-z$, because b may possibly come after x. The chains $a-b-y-z$ or $a-w-x-y-z$ or $a-b-c-z$, on the other hand, could be valid once we add the missing edges. Similarly, in figure 5-7, the chains must go from a or w to z or d; in figure 5-8, the chains must form a cycle. We therefore need some clean way of determining and expressing the order of the vertices around the boundary.

We apply the following three rules to determine the relative order of the vertices on the two input chains:

1. If bound p matches into bound q, then TAIL (p) precedes HEAD (q), and vice versa.

2. If there is a joint connecting corner c through bound p to TAIL (p) and the parallel length (PAR-LEN) of the joint in the direction antiparallel to the bound is definitely greater than 0.0, then TAIL (p) precedes c.

3. If there is a joint connecting corner c through bound p to HEAD (p) and the parallel length (PAR-LEN) of the joint in the direction parallel to the bound is definitely greater than 0.0, then c precedes HEAD (p).

The latter two rules are not strict deductions, but they are almost always valid.

The ordering information derived from these rules is used to splice together the PCO's of the two merged clumps into a single PCO. See Table 5-1 for the construction of the PCO in figure 5-6, and see section A.7 for a discussion of how to manipulate a PCO.

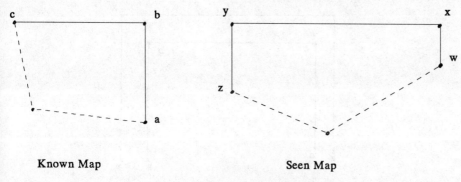

Known Map   Seen Map

Figure 5-6: Splicing Bounds: Example 1

PCO 1: $a \to b \to c$
PCO 2: $w \to x \to y \to z$

edge matches: $w - x \Rightarrow a - b$, $b - c \Rightarrow x - y$
joints: $w \Rightarrow b - a$, $x \Rightarrow a - b$, $b \Rightarrow w - x$, $b \Rightarrow y - x$, $c \Rightarrow x - y$

From edge-match $(w - x, a - b)$ deduce $a \to x$, $w \to b$.
From edge-match $(b - c, x - y)$ deduce $b \to y$, $x \to c$.
From joint $w \Rightarrow a - b$ having strictly positive PAR-LEN, deduce $a \to w$
From joint $c \Rightarrow x - y$ having strictly positive PAR-LEN, deduce $c \to y$

Final PCO

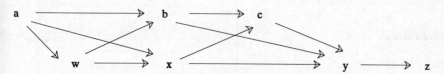

Table 5-1: PCO splicing: an example

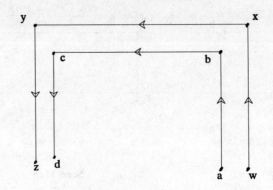

Figure 5-7: Two chains covering the same boundary

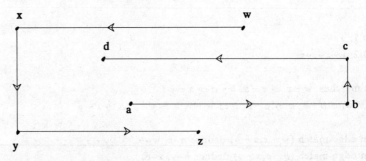

Figure 5-8: Two chains must be combined to a cycle

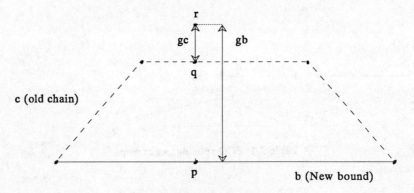

q - point corresponding to p on c

r - point on curve corresponding to q

g_c - grain-size of c

g_b - grain-size of b

Figure 5-9: Determining the Grain-Size of a New Edge

We will need new bounds to connect vertices from different chains. For example, in figure 5-6, some bound will have to connect a, b, or c to w, x, y, or z. The length and orientation fuzz of such bounds can be found readily from the measurements of connecting joints and edges. (See section 5.3.3.) Finding the grain-sizes is trickier. As figure 5-9 illustrates, the new grain-size of bound b is the maximum over all points p on b of [the minimum over all input bounds c covering p of [the grain-size of c plus the distance from p to the point on c corresponding to p]]. We have written a routine to calculate this using interval arithmetic for bounds which connect endpoints of two matched bounds. For more complicated cases, like figure 5-9, we would have to call the sketcher.

5.3.2. Polygon Splicing

Polygon splicing is much harder than bound splicing. Ideally, each output region should have polygons satisfying the following:

1. They should contain exactly that area covered by input polygons. If they cover less, they have lost information; if more, they have made invalid inferences.

2. They should be disjoint, except at edges.

3. If the bounds for the region have already been chosen, then each bound edge should be a polygon edge, and no other polygon edges should lie on the boundary.

4. They should be convex.

5. They should use only vertices already in one map or the other.

The disjointness condition implies that the polygons fit together in jigsaw puzzle fashion.

All these can be easily satisfied given a fixed set of coordinates. However, it is impossible to do so if we have only fuzzy relations between coordinates. Depending on details of measurement, the overlapping regions may create quite different shapes; and a division of polygons which works for one will not work for the other. Without keeping track of all the separate cases, there is no way to achieve the first two conditions in the presence of fuzzy measurements. (See figure 5-10.) In fact, under extreme conditions like figure 5-11, removing the risk of overlap effectively means excluding one or the other polygon entirely. As with MERCATOR maps as a whole, there is a trivial method of merging polygons which preserves all the information; merely save all the polygons. Of course, if we did this there would soon be a motley collection of polygons unusable for any calculations.

The prohibition against creating new vertices and the requirement of using edges of bounds in the same region, taken together, greatly restricts the range of polygons which can be created. In fact, they practically ensure that the polygon splicer cannot be deductive, since the lines which can be constructed typically lie outside the input polygons. This can only be avoided by the use of degenerate polygons. (See figure 5-12.)

111

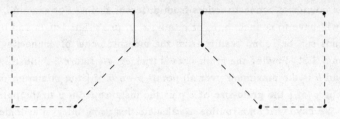

Two partial regions for the same object

If measurements are fuzzy, then the overlap can look like any of the following

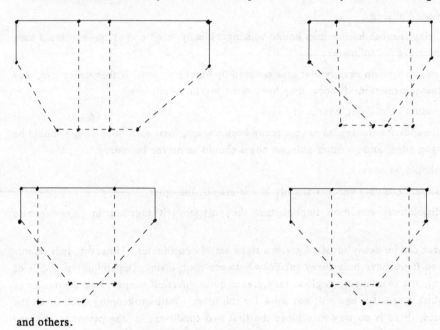

and others.

Each of these requires a set of polygons of different structure.

Figure 5-10: Overlapping Polygons

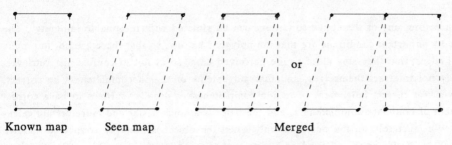

Known map	Seen map		Merged	

The two polygons could overlap or not.

Figure 5-11: Overlapping Polygons: 2

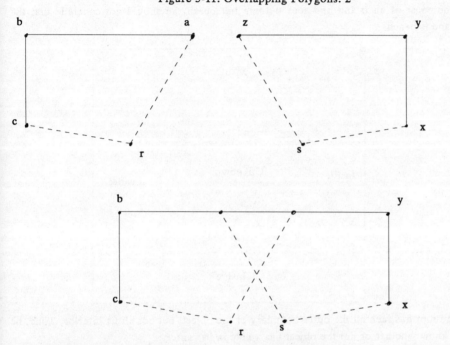

The merged polygons are supposed to use only vertices x, y, b, c, r, and s. The only polygons of this kind which stay entirely within the known area are $s - x - y$, $r - b - c$, and degenerate single edges.

Figure 5-12: Restricting Polygon Vertices

The situation would be hopeless, except that polygons are unimportant in MERCATOR. In fact, polygons as such are not used anywhere outside the merger. The merger uses polygons to help generate knowledge bounds and internal edges. The internal edges are important to connect nearby region vertices. Knowledge bounds are used to retrieve the extent of incompletely known objects and to distinguish between complete and incomplete regions.*

---

* Note, however, that polygons play a much more important role in other retrieval functions, such as path finders, and in systems with completeness information. If MERCATOR were extended to handle

113

Therefore, any of the above conditions can be violated with reasonable impunity. The only really important conditions are that the polygons be few, so that there are not too many internal edges; that they stay close to the perceived area, so as not to confuse the retriever; that they not intersect themselves; and that judgements of region completeness be correct. Moreover, for correct judgement of region completeness it usually suffices to have correct judgement of boundary completeness, and the latter is a much easier and more certain calculation. We must rely on the polygons only when the object is multiply connected and we have seen the entire exterior boundary but no part of some internal boundary. (See figure 5-13.) This case is rare, but worth keeping in mind. For example, if the robot wanders all around the coast of an island and sees nothing but beach, he should not conclude that the entire island is beach.

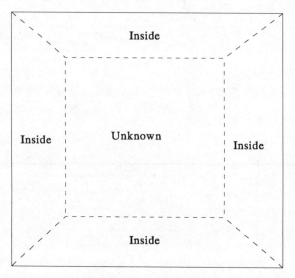

The robot has seen all the outer boundary of the object, but not all its interior. Thus, he does not know whether or not the object has a hole in its center.

Figure 5-13: Polygons used to determine completeness

It is not critical that the polygons created be deductively valid. The actual MERCATOR merger creates polygons which are contained within the convex hull of the seen area, thought not necessarily within the seen area. If the object is convex, this is wholly legitimate; even if it is not, it is unlikely to cause trouble. It can cause the retriever to assume a slightly larger object than is actually valid. However, for many computations, including relative position (see Section 3.5) the answer depends only on the convex hull, so no false information will be produced. The program will sometimes falsely conclude that it has seen the entire object after it has seen the boundary. However, this conclusion will make trouble only in the rare case that there is a hole in some unseen part of the object.

these, our rather casual attitude might not suffice.

5.3.3. Preserving Measurements

There are three ways to improve the measurements — relative positions or object dimensions — in the cognitive map. The first is *splicing*, bringing an edge or joint or several from the scene description into the cognitive map. The second is *fuzz constriction*, tightening the fuzz ranges on measurements of edges or joints already in the map. The third is *edge creation*, building an edge or joint between two vertices in the map which lies close to some edge between vertices not in the map. Splicing requires no numeric computation, but a lot of thought. Fuzz constriction and edge creation require a lot of computation and little thought.

If an edge or joint connecting the boundaries of two objects is strikingly precise, then it may be worthwhile to splice the vertices and the edge or joint into the map in order to capture the relative position of the two objects. (See figure 5-14.) But caution is necessary. For one thing, we will have to build regions which include the boundary vertices. This may be more trouble to the region builder than is worthwhile. For another thing, the mere fact that a measurement is unusually precise does not mean that it carries particularly valuable data. We mentioned above the difficulties of determining what is information in a MERCATOR map. One case where it is particularly hard is for edges connecting two objects. (See figure 5-15 for an example where apparently good measurements in fact express no more than apparently poor measurements.)

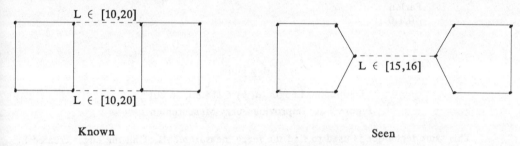

Known   Seen

Figure 5-14: An edge which carries a measurement

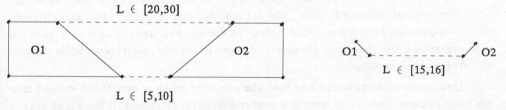

The seen map adds no new information. In any model of the known map, there exists a line from O_1 to O_2 of length between 15 and 16.

Figure 5-15: An edge which does not carry a measurement

Fuzz constriction and edge creation are similar operations. We calculate the distance between two vertices from a path of edges and correspondence joints using Monte Carlo techniques. (See figure 5-16.) If the two vertices are already connected by an edge, and this technique give more accurate measurements of the quantities, then we can record as the new measurement the intersection of the old measurement with the calculation. If the two vertices are not connected by an edge, then an edge can be created with these measurements.

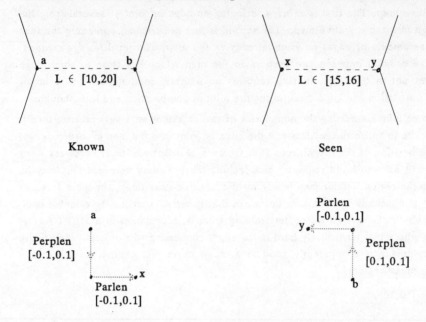

Connecting joints

Deduction: Length $(a, b) \in [14.80, 16.20]$

Figure 5-16: Improving Fuzzy Measurements

This same technique is used to find the fuzzy measurements of all the edges created by the merger.

Fuzz constriction is actually better done as part of the matcher, as discussed in section 4.11. For reasons discussed there, we did not take that approach. The above method requires duplicating calculations already done in the matcher, and it passes over potential improvement to the matcher. However, the quality of the actual constriction done is not usually much impaired.

These techniques are called into play when an edge which is outside the merged map has fuzzy measurements which seem to be unusually tight in its context. If there is an edge in the map that lies close to it, or is tightly connected to it, we can apply fuzz constriction. If there are two vertices unconnected by any edge which lie close to its endpoints, we can create a edge between them. Otherwise, we must apply splicing.

5.3.4. Crude Estimates

The issue of keeping crude regions is a direct clash between the needs of efficiency and the need to avoid redundancy. Crude regions — that is, simple regions with large grain-size — are, by definition, redundant; almost their only *raison de etre* is to render certain algorithms more efficient. (Occasionally, they also make the matcher more effective.) No other issues are involved here. Keeping crude regions does not conflict with the regularity conditions, and it is fully compatible with the bound and polygon splicer. However, it turns out to be extremely difficult to come up with a set of criteria for constructing crude regions which is both sensible and general. In large measure, this is due to inadequacies in the region construct. (See section 8.5.2.) Owing to this difficulty, we have decided to keep only a single region — the finest — in the actual MERCATOR program.

Maintaining simple topological relations, particularly region adjacency, is still more problematic. It involves choosing adjacent or closely related regions from two different clumps. It is difficult to do this without generating large numbers of inferior regions.

5.3.5. Second Order Problems

The solutions which we have proposed to the above problems interact in a number of ways, mostly harmful. Measurement preservation by splicing edges places demands on the bounds splicer. Choosing bounds places demands on the polygon merger, and vice versa. Picking crude regions interacts with both of these. There is no general scheme for resolving these interactions. Rather, we must simply decide priorities, and force the lower priority processes to make do with the results of the higher priority processes.

5.4. The MERCATOR merger

In this section we will present the algorithms that we have actually implemented in MERCATOR, with examples. We will also indicate what additional features could easily be added, and how.

Algorithm 5-2 shows the overall structure of the merger. It is rather minimal. It saves only one region per clump, as discussed above, and does not do any kind of measurement preservation. Fuzz constriction and edge creation could easily be added at the end. I left these out for want of time.

Input : a cognitive map, a scene description, and a set of matcher correspondences.
Output: an updated cognitive map.

Add unmatched seen clumps to map.

Add properties of matched seen clumps to those of matching known clumps.

Adjust clump containment hierarchy to reflect clump matches and new clumps.
   (See algorithm 5-6.)

Loop for each clump match:
  Use the edge-matches to merge the PCO's of the matched clumps.
  Find the "finest" complete chains of bounds in the PCO's using
    existing vertices. (See algorithm 5-3.)
  Merge the polygons to fit the chosen set of bounds and the existing
    vertices. (See algorithm 5-5.)
  Note the knowledge bounds as the polygon edges which are not
    real bounds and not shared with another polygon.
  Put the chains and polygons together into a region.
  Save the region as the only region of the merged clump.
endloop;

(In saving the constructed regions, all their vertices and connecting
  edges are saved (transferred to the cognitive map) automatically.)

Eliminate
  a) Vertices not in a polygon or bound of an approved region
  b) Edges or joints not connecting two approved vertices
  c) PCO relations on unused vertices

Fix all the back pointers. These are pointers from bounds to regions,
  from vertices to edges, etc. which allow quick retrieval.

Algorithm 5-2: Merger: Overall Structure

Merging more than two clumps together requires almost no modification in the algorithm. This feature is implemented in the MERCATOR program.

Fixing back pointers (the last step of the algorithm 5-2) and insuring that decisions taken by one section of the algorithm are available to the next, though theoretically trivial, occupy a good third of the merger code.

The algorithm refers to three subroutines: to find the bounds, to find the polygons, and to fix the clump containment graph. These are shown in algorithms 5-3, 5-5, and 5-6, respectively. (Algorithm 5-4 is a subroutine of algorithm 5-3.)

118

Input: A PCO of vertices, with chains of bounds connecting some of the vertices
Output: The finest complete chain of bounds

For each PCO link connecting two consecutive vertices which does not
  have a bound associated, create a bound. Find the fuzzy measurements
  of the bound as described in section 5.3.3. Find the grain-size of
  the bound as described in section 5.3.1.

Assign a "weakness" score to each bound in the PCO. The weakness score
  should be an increasing function of the grain-size of the bound, the
  length of the bound, and the fuzz in the measurements of the bound.

Find the complete chain with the minimal total score using algorithm 5-4.

Algorithm 5-3: Splicing Bounds

Input: a PCO with score attached to its arcs.
Output: the complete chain with minimal score

Assign each starting PCO node (node without a predecessor) a total
    score of 0.0, and mark it as explored but unexpanded.
Assign all other PCO nodes a total score of infinity.
Loop until all nodes are expanded:
   Choose a node n which is explored but not expanded and all of
      whose predecessors are expanded;
   Loop for each bound b leaving n
      Let m be the far end of b;
      Let new-score be the total score of n plus the score of b;
      If the total score of m is greater than new-score then
         set the total score of m to be new-score;
         mark m as explored;
         attach a back-pointer from m back to n;
      endif
   endloop
   Mark n as expanded
endloop;
Find the ending vertex with minimal score. Find the minimum score path
  by following back pointers.

Algorithm 5-4: Finding Optimal Chain

Algorithm 5-4, above, assumes that the PCO is not closed; the case where the PCO is
closed is an easy modification. The algorithm is an adaptation of the standard algorithm for
finding the longest path in a DAG. It has a useful incidental property. Suppose we have to

merge two regions which are each accurate in one section of the boundary, and inaccurate in another. We wish to merge these together into a single chain incorporating the best part of each. This same algorithm will do that for us. We use the edge-matches and elbows to arrange the vertices in a PCO; we add the crossing edges; and then we find the best complete cycle of edges.

Modifying algorithm 5-3 to produce chains of bounds other than the finest requires two changes. Firstly, we will wish to form bounds connecting unconnected vertices which are not consecutive; criteria must be found for choosing such vertices. Secondly, scores must be assigned to each bound. The first is a hard problem. Its difficulty is a major reason that we have not implemented the creation of crude regions. Moreover, finding grain-sizes for bounds which connect non-consecutive vertices is quite a difficult computation.

Algorithm 5-5 constructs a new set of polygons for a region:

Input: Sets of polygons, a set of PCO's, designated chains of bounds in the PCO's

Output: A good set of polygons

Expand each polygon by replacing each boundary vertex with the corresponding vertex or vertices on the chain in the outward direction.

Remove duplicate polygons.

For each polygon with non-boundary vertices, but with three or more consecutive boundary vertices, create a new polygon by connecting up the consecutive boundary vertices cyclically. This is called a *nook* polygon.

Group the polygons into sets according to the boundary chain or chains containing their vertices. Take each set of polygons all of whose vertices lie on one or two chains, and string them into a set which fits together jigsaw puzzle fashion. Again, remove duplicates.

For each set of polygons all of whose vertices are on a single chain or on two chains, string them together into a set which fits in jigsaw puzzle fashion. Again, remove duplicates.

If the region is complete, then quit.

Call the sketcher to assign a consistent set of coordinates to the vertices of all the remaining polygons

Fix polygons which overlap edges.

Remove any polygon which is wholly contained within other polygons, or which is not a true polygon.

Algorithm 5-5: Merging Polygons

We illustrate algorithm 5-5 with three examples, illustrated in figures 5-17, 5-18, and 5-19, and tables 5-2, 5-3, and 5-4 respectively.

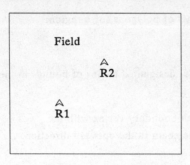

Real World. Two successive robot positions shown

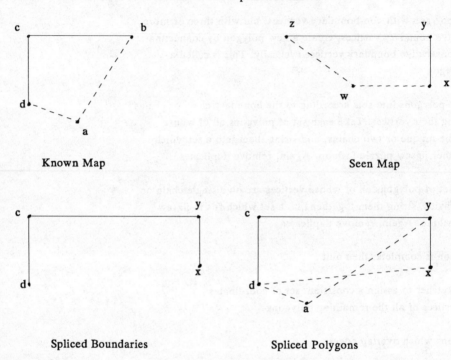

Known Map   Seen Map

Spliced Boundaries   Spliced Polygons

Figure 5-17: Polygon Splicing: Example 1

Input polygons: (a,b,c,d); (w,x,y,z)
Input region bounds: $x \rightarrow y \rightarrow c \rightarrow d$

Expand polygons: $(a,b,c,d) => (a,y,c,d)$
                     $(w,x,y,z) => (w,x,y,c)$

Duplicate polygons: None
Nook polygons: (y,c,d) and (x,y,c)
Jigsaw bounded polygons: (y,c,d) and $(x,y,c) => (x,y,c,d)$
Redundant polygons: (w,x,y,c) is contained in (x,y,c,d)

Output polygons: (x,y,c,d), (a,y,c,d).

Table 5-2: Splicing Polygons: Example 1

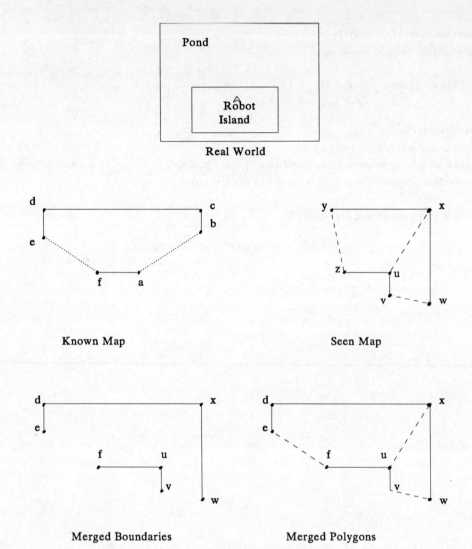

Figure 5-18: Polygon Splicing: Example 2

Input polygons: (a,b,c,d,e,f); (u,v,w,x) and (u,x,y,z)
Input region bounds: $w{\rightarrow}x{\rightarrow}d{\rightarrow}e$; $f{\rightarrow}u{\rightarrow}v$

Expand polygons: (a,b,c,d,e,f) => (u,w,x,d,e,f)
                            (u,v,w,x) => (u,v,w,x) (unchanged)
                            (u,x,y,z) => (u,x,d,f)

Duplicate polygons: None
Nook polygons: (x,d,e)

Jigsaw bounded polygons: (u,w,x,d,e,f), (u,v,w,x),   and
                                       (u,x,d,f)
                            => (u,v,w,x) and (u,x,d,e,f)

Redundant polygons: None

Output polygons: (u,v,w,x), (u,x,d,e,f)

Table 5-3: Splicing Polygons: Example 2

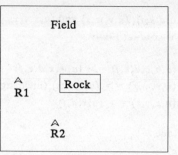

Real World: Two robot positions shown

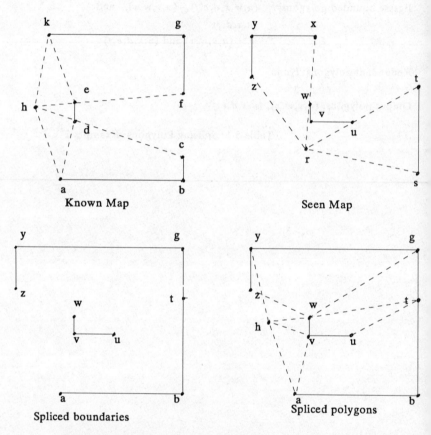

Figure 5-19: Polygon Splicing: Example 3

Input polygons: (e,f,g,k), (h,e,k), (h,d,e), (h,a,d), (a,b,c,d)
                     (r,v,w,x,y,z), (r,u,v), (r,s,t,u)

Input region bounds: $a \rightarrow b \rightarrow t \rightarrow g \rightarrow y \rightarrow z$

Expand polygons: $(e,f,g,k) => (w,t,g,y)$
                     $(h,e,k) => (h,w,g,y)$
                     $(h,d,e) => (h,v,w)$
                     $(h,a,d) => (h,a,v)$
                     $(a,b,c,d) => (a,b,t,v)$
                     $(r,v,w,x,y,z) => (r,v,w,g,y,z)$
                     $(r,u,v) => (r,u,v)$ (unchanged)
                     $(r,s,t,u) => (r,b,t,u)$

Duplicate polygons: None
Nook polygons: (t,g,y), (a,b,t), (g,y,z)
Jigsaw bounded polygons: (t,g,y) and $(g,y,z) => (t,g,y,z)$

Fix polygon: (t,g,y,z) to (t,g,y,z,w)
                 (a,b,t,v) to (a,b,t,u,v)

Redundant polygons: (t,g,y,z,w) contains (w,t,g,y)
                        (t,g,y,z,w), (h,w,g,y),
                        (h,v,w), and (h,a,v) contain
                        (r,v,w,g,y,z)
                        (h,a,v) and (a,b,t,u,v) contain
                        (r,b,t,u) and (r,u,c)

Output polygons: (t,g,y,z,w), (h,w,g,y), (h,v,w), (h,a,v),

                                          and (a,b,t,u,v)

Table 5-4: Splicing Polygons: Example 3

The polygons produced by this merger have the following properties:

1   The area covered by the output polygons contains the area covered by the input polygons, and is contained in its convex hull. The algorithm is not deductive but it does preserve information.

2. Each bound on the chosen chains is a bound of a polygon.

3. The polygons all of whose vertices lie on one or two chains are non-overlapping. This is easy to enforce on these polygons, since it can be characterized topologically.

4. Each polygon covers some area not covered by any other polygon.

5. It is very rare, though possible, for this algorithm to produce a polygon which is invalid in the sense that its edges necessarily intersect each other.

Finally, there is algorithm 5-6, which maintains clump containments. After the last couple of algorithms, this should be pleasantly simple:

Input: Two containment hierarchies of clumps (known and seen) and a set of clump-matches

Output: An updated known containment hierarchy.

Out of each set of clumps which are matched together, let one clump be the designated clump, and the others be the matching clumps. If clump c is a matching clump, desig (c) is the designated clump matched with c.

For each unmatched or designated clump c,
  for each clump d, a container or content of c
    replace d by desig d as a container or content of c.

For each matching clump, c,
  for each d, a container or content of c,
    add desig (d) is to the containers (contents) of desig (c).

Algorithm 5-6: Preserving Clump Containment

6 Review of Previous Work

6.1. Introduction

Spatial representations, spatial reasoning, and geometric calculations have been the subjects of an overwhelming body of study. In AI, these questions constitute a large part of research into vision, robotics, and naive physics. Spatial reasoning has been studied from many different angles in cognitive psychology — in terms of development, memory, inference, imagery, problem solving — and is a favorite domain for work in animal psychology, because of the relative ease of devising experiments to test it. Spatial representations and calculations constitute nearly the entire subject of computational geometry, and a very large part of computer graphics. In a slightly different sense, it is a large part of all the graphic arts. Finally, space is the subject of a substantial fraction of mathematics, including much of geometry, topology, and real and complex analysis.

In the face of this enormous literature (of which I know only a small part), I will largely concentrate in this chapter on work in AI which have addressed the problem of cognitive mapping. I will also briefly discuss the work in psychology on cognitive mapping, the work in AI on vision and on naive physics, and work in computational geometry on polynomial approximations most directly relevant to MERCATOR.

6.2. McDermott's SPAM

Drew McDermott [McDermott and Davis, 84] developed the SPAM program (short for SPAtial Module) as a knowledge base manager for spatial information, acting as a autonomous module of an arbitrary reasoning system. The overall structure is like that of MERCATOR, consisting of an assimilator, which assimilates a sequence of geographic facts into a cognitive map; a quantity retriever, which answers user queries about specific objects using the information in the cognitive map; and an object retriever, which enumerates all objects with specified properties.

For example, one can tell SPAM, "the distance from DESK1 to CHAIR52 is less than 4 feet" and "the distance from CHAIR52 to ME is less than 6 feet", and these facts are assimilated into a cognitive map. If one then queries SPAM "How far is DESK1 from ME?", it will answer "From 0 to 10 feet". (SPAM will actually succeed on this particular problem.)

The positional representation in SPAM is based on the idea of associating a frame of reference with each object. Each frame of reference has its own origin, scale, and orientation. The positional part of the map consists of facts of a particular kind relating pairs of reference frames. Three kinds of relations are recorded: the coordinates in one frame of reference of the origin of another frame; the difference between the orientations of two frames; and the ratio between the scales of two frames. Constant ranges (fuzz ranges) are used for each of these. For example the map might record "the coordinates of the origin of TREE1 in the reference frame of YARD5 lie in [5.0, 7.0], [2.0, 3.0]," "the orientation of

HOUSE5 is between -0.1 and 0.3 counterclockwise from the orientation of STREET14," or "the scale of ROOM23 is between 5.0 and 7.0 times that of DESK12." Such a relation is called an *mquant*. (See figure 6-1.) The mquants are constrained to correspond to three trees (for position, orientation, and scale) on the reference frames.

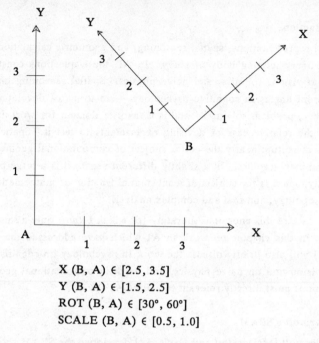

X (B, A) ∈ [2.5, 3.5]
Y (B, A) ∈ [1.5, 2.5]
ROT (B, A) ∈ [30°, 60°]
SCALE (B, A) ∈ [0.5, 1.0]

Figure 6-1: SPAM Mquants

Shapes in SPAM are described in terms of hierarchies of "circyls", cylinders with spherical endcaps (see figures 6-2 and 6-3.) Circyls are characterized by length, cylinder radius, and endcap radii. Mquants relate these lengths to each other and to other scales. Objects are described as a single circyl to first order, and as sets of circyls to higher orders.

Figure 6-2: A Circyl

Quantity retrieval in SPAM is performed similarly to MERCATOR. The organization of the mquants in trees insures that any specified quantity can be expressed in a unique way in terms of mquants, and that this expression can be easily found. The problem is then reduced to finding to the maximum and minimum of the function, given the bounds on the mquants. This can be done, either using Monte Carlo search or using hill-climbing.

Assimilation is done in one of two ways. The less drastic way is called *fuzz constriction*. The new fact may imply new and tighter bounds on one or more of the mquants. If so, these new bounds can be recorded. If fuzz constriction fails, it is sometimes possible to assimilate

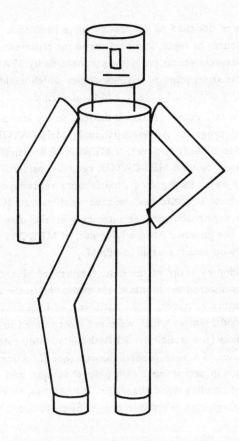

Figure 6-3: Multiple Circyls

the fact using *remapping*, a restructuring of the mquant trees, including possibly introducing new frames of reference.

SPAM ran into a host of technical problems, which are described in the references. In my opinion, these were fundamentally due to two underlying problems. The first was that the shape representation is not integrated with the positional representation. For example, there is no way in SPAM to specify the distance between two facing sides of two objects precisely, while leaving their sizes vague, because there is no way to refer to the object boundaries. There is no way to enumerate a row of shops on a street and specify that they fit together tightly from one end of the street to another without specifying the exact size of each. There is no natural way to assert that four objects lie at the corners of a rectangle, without specifying the dimensions of the rectangle. (See [Davis, 81].)

The second major problem with SPAM was its very generality and abstraction. It was supposed to do inference and answer queries for an arbitrary domain, but, as discussed in appendix A.5, performing arbitrary geometric inference is intractably hard. Since SPAM was conceived *invacuo*, without context, there were no guidelines for imposing normalcy conditions on the input, or for restricting the range of inferences to be performed.

MERCATOR was designed to get around these problems. I chose vision as a natural and understandable source of input, and I reformed the representation to be boundary based, and thus avoid the inexpressiveness problems encountered by SPAM. The switch in representation also enabled the description of various shapes which could not be cleanly handled in SPAM, such as multiply connected objects, and the description of partially occluded objects.

The difference in task domain makes it difficult to say whether SPAM or MERCATOR was a better working program. An assimilation in MERCATOR, for example, takes ten times as long as one in SPAM; however, a MERCATOR assimilation involves much more input information. In my opinion MERCATOR can be considered an advance on SPAM in a number of significant ways. Its representation is more expressive, more flexible, and better defined. The hierarchical structure has semantic significance. Its normalcy conditions have been formulated. Its asymptotic time requirements as the map grows large seems to be better, though this is not proven. Also, a large part of MERCATOR deals with scene recognition, which is wholly outside the scope of SPAM.

MERCATOR adopted many of the basic features of SPAM, most notably the use of fuzz ranges to express uncertainty; Monte Carlo evaluation in the retriever; and the choice of basic modules — quantity retriever, object retriever, and assimilator. However, SPAM has quite a number of good features which were not incorporated in MERCATOR. SPAM has size and orientation trees (see section 8.5.3.) Both the quantity retriever and the object retriever will answer queries of a very general format. (See [McDermott, 80] and [McDermott, 81].) The assimilator will accept input of a general format, and when it can do something with it, it will. SPAM handles three dimensions. SPAM has, to a limited degree, the ability to reorganize the cognitive map in order to group objects found to be physically close.

6.3. Kuipers' TOUR

The task domain of the TOUR program (see [Kuipers, 77], [Kuipers, 78]) is the same as MERCATOR's: to create a cognitive by moving about and piecing together local descriptions. The conception of maps and descriptions is wholly different.

Kuipers' maps are called "route maps" in psychology (see section 6.10); they contain mainly topological information. A map consists of PLACES (points); PATHS (curves); REGIONS (areas); and ORIENTATION-FRAMES (local reference frames). A PLACE description consists of (1) a standard ORIENTATION-FRAME; (2) a set of PATHS intersecting at the PLACE, together with the angles of the PATHS relative to the ORIENTATION-FRAME; (3) a set of distances and directions to other PLACES which are presumably visible from the base PLACE. A PATH description consists of (1) a partial ordering of PLACES on the PATH; and (2) REGIONS bounded by the PATH on the left and the right. The description of an ORIENTATION-FRAME consists of its orientation relative to other frames. A REGION description is a list of PLACES contained and bounding PATHS.

The position of the robot is described in terms of its current PLACE and PATH, and its direction on the PATH.

The simulated robot performs two types of actions; TURN and GO-TO. These inputs take a number of fields, some of them optional. The program tries to fill in open slots. For example, if the robot is instructed to GO a specified distance along a known path, and he knows what lies at the end of that distance, then he will fill in the destination slot of the GO command. The program also tries to deduce facts about the world from the filled slots. For example, if he is at Providence on Route 95 going south, and he is told to GO-TO New Haven, he will deduce that New Haven is a PLACE incident to 95, and that it comes after Providence on 95. These are the two actions of the program: to build up the cognitive map, deducing PLACES, PATHS and ORIENTATION-FRAMES from the input arguments to the actions; and to deduce missing arguments of the action from the cognitive map.

Kuipers also discusses how to calculate position using dead reckoning from distances and directions, and how to plan routes by using the hierarchy of regions, but he did not implement either of these.

Clearly, topological maps of this kind cannot express the metric information of a MERCATOR map. On the other hand, it is worth noting that MERCATOR has no equivalent of the PATH primitive, and therefore is less able than TOUR to represent situations where only topological information is available.

6.4. Lavin's DYNAVU

Another view of cognitive mapping was presented by Mark Lavin in [Lavin, 77] and implemented in his program DYNAVU. Like TOUR and MERCATOR, Lavin simulates a robot wandering in a world and incrementally creating a cognitive map from a sequence of descriptions The world of DYNAVU consists of unimodal hills. The robot moves through this world, taking frequent snapshots. The vision simulator provides schematized descriptions of these snapshots with slight inaccuracies introduced randomly. (See figure 6-4.) No information is provided about the motion of the robot. The object of the program is to identify the 3-D coordinates of every mountain peak, and the coordinates of the viewpoint of each snapshot.

DYNAVU contains four basic modules:

1. MATCHER: This matches two snapshots and finds hills common to each. It uses four criteria: matches must be 1:1, the image coordinates must be close, IN-FRONT-OF relations must be preserved, and hills in the foreground should be matched before hills in the background. (See figure 6-5.)

2. DPMF5: Given two scenes with two or more matched hills of known coordinates, determine the viewpoints of the snapshots.

3. DPMF6: Given two scenes from two viewpoints with known coordinates, deduce the coordinates of the matched hills

4. DPMF7: Given two scenes with at least three matches, deduce the positions of the matched hills and the two viewpoints.

DPMF5, DPMF6, and DPMF7 use involved trigonometric formulas which to find the 3-D point which will minimize the error in the 2-D views. They also return confidence ratings.

133

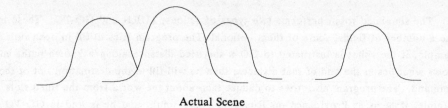

Actual Scene

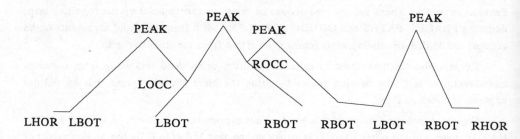

Schematized Description of Input

Description shows structure of image features, with image coordinates.

Image features: LBOT, RBOT — left, right bottom of hill
       LOCC, ROCC — left, right occlusion point
       LHOR, RHOR — left, right limits of horizon
       PEAK — peak of hill

Figure 6-4: Input to DYNAVU

DYNAVU combines these in algorithm 6-1:

Apply matcher to first two inputs.

Apply DPMF7 with matches to first two inputs to get coordinates of matched hills and two viewpoints

Loop through subsequent inputs:

 Match new input against previous input

 Take matches involving hills already located.

 Use DPMF5 to locate new viewpoint.

 Use DPMF6 to locate newly matched hills.

Algorithm 6-1: DYNAVU Algorithm

(This description is considerably simplified. In particular, Lavin contains some functions to deduce the radius of the hills, and he has various devices for modifying tolerances or picking new scenes to match if the requisite number of matches cannot be found.)

134

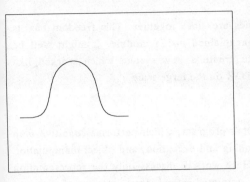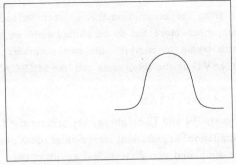

No match — image coordinates too far apart.

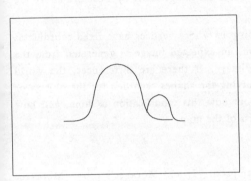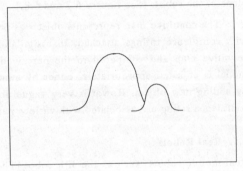

No match — IN-FRONT-OF relation reversed.

Figure 6-5: Matching in DYNAVU

Lavin's model has notable similarities to MERCATOR. The cognitive map is metric. Uncertainty in position is explicitly represented. Assimilation is reduced to matching and merging, though DYNAVU's merger is rather trivial. Several of the omissions which Lavin points out in DYNAVU have been fixed in MERCATOR. These include the ability to handle broken contours (see figure 6-6) and the optional use of explicit motion information.

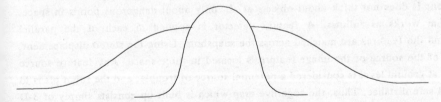

Figure 6-6: Broken Contour

However, the two programs are really analogous rather than parallel. The great difference is in the inputs. DYNAVU starts with a processed image while MERCATOR starts with a small cognitive map. This frees MERCATOR from the difficulties of image interpretation

135

and from the assumption that consecutive scenes are close together. This freedom has its price; much more has to be shifted onto an unexplained vision module. It might well be worth trying to combine the two programs to create a new system which worked like DYNAVU on the small scale and like MERCATOR on the large scale.

6.5. Rowat's UTAK

[Rowat, 79] and [Rosenberg, 81] present the Utak program, which performs cognitive map assimilation, exploration, incremental route planning and execution, and object manipulation in a simulated two-dimensional environment. Here we will discuss only the representation and assimilation. The input to the assimilator is simulated retinal input, in terms of grey levels on a grid. The retina has high resolution at the center, and low resolution at the periphery, in imitation of a real retina. Conceptually, it is the image taken by a camera above the plane of the robot. (See figures 6-7 and 6-8.)

The cognitive map represents objects as polygons whose vertices have fixed coordinates with confidence ratings attached. In assimilation, an expected image is generated from the cognitive map and compared to the perceived image. If there are differences, the world model is adjusted appropriately, either by modifying the shapes recorded for the objects or by adding new object. Rowat is very vague about how this modification is done, and how confidence rating are associated with various parts of the map.

6.6. Real Robots

Real mobile robots, such as the JPL robot [Thompson, 77] and Moravec's robot [Moravec, 81] necessarily face the problem of constructing a cognitive map. However, other difficulties usually loom much larger, and consequentally cognitive mapping is performed somewhat crudely.

Moravec's cart is a mobile robot equipped with a movable camera. Its task is to get to a given destination without bumping into obstacles. It executes a run by first taking camera snapshots from nine different positions for super stereo information; then lurching forward some safe distance; then looking again; and so on.

Remarkably, the cart manages to carry out its task without doing any kind of object discrimination. It does not think about objects at all, only about dangerous points in space. The algorithm works as follows. A feature detector is applied to each of the parallel snapshots, and the features are matched across the snapshots. Using the stereo displacement, the location of the source of the image feature is located in three-space. Any feature source which is not at ground level is considered a potential source of trouble, and the robot plans to avoid it by a safe distance. Thus, the cognitive map which is built up consists simply of 3-D coordinates for worrisome points.

After the robot moves, its position and orientation is calculated by comparing the feature points in the new set of snapshots with the feature points in the old cognitive map. The program finds the maximal set of feature matches which preserves distances.

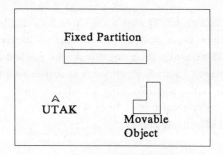

Figure 6-7: World for Utak

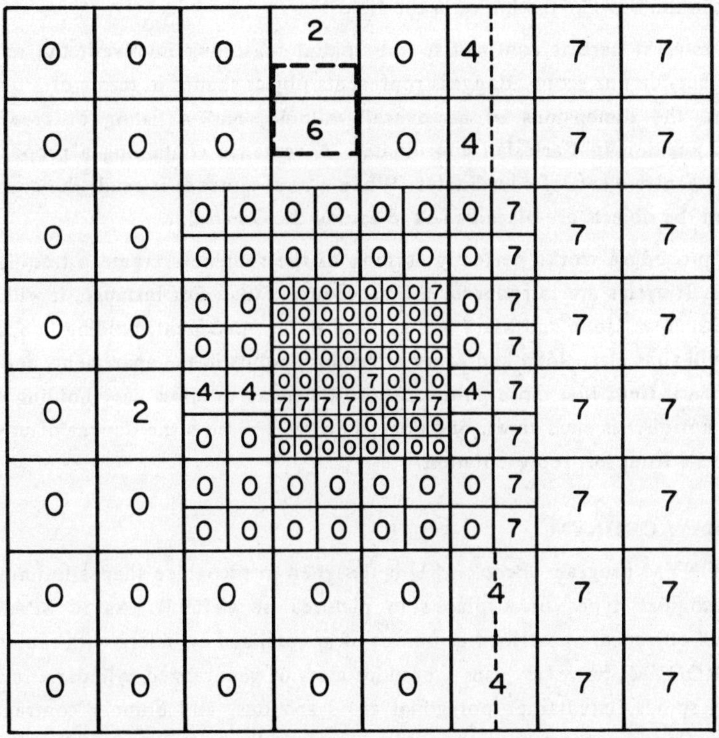

			2				
O	O	O	⌐‾‾¬	O	4	7	7
O	O	O	6	O	4	7	7
O	O	O O O O O O O 7 / O O O O O O O O 7				7	7
O	O	O O / O O	O O O O O O O 7 / O O O O O O O O / O O O O O O O O / O O O O O O O O	O 7 / O 7		7	7
O	2	4‑4 / O O	O O O 7 O O O / 7 7 7 0 O O 7 7 / O O O O O O O O / O O O O O O O O	4 7 / O 7		7	7
O	O	O O O O O O O 7 / O O O O O O O O 7				7	7
O	O	O	O	O	4	7	7
O	O	O	O	O	4	7	7

Copied from [Rowat, 79]

Figure 6-8: Retina for Utak

137

The JPL robot [Thompson, 77] uses a cognitive map divided into square sectors. The map marks non-traversible areas and unknown areas in terms of polygons with vertices of fixed coordinates. Their article does not discuss the method of assimilation used. However, in this representation, a simple algorithm will suffice. All that must be done is to find how the unknown areas in the cognitive map are marked in the corresponding sector of the visual input, and fill them in accordingly. Since the map uses coordinates in a fixed reference frame, this can be done effectively and easily.

6.7. Boggess

[Boggess, 79] discusses assimilation of spatial information from natural language texts; in particular, the dependence of the meaning of prepositions on the objects they relate. For example "in" means three different relationships in the three phrases "the soup in the bowl", "the crack in the bowl", "the house in the field".

Our interest here is confined to the spatial reasoning involved; the natural language issues are outside our scope. Boggess represents object shapes in terms of a qualitative shape description, the dimensions of an overall volume, and a listing of free surfaces. She represents position in Cartesian coordinates. A sentence containing a preposition is a constraint between two sets of coordinates. When a new sentence is read, the constraint is interpreted, and the objects are placed so as to satisfy the constraint.

This procedure works perfectly as long as the sentences create a tree-like structure of constraints. If cycles are introduced, the procedure fails. For instance, it will not work with a sentence such as "John and Mary were sitting in his apartment, holding hands," because the program will first place John and Mary at random points in the apartment, and not be able to correct when it finds that those points are too far away to allow easy holding of hands. Boggess does not discuss such cases. She does, however, discuss the danger of unwarranted precise retrievals from this representation.

6.8. Brooks' ACRONYM

The ACRONYM program [Brooks, 81] is designed to recognize shapes in images; in particular, to recognize types of airplanes in pictures of airfields. As in SPAM, specific 3-dimensional objects are described as unions of generalized cylinders with real-valued parameters. ACRONYM, however, uses a broader class of generalized cylinders, including straight or circular spines, circular or polygonal cross sections, and bilinear contractions in either dimension. Generic object models are described similarly, with symbolic constraints on the parameters. Relative positions of generalized cylinders are specified by linear transformations (rotation of the principal axis and translation of the origin). Two dimensional images are described as unions of ribbons and ellipses, which are the projections of generalized cylinders. The three-dimensional object models are used to calculate predictions of potential features of the image in terms of ribbons and ellipses, including constraints on the measurements of these features. These predictions are matched against the image, and the measurements taken from the image are checked for consistency with the original model

Of primary interest to us is Brooks' constraint manipulation system (CMS), which finds upper and lower bounds of a quantity under a set of symbolic constraints. CMS accept a very broad class of constraints. A constraint must be expressible in normal form, as an inequality with a single variable on one side, and an expression using an arbitrary combination of other variables and the functions $+$, $-$, $\times$, $\div$ min, max, sin, and cos. It uses an extension of the SUP-INF algorithms given in [Shostak, 77]. These algorithms are provably correct, in that they always terminate, and they always return upper and lower bounds.

Our major objections to generalized cylinders in SPAM, that they made it difficult to constrain object boundaries, does not apply here, owing to the generality of the constrain language. ACRONYM allows the expression of practically any constraints at all. The class of expressible facts in ACRONYM — its epistemological adequacy, in the terms of [McCarthy and Hayes, 69] — is considerably greater than MERCATOR's .

Extending ACRONYM to cognitive mapping would be difficult. It would require a well defined semantics for matching objects, like MERCATOR's grain-size; a representation for partially known objects; a method of splicing together partial descriptions of objects; and an organization of constraints which makes it possible to extract the relevant constraints in particular problems. The program obviously cannot consider all the constraints in the map for each calculation; it must heuristically choose a set of important constraints before presenting the problem to the SUP-INF algorithm. When this was done, there would be no assurance that it would work. Brooks states that he believes that the SUP-INF algorithm is complete for linear problems, but those are rare in MERCATOR. Almost every problem is quadratic, and as we will show in appendix A.5, there is no efficient complete algorithm for these.

It might be more promising to add the CMS to MERCATOR. It could be used instead of, or in addition to, the Monte Carlo evaluator or the sketcher. It would also allow the addition of constraints not currently available in MERCATOR, of the sort which come from natural language or general rules (see section 9.4.6), though this would again raise the problem of isolating the relevant constraints in a given situation.

6.9. Approximating Curves by Polygons

Chains of straight lines are probably the simplest approximations for curves, and they have been extensively studied in image processing. One popular line-based scheme is *chain encoding*, which uses a sequence of lines of fixed lengths in grid directions to approximate the curve. (See figure 6-9.) When this scheme will suffice, it is very efficient in both space and time, because a chain can be recorded merely as a sequence of grid directions. [Freeman, 74] gives a thorough review of chain encoding. He presents methods to convert an array image into a set of chain encoded curves, and algorithms which calculate standard functions — area, length, etc. — on chain encodings. In particular, the problem of matching two curves is easy, not surprisingly.

Chain encodings will not serve for MERCATOR; the grain-size is half the length of the side. A number of researchers have studied the problem of approximating curves with lines of arbitrary length and orientation. In particular, [Montanari, 70] presents an algorithm which calculates the minimum length polygons within a given tolerance of a input chain

139

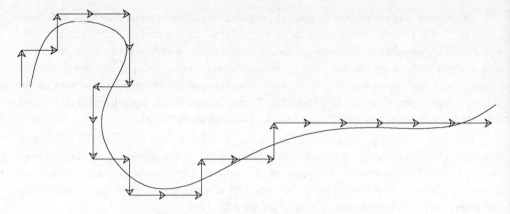

Figure 6-9: Chain Code Approximation

encoding. He asserts that for his sample images, (of grain chromosones), the minimum length polygon within half a grid length of the chain had usually about one quarter as many sides as the chain. Even this is hardly adequate input for MERCATOR. Assuming that the angle of the side of the polygon are distributed evenly, then the average length of the output polygon side would be about 3.5 grid lengths, while the tolerance is 1 grid length (half a grid from the curve to the chain, and half from the chain to the polygon.) However, I feel certain that one can do better than that with larger tolerances from the chain.

[Ballard, 81] presents the strip tree representation for curves. This representation resembles MERCATOR's edges with grain-size in some ways, though its purpose is quite different. A strip tree consists of rectangles hierarchically organized by containment. Each rectangle contains a section of the curve, and runs parallel to the starting and ending points of that section. The rectangle is characterized by the coordinates of the starting and ending points and by the width of the rectangle on either side of the connecting line. At each level of the hierarchy, the ending point of one rectangle is the starting point of the next. (See figures 6-10 and 6-11.)

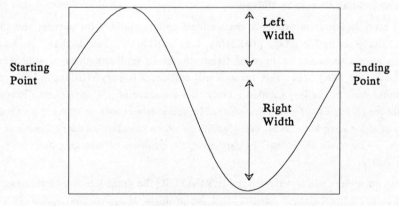

Figure 6-10: Strip Tree Rectangle

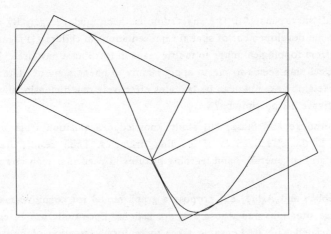

Figure 6-11: Strip Tree

Ballard gives algorithms for doing a variety of calculations using strip trees: finding curve length, finding distance from a point to a curve, determining the union and intersection of two curves, determining whether a point is in an area, etc. The hierarchical structure of the strip tree allows all these to run quickly. He does not, however, discuss the problem of matching two different strip trees for the same curve.

A strip tree rectangle looks very much like an edge with grain-size. (See figure 6-12.) The only differences are that the strip tree rectangle is assymetrical, and that the edge with grain-size is rounded at the vertices. The latter is the critical point in terms of MERCATOR. The fact that the strip tree rectangle stops dead at the curve point means that it cannot be used to represent uncertainty; the curve point must be known exactly. There are always points arbitrarily close to the curve which are outside the strip tree. On the other hand, I would guess that Ballard's algorithms do not require this feature, and could be adapted to MERCATOR edges with slight modifications. If this is the case, and if Ballard's algorithms are amenable to fuzzy quantities, then it might well be worth adding them to MERCATOR to render calculations with multiple regions more efficient.

Edge with grain-size   Strip tree rectangle

Figure 6-12: Grainy edge vs. Strip Tree Rectangle

6.10. Cognitive Mapping: Psychology

The psychological literature on cognitive mapping, though extensive, contains relatively little on assimilation. In 1973 Hart and Moore described research into learning of cognitive maps as "relatively uncharted" [Hart and Moore, 73] and the description still seems apt. Studies have revealed a distinction between topological and metric maps (sometimes called "route-maps" and "survey-maps"). The suggestion has been made, largely by analogy with Piaget's theory of the developement of spatial representations in children [Piaget, 67] that individuals progress from topological maps to metric maps in learning a new area. The whole concept of a topological map seems to me to apply mainly to phenomena of quite a large scale, a scale where streets, for example can be taken as effectively one dimensional. What could a "route-map" of figure 2-1 possibly be?

[Thorndyke and Stasz, 80] study knowledge acquisition from maps, with particular attention to the effectiveness of learning strategies. Their results are more suggestive as regards learning generally, and learning pictures in particular than as regards cognitive mapping.

[Lieblich and Arbib, 82] propose a graph model for cognitive maps, whose nodes are identifiable situations and whose arcs are actions. Each node has an expected "drive reduction" associated with it. Learning takes three forms: creation of nodes and arcs, when an action brings the creature to an unrecognized situation; merging of nodes, when two situations prove to be geographically or functionally equivalent (if a rat is consistently rewarded at a door with a "+" sign, which is sometimes to the left and sometimes to the right, he will generate a node for "+" doors with no geographic labelling); and modification of the expected drive reductions, which occurs according to whether the expectations are met or not. Lieblich's and Arbib's are mainly concerned with the last.

There is a great body of work on retrieval from cognitive maps. I mention a few examples which have caught my interest; a systematic survey is beyond the scope of this thesis. [Hintzman et. al., 81] studied reaction times in calculating directions, using experiments reminicent of the imagery experiments of [Kosslyn, 77] and got results which are largely compatible with Kosslyn's, though not entirely so. [Tversky, 81] studies distortions in recall and recognition, and found that scenes are remembered as more regular and symmetric than they really are. In a related effect, the relative position of two objects was misremembered as the relative positions of their containers; for example, Reno was misremembered as east of San Diego because Nevada is east of California. [Lynch, 60] studied (among other things) the drawing of sketch maps of cities, and found regularities in the order of drawing, in the choice of objects shown, and in the errors made. [Cheng and Gallistel, 83] show that a rat's cognitive map requires a metric space.

However, though the processes being studied are basically those modeled in MERCATOR, the difference in approach makes direct comparisons difficult. These results, though intriguing, are not particularly suggestive of either representations or processes. Almost any representation and process can be jerry-rigged with *ad hoc* features which will produce any one of these results; no known representation or process will give many of these results in a natural way. The truth is that it would be very difficult to design an experiment which could show that MERCATOR is false, especially since MERCATOR is admitted to be inadequate. The results of [Cheng and Gallistel, 83] are an exception; if it were shown that cognitive maps did not require a metric space, then MERCATOR could not be true. But beyond such basic point MERCATOR may not be falsifiable, in the sense of [Popper, 59], as a psychological theory. Of course, psychology is not its primary intention.

6.11. Interval Arithmetic

There is a substantial mathematical literature on computations with intervals. ([Alefeld and Herzberger, 83] gives an introduction. It is not clear to me whether there are techniques here which would substantially increase the power of MERCATOR to carry out its research. This is a subject for future research.

6.12. Computer Vision

There has been surprisingly little research in computer vision to date which is directly relevant to cognitive mapping. Shape representations in vision research are geared to facilitate matching images with models rather than doing geographic computations. Therefore, a strong emphasis is placed on uniqueness of representation, on ease of indexing, and on the development of quick matching algorithms. Little thought has been given to integrating shape descriptions with position descriptions. ([Ballard and Brown, 82] chapters 8 and 9 give a good overview of shape representations in computer vision.)

Vision research has left the problem of representing scenes of several objects almost unaddressed. No representations have been developed with a level of precision intermediate between exact coordinates and very qualitative relations such as "BEHIND", "LEFT-OF", etc. (The issue is hardly discussed in surveys of the field such as [Brady, 81], [Ballard and Brown, 82], or [Marr, 82].) A number of programs have been written which determine the structure of scenes from visual input, particularly line drawings (e.g. [Waltz, 75]). Here, however, the major issue is patterns of connectedness and occlusion, rather than using known facts about one object to determine the interpretation of the second.

The problem of matching images produced in temporal succession or by stereo vision might seem analogous to the problem of scene matching in MERCATOR. However, since there is every reason to believe that the former tasks are performed on very low-level representations, it seems unlikely that the two processes have much in common. (See [Marr, 82], p. 146.)

6.13. Spatial Representations in Naive Physics

Physical reasoning, both at the "naive" and at the expert levels, involves deep spatial reasoning and geometric representations. However, the requirements on spatial reasoning in this domain are apparently different from those in cognitive mapping, in a number of respects:

- Physical reasoning generally involves small numbers of objects. When there are large numbers, they are generally grouped together into "collections", such as heaps of sand. Thus, object retrieval is not generally a problem.

- Unlike in cognitive mapping, small grain-size changes in the shape of an object can make a great difference to its physical behavior. An object can get caught on a very small hook that hardly projects from the surface. A different idea of shape approximation must therefore be used. ([Requicha, 83], [Davis, 86]).

- Topological properties of objects (being solid or hollow, having holes through or into them) are much more important in physical reasoning than in geographic reasoning.

([Hayes, 79], [Davis, 84b])

- The vertical direction is strongly distinguished by gravity. Likewise, the orientation and convexity of surfaces with respect to the vertical is particularly important. ([DeKleer, 75], [Hayes, 79])

- Free space must be represented explicitly, and divided into regions of physical significance. ([Forbus, 79])

- In reasoning about the manufacturing of physical objects, the shape representation must be easily related to the actual matnufacturin techniques. It is therefore important to use a vocabulary of standard shapes which can be cast or bored. ([Requicha, 80])

In view of these many differences, it seems likely that the spatial representations and computational techniques required for physical reasoning are quite separate from those required for cognitive mapping.

7 Running the Program

7.1. Implementation

The theory described in this thesis has been fully implemented in a running computer program called MERCATOR. This program includes functions for retrieval and assimilation, as well as simulator and utility functions. The program has been largely debugged and tested. This chapter describes the implementation, the simulator functions, and the results of the tests.

MERCATOR is implemented on the Yale Research DEC-2060. It is written in NISP, a dialect of LISP providing data-types and efficient arithmetic, developed by Drew McDermott. [McDermott, 83] NISP is implemented as a set of macros on top of another LISP implementation. In this case, the base dialect is TLISP, the local variety of UCI LISP. [Meehan, 79]

Table 7-1 shows the various parts of the MERCATOR program and their lengths.

Section	Lines of code	Compiled?
Arithmetic:	2576	Yes
Type definitions and utilities:	1760	No
Fact Retrieval:	2355	No
Object Retrieval:	88	No
Assimilation:	3923	No
Matching:	1739	No
Merging:	2164	No
Vision Simulation:	2112	No
Motion Simulation:	191	No
State preservation and restoration:	1141	Largely
Total	18079	

Table 7-1: Sections of the MERCATOR program

The state preservation and restoration functions allow the user to save a MERCATOR map and a set of correspondences, which he has built in core, onto disk, and to recreate them from disk.

It is possible to load all of MERCATOR simultaneously into a DEC-20 LISP core image with about 140,000 free words, but doing so leaves very little free space for running the program. Therefore, we use two forks to run MERCATOR. The first contains the simulator functions; the second contains the assimilator and retrieval functions. They communicate via disk files. This problem could be alleviated by compiling more of MERCATOR and thus reducing its space requirements, or by moving to a machine with a larger address space.

7.2. Differences between Implementation and Theory

The MERCATOR program implements almost exactly the algorithms described in chapters 2 - 5. There are, however, a few exceptions:

One Dimensional Objects. The correct representation for one dimensional objects is discussed in section 2.7. The representation used in the program is considerably clumsier, with no corners, and using no bounds per edge, rather than two bounds per edge. The difficulties of using this representation are substantial. In the current implementation, the vision simulator, the retrieval functions, and the matcher handle the representation correctly. The merger does not. Therefore, we have included no one-dimensional objects in our test cases. (See section 7.5.)

Path Finding. It turns out that the hierarchical path finding algorithm presented in section 3.3 is only worthwhile in very large maps with many levels of hierarchy. Therefore, though we implemented this feature to test its feasibility, we have removed it from the actual code, and instead use simply bidirectional search on edges and joints.

Choice of tree in sketcher. The description of the sketcher (section 3.4) asserts that a tree of edges and the sequence of vertices to be assigned coordinates is chosen at the beginning. The program does not do this. Instead, it chooses the vertices on the fly, picking the most constrained vertex and assigning it a coordinate at the appropriate point in the algorithm. I believe that the algorithm in the text is both more efficient and more effective, but I have no proof, and I doubt that it generally matters much.

7.3. The Vision Simulator

In a complete system, the MERCATOR assimilator would get its input from a vision module, which took sensory data and interpreted it as a MERCATOR map. Our system replaces this with a simulator. The simulator maintains a world model, and creates the scene descriptions for the assimilator by calculating what the robot would see in that model. As table 7-1 indicates, the vision simulator is as substantial a piece of code as the other modules of MERCATOR; it performs a non-trivial calculation. However, it has no significance for AI, since it models the physical world rather than any reasoning process. For that reason, it does not deserve the full exposition given to the other modules of the system. The algorithm used is entirely *ad hoc*. We describe the module here in brief.

The task of the vision simulator is to generate a scene from a world description. Computer graphics struggles with this problem in real earnest; fortunately, we can be relatively irresponsible about it. Firstly, we have a much simpler world. Secondly, we are developing a symbolic, rather than an analog representation. Thirdly, the object of our vision simulator is to conceal information rather than to reveal it, to encode the uncertainties of vision in a MERCATOR map.

The major issue in designing the simulator is the structure of the world model and the specification language for it. There are three major objectives in designing this language: flexibility, simplicity, and security. The user should be able to input any possible world, and

146

have the system produce any correct MERCATOR map for it; the user should be able to input and modify worlds easily; and the system should not allow the user to input incoherent worlds or produce incorrect maps. We have chosen to emphasize flexibility over simplicity or security. Thus, worlds are difficult to input and require debugging, but there is a lot of freedom in their construction.

In setting up the world model, the user has control over the following:

- Objects and properties. The user can place any objects in any place. He may designate some of them as opaque cliffs.

- Visibility. The user can determine arbitrary conditions under which an object which is within the range of vision and which is not occluded may be visible or invisible. He may, for example, specify that some particular object can only be seen from two feet away, or from one particular side.

- Shape. The user can have any shape reported for any given object, with any grain-sizes. He can have different shapes reported under different circumstances, including random circumstances. It is left up to the user to insure that the shape description is correct and coherent.

- Adjacency. The user may have different objects seen as adjacent under different circumstances.

With each call to the vision module, the user can set the following parameters:

- Fuzz uncertainties. Two real numbers which indicate the typical uncertainties of length and orientation fuzz ranges to be produced. The fuzz ranges are chosen randomly as intervals around the true value, with average range as specified.

- Range of vision. Minimal angle, maximal angle, and maximal distance that the robot is looking.

- User chosen parameters to guide the choices enumerated above of visibility, shape descriptions, and adjacency. In setting up my test worlds, I have found it most convenient to decide these on the basis of two parameters — a typical grain-size and a typical number of sides per object — together with a large number of choices left up to a random number generator.

The vision simulator then proceeds to carry out the following steps:

1. Calculate the visible area from the range of vision and the cliff occlusions.

2. Find all objects in the visible area satisfying the visibility criteria.

3. Find the visible real bounds of objects using shape descriptions, adjacency relations, and the limits of vision.

4. Create regions and clumps for each connected part of each object. If some object is apparently broken in the middle by occlusion, create two clumps and regions.

5. Determine the knowledge edges for each region.

6. Determine the internal edges. Two vertices A and B are connected by an internal edge if they lie in a clump tiling, and given any other vertex C in the tiling the angle A-C-B is acute. This criterion ensures that the tiling is connected and that close points are

connected.

7. Find polygons and PCO's for each object.

7.4. Motion

MERCATOR handles robot motion as follows. The omniscient user specifies the exact distance and direction of motion, and a region which directly contains the destination of the robot. The world model is updated appropriately. In the MERCATOR map, a new clump, region, and vertex are created for the new robot position. It is connected to the old region by an edge with fuzzy measurements randomly chosen around the input values. We then use that edge to calculate the distance and direction of the new robot position to the vertices of the containing region, and edges are created expressing that distance and direction. (This is necessary to preserve the tiling condition.) Finally, we eliminate the old robot clump and region.

This procedure is a slight cheat, in that the destination region is part of the input. It would be slightly more kosher to input only the distance and direction and have the program calculate the destination region, or see the destination region in the next assimilation. However, the first approach requires either that measurements be quite precise or that movement be quite slow. The second approach runs into a variety of ugly technical problems in the programs. Since the point is not crucial, we allowed ourselves this evasion.

7.5. Test Cases

Figures 7-1 and 7-2 show the two world models on which most of our testing has been done. Figure 7-1 was designed as a plausible real world model, and was used to test the behavior of the program with a substantial number of clumps. Figure 7-2 was designed to test a variety of the special cases which the program can handle (curved objects, adjacency relative to grain-size, multiply connected objects, overlapping objects). The single major untested feature of the MERCATOR program is the ability to cope with multiple regions, because neither the merger nor the vision simulator was designed to produce them. Three features of the "worlds" should be noted. In figure 7-2, the blue object becomes invisible when the grain-size drops below 0.05, and the red and black objects are seen as adjacent. In figure 7-1, the furniture is invisible to the robot except when he is in the same room. Both these are very crude approximations of the difficulty of seeing small, far away objects. Also, in figure 7-1, the furniture is presumed not to obstruct vision, including vision of the floor; that is, the robot can be certain that the floor continues under the furniture.

148

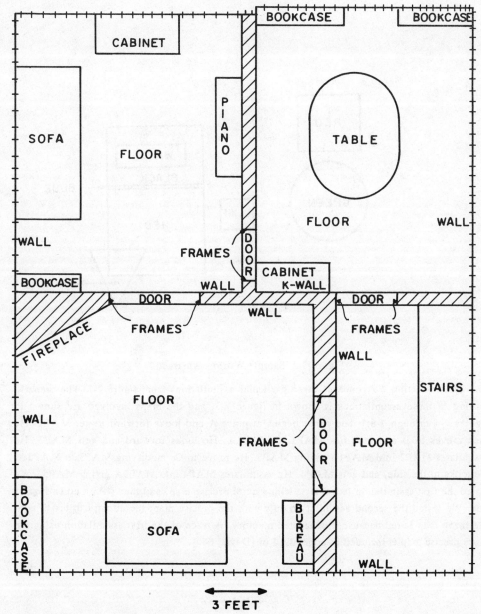

Solid lines are object boundaries.
Hatched lines are opaque objects.

Figure 7-1: Sample World - House

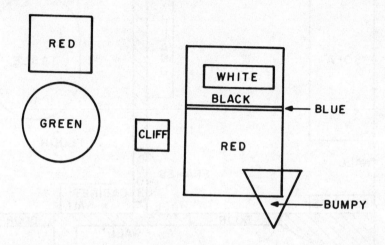

Figure 7-2: Sample World - Abstract

The data in section 7.7 concerns three particular assimilations from figure 7-1. The scenario leading to these assimilations is shown in figure 7-3, and the maps involved are shown in figures 7-4 through 7-8.* The robot begins at point A and looks forward to get MAP1. He then moves to B and modifies MAP1 to MAP1A. He looks forward and gets MAP2. He assimilates MAP2 into MAP1A giving MAP3. He move to C, modifying MAP3 to MAP3A. He looks to the side, and gets MAP4. He assimilates MAP4 into MAP3A giving MAP5. We tested the first assimilation twice, first with a quite precise map, and then with a much fuzzier one. We tested the second assimilation only with the precise map; the attempt to test it with the fuzzy map failed because it exhausted memory. A trace of the first assimilation using the more precise map is included in appendix I of [Davis, 84a].

---

* There is no diagram for MAP5, because it is too confused to be drawn.

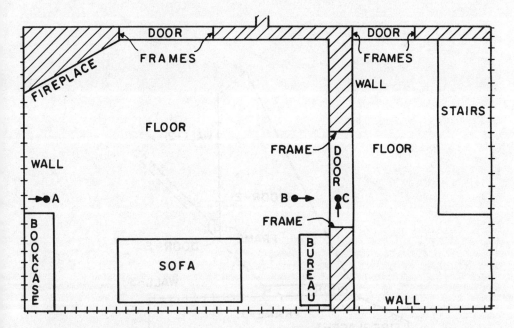

A, B and C are successive positions of the robot.
Arrows indicate the robot's orientation.

Figure 7-3: Sample Tour

151

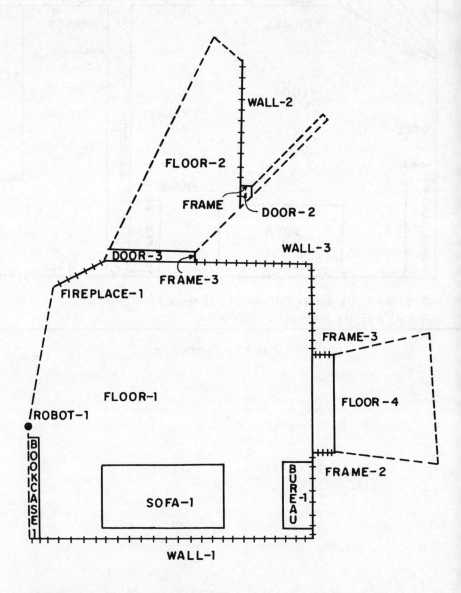

Solid lines are object boundaries.
Hatched lines are cliffs.
Dotted lines are knowledge edges.

Figure 7-4: Map 1

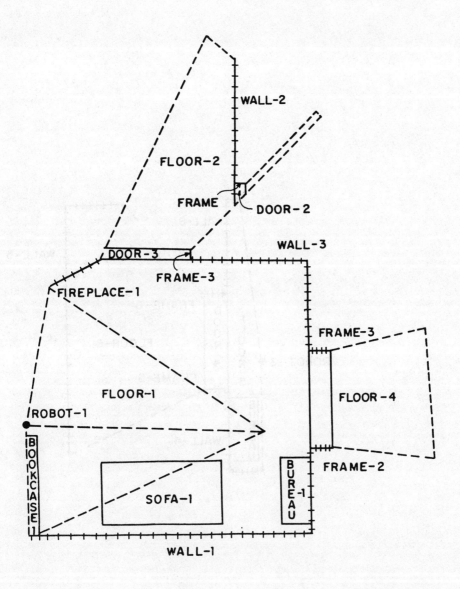

Figure 7-5: Map 1A

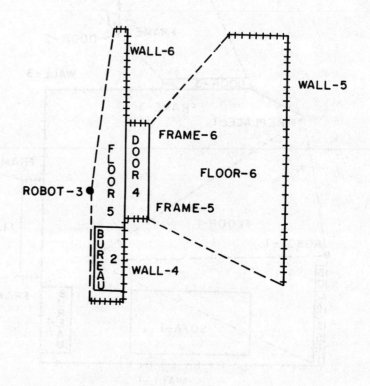

Figure 7-6: Map 2

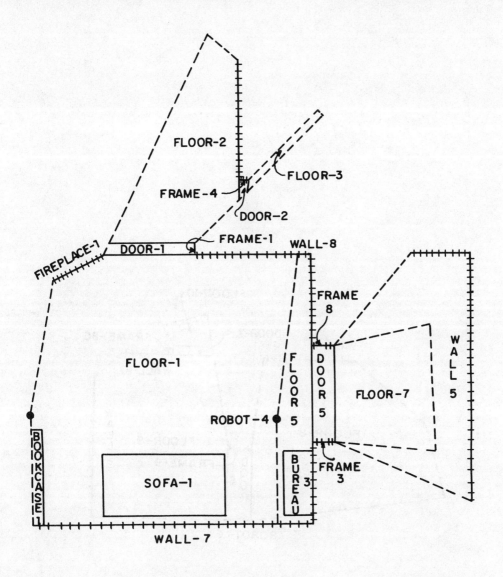

Figure 7-7: Map 3

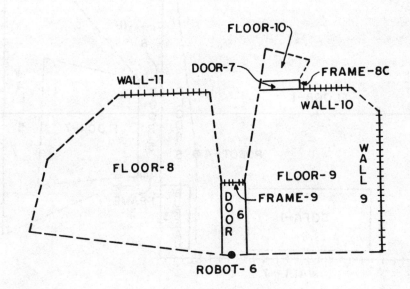

Figure 7-8: Map 4

In the precise map, length fuzzes were typically 10% of the length (i.e. if the true length was 100, the fuzz would be [95, 105]); orientation fuzzes were accurate to within 5 degrees; grain-sizes were randomly chosen in a bimodal distribution to be either about 0.1 feet (with 25% probability) or about 0.001 feet (with 75% probability). In the fuzzier map, length fuzzes were 30% of the length, orientation fuzzes were accurate to 10 degrees, and grain-sizes were chosen to be about 0.1 feet.

Other tests were performed in other parts of the house and in figure 7-2. The results were comparable to those discussed here.

7.6. Results

There is good news and there is bad news. The good news is that, generally, the program works. Most of the time, the program will handle the range of shapes and shape representations claimed for it. It will usually match two very dissimilar shape descriptions of different objects and reject similar but incompatible descriptions of different objects. It uses relative position of objects, both with respect to the robot and with respect to other objects, to disambiguate ambiguous matches. In merging, it chooses or creates good regions, covers the combined area of partial objects, combines partial views into complete objects when possible, combines separated views when the connecting section is seen, and preserves most of the normalcy conditions. As we shall see below, degrading the precision of the input slows the program down, but does not seriously hurt its behavior. Most of what the program does is correct.

The bad news comes in three parts. Firstly, the program is abysmally slow. Secondly, it sometimes makes unbelievable mistakes. Thirdly, and most seriously, the program is not robust. Once one major mistake has been made, behavior deteriorates very quickly. Some of this is due to random programming bugs, but on the whole it reflects serious design inadequacies.

Many of the mistakes made come from the two flaws in the matching algorithm discussed in section 4.11. The non-robustness of the system derives from several sources. In the matcher, it is the natural result of using a deterministic search for the best set of correspondences together with very careful checking of geometric consistency. Once a invalid match is accepted, it throws off all the rest of the matcher, because everything has to be consistent with that invalid match. Probably, both features of the matcher should be modified. The search should be made somewhat non-deterministic while the consistency check should be weakened. Indeed, a non-deterministic search would be unacceptably expensive computationally unless the consistency check can be made much more quickly.

In the merger, the main problem arises from unformulated normalcy conditions, implicit assumptions about the input to the merger. In particular, the merger sometimes assumes a high degree of structure on the correspondences produced by the matcher, which the matcher does not necessarily provide. These assumptions need to be identified, and the code must be modified either to provide them or not to require them.

The slowness of the program (half an hour CPU time to assimilate a medium-sized map) is, I believe, a correctable condition. I feel reasonably certain that, if the problem with chain matches described in section 4.11 is fixed and the code is rewritten for efficiency and compiled, then execution time can be reduced by at least an order of magnitude.

Another problem, less important at this stage, but potentially troubling, is the rate of growth of the maps. This is illustrated in table 7-2. MAP1A, for example, has fifty-five edges for twenty objects. After two assimilations, MAP5 has twice as many edges, and only three more objects. To a substantial extent, this is because the vision simulator creates single edges bounding two objects, and the merger tends to replace these by separate edges connected by joints. This in itself would not be reason for concern. However, our preliminary study suggests that the problem goes beyond this. In particular, there is reason to suspect that the pruning of redundant polygons and internal edges is inadequate. I do not have enough data to determine this for certain.

7.7. Data

Tables 7-2, 7-3, and 7-4 show some statistics for the assimilations shown in figures 7-4 through 7-8 above. MAP2 is assimilated into MAP1A to produce MAP3; MAP4 is assimilated into MAP3A to produce MAP5. We refer to three tests. Test1 is assimilating the precise MAP2 into MAP1A. Test2 is assimilating the precise MAP4 into MAP3A. Test3 is assimilating the imprecise MAP2 into MAP1A.

Sizes of Input and Output

Map	MAP1A	MAP2	MAP3A	MAP4	MAP5
# of objects represented	20	11	21	11	23
# of clumps	20	11	22	12	27
# of regions	20	11	22	12	27
# of edges	55	24	84	26	117
# of vertices	35	16	48	17	65
# of polygons	14	10	21	8	24
# of bounds	77	40	65	43	82
# of joints	3	3	11	1	23
# of pco's	19	10	22	13	29
# of pco-nodes	59	32	71	31	91
# of pco-arcs	43	24	52	18	65
total # of elements	345	181	429	181	550
# of freewords used	2531	1217	3194	1305	4042

(# of vertices does not include the pseudo-vertices associated with joints.)

The figures for MAP1A, MAP2, and MAP3A apply to both the precise and the fuzzy maps.

Table 7-2: Map Sizes

158

Assimilation	Test1	Test2	Test3
# of clump matches			
Pairs matching in properties	25	37	25
Accepted / rejected by position checker	16 / 9	23	24 / 1
Accepted / rejected in consistency check	9 / 7	9 / 14	9 / 15
Incorrect matches accepted	0	2	0
Correct matches rejected	1	3	1
# of edge matches			
Proposed	76	77	110
Accepted / rejected in consistency check	22 / 54	12 / 65	22 / 88
Incorrect matches accepted	0	3	0
Correct matches rejected	0	10	0
# of chain matches			
Proposed	25	33	49
Accepted	7	8	7
Incorrect and accepted	0	2	0
Correct but not proposed	1	5	1
Correct, proposed, and rejected	0	1	0

Table 7-3: Correspondence Generation

Task	Time (cpu secs)
Sketching (4 coordinate sets, on a 4 vertex object)	5.3
Position retrieval	
two far away small objects	4.0
two nearby large objects	9.2
Object Retrieval	2.9

Times are given for typical examples, without counting time for macro expansion or garbage collection. Garbage collection usually takes a third as long as the rest of the execution.

Assimilation: (These figures include macro expansion time, but not garbage collection. Over an entire assimilation, macro expansion takes about 100 cpu seconds.)

Test 1:

Matching:	900	cpu seconds (approximate)
Merging:	137	
Total Assimilation	1050	(approximate)

Test 2:

Building clump matches	164	cpu seconds
Building edge matches	54	
Building chain matches	144	
Consistency check	380	
Total matching	742	
Merging	133	
Total assimilation	875	

Test 3:

Total assimilation	1412	cpu seconds

Table 7-4: Run Times

Tests 1 and 3 were successful, test 3 being a quite impressive success. In both, the matcher succeeded in choosing the 22 correct edge matches out of 110 which were possible a priori. Notably, although the increased fuzziness of test 3 allowed for much less initial pruning, and it created twice as many correspondences, nonetheless the output of the assimilator was identical in structure, and it required only 1.5 times as much CPU time. This suggest that the time required by MERCATOR need not grow very quickly with the size of the problem.

Test 2, however, was a failure, mainly due to bugs in the chain match logic. The chain match builder proposed only 9 of the 14 true chain matches, while proposing 25 false chains. The consistency checker went on to reject one of the true chains, and accept two of the false chains. Clearly, this section of the program needs extensive revision.

7.8. Conclusions

The development and testing of the program was definitely worthwhile. The entire theory takes its form from the fact that a program was built; without it, the theory would have been considerably more nebulous and less coherent. The need for much of the details of representation and algorithms and many of the normalcy conditions could not have been seen *a priori*, even though, once seen, they can be justified on theoretical grounds.

The MERCATOR program is clearly too slow and too buggy to be of practical interest in its current implementation. However, there are some very promising aspects to its behavior which encourage further work and optimization.

8 The Significance of MERCATOR to AI

8.1. Introduction

AI has its own set of standards for judging theories. An AI theory is broad if it describes a broad class of knowledge and inference. It is coherent if its sub-parts fit together well. It is resonant if it introduces ideas which are relevant to other AI problems. It is robust if it can be extended to handle more knowledge and more inferences, and if it will interface cleanly with other AI theories. This chapter evaluates MERCATOR in these terms.

The major emphasis in developing MERCATOR has been on coherence. The algorithms and data structures — retriever, matcher, merger, MERCATOR maps, and correspondences, together with normalcy conditions — all fit together in a clean theory. Each module uses nearly every aspect of the map which is in principle relevant. The normalcy conditions necesary for the running of each module have been tabulated, and the merger tries hard to preserve them. The matcher correspondences serve well both in the internals of the matcher and in communicating between the matcher and merger.

The scope of MERCATOR is deep rather than broad. It describes only a very small part of the world, the location of objects in two dimensions; but it can describe almost the entire possible range of two-dimensional locations, and an impressive class of states of partial knowledge. Its algorithms carry out only a small class of inferences — one type of assimilation, and three types of retrieval — but, owing to the incompleteness of the knowledge, to do so they must make surprisingly sophisticated inferences using many different types of information. Emphasizing coherence limited the scope of problems which could be studied, since it demanded that no feature be added to MERCATOR maps unless its full implications for representation, retrieval, matching, and merging were understood.

8.2. The Implications of MERCATOR

In any integrated computer system, many or most of the design decisions, including the program specifications, are made largely to fit in with other design decisions. In learning from such a system, it is important to separate the chaff from the wheat, and decide what features are valid outside the system, and what is their scope. At the most specific level, MERCATOR builds cognitive maps from visual input. More generally, it does spatial reasoning; it manages a knowledge base; it is an AI system. At each of these levels, it has something to say.

Several aspects of MERCATOR are relevant to spatial reasoning in general. The most important of these is the separation of the topological level and the geometric level. In this way, MERCATOR avoids a common dilemma. Most spatial representations have to choose between generality in the situations they can describe, on the one hand, and the ability to express imprecision, on the other. Representing area in terms of geometric entities (points, lines, splines, etc.) gives generality, but not imprecision, or only very limited imprecision.

162

Representing shapes and relative positions of objects directly allows the expression of general types, but requires a special vocabulary of shapes and relative positions which is difficult to make in any sense complete. MERCATOR combines the two approaches. Objects are located in terms of vertices, which correspond to points, and the relative positions of vertices is described in fuzzy measurements.

Another advantage of this scheme is that shape is fully integrated with position. It is as easy to express the position of the north end of one field with respect to the south end of another field (a fact about relative positions) as to express its position relative to the south end of the same field. Both ends are represented by sets of edges, and their relative positions are connecting edges. In most schemes which record relative positions of objects, the ends of the fields will be parts of a shape description. Retrieving the relative positions of the two ends of the fields will involve composing information from the shape description with the relative position information; and, since each of these is imprecise, the composition may have no useful information. (See section 6.2.)

A significant feature of MERCATOR is that almost all the reasoning involves the object boundaries rather than their interiors. Boundaries are much easier to deal with, primarily because one-dimensional topology is much simpler than two-dimensional. Reasoning about boundaries proves to be adequate for a large class of inferences across a broad range of physical situations.

Two of the technical devices introduced in MERCATOR may be of general value in computational geometry generally as well as in AI spatial reasoning. The definition of the grain-size approximation, though similar to previous schemes, has particular advantages in representing partially known curves. (See section 6.9) We have developed soundly based schemes for dealing with them. PCO's may have general use in building up specifications of cyclic structures.

Within the particular domain of constructing a cognitive map from visual input, many aspects of the MERCATOR algorithms have general validity beyond the scope of this particular program. Specific ideas that seem to derive naturally from the problem include the use of an object hierarchy to find a connection between objects, the division of assimilation into matching and merging (though admittedly a simplification), the use of local geometrical consistency to constrain the matcher, and the use of clump matches, edge matches, and joints as the output of the matcher.

The success in using intervals in MERCATOR also holds out promise for their use in other AI programs which must reason about uncertain real quantities, such as naive physics programs which deal in uncertain quantities, or planning programs which deal in uncertain times. (See [McDermott, 82], [Davis, 85], [Dean, 85].)

It is more difficult to assess the significance of MERCATOR for knowledge base managers generally. MERCATOR keeps track of a few simple, well-defined aspects of the structure and relations of a large number of entities. Most AI knowledge bases, by contrast, deal with entities which are related by an indefinite class of relations, and must accept the addition of new rules of inference. They therefore require a looser structure and a more general inference engine.

A second important difference between MERCATOR and other AI knowledge base managers is the "adequate input" assumption; the assumption that any key fact will eventually be perceived directly and therefore need not be deduced by a forward inference procedure. Of course, forward inference is necessary in the vision module in order to construct a MERCATOR map from images, but the point is that there is a level at which assimilation can be viewed as matching and splicing. This is generally far from the case. For example, story understanding, which can be viewed as the construction of a data base from natural language text, has been shown to require extensive forward inference before a sentence can be connected to the representation of the previous text [Dyer, 83].

Finally, the ontology underlying MERCATOR, Euclidean space, is very well understood and investigated. Most other knowledge bases fish in much murkier waters: naive psychology, naive physics, etc.

These three properties determine many of the features of the MERCATOR map, including the isomorphism of the input to the knowledge base; the reduction of merging to splicing; the absence of universal quantifiers, negation, sets, prototypes, or IS-A links; the use of a non-propositional representation and inference rules; and the ease of finding a semantics for this representation. Very few, if any, other AI tasks have all three properties; however, it is worth considering an analogy with tasks with even one such property. For example, the task of assimilating an episodic memory from individual events might have either or both of the first two properties. Therefore, it might be worthwhile to construct such a system which reduced merging to splicing knowledge bases, and which lacked negations, universals, and prototypes. (CYRUS [Kolodner, 80] used a (very simple) knowledge base input and lacked negation and universals; however, it used prototypes.)

8.3. The Vision Module

MERCATOR works on the hypothesis that a vision module can analyze what it sees and describe the scene as a MERCATOR map. This, I will argue, is a plausible model for simple scenes. However, there will be cases where even a sophisticated vision system will not be able to create a correct map, and cases where a good vision system will be able to give information not representable in a MERCATOR map.

A MERCATOR map involves requires three kinds of information. Objects must be identified and described. They must be approximated by polygons, and an upper bound on the error must be evaluated. Finally, physical distances and directions between points in the scene must be estimated between bounds.

Current vision systems can provide all this information to some extent in restricted environments, and there is every reason to believe that, in the future, they will provide more information in more general enviroments. Object identification and description is a major thrust of vision research. (See [Brooks, 81], [Hollerbach, 75], [Marr and Nishihara, 76].) [Montanari, 70] discusses constructing polygon approximations to curves. (see section 6.9.) Determining distances and orientations is a large part of constructing 2-1/2 D sketches. In particular, distance estimates can be derived from stereopsis, motion, directional selectivity, optic flow, occlusion, texture, and *apriori* knowledge of physical size; orientation estimates can be derived from stereopsis, motion, optic flow, surface contours, texture contours, and shading. (see [Marr, 82] p. 276.) Most of these give information which is quite imprecise, and which can reasonably be represented by a fuzz range.

The most difficult case for a vision module to handle is where there is a small, deep hole in a cliff. (Figure 8-1). Any plausible vision system will skip the hole, and interpret the wall as extending all the way across. However, this is not a valid MERCATOR map. By definition of grain-size, an accurate approximation must go in and out of the hole, and an approximation which goes across the hole has a grain-size as large as the depth of the hole.

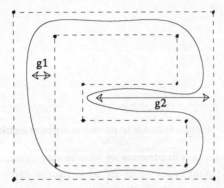

Two regions, in dotted lines, approximating an object in solid.
The inner region is fairly accurate, with grain-size g_1.
The outer region is very inaccurate, with grain-size g_2.

Figure 8-1: Object with Small Hole

Intuitively, it might seem that we have the wrong definition of grain-size. The approximation which crosses the hole *should* be a good approximation. However, it is difficult to frame a definition of grain-size which allows this but excludes a number of very poor cases. (See Section 2.4)* Another approach is to say that this is a problem for the contradiction handler. (See Section 8.4.10.) Originally we erroneously omit the hole. When we come closer and see the hole, the contradiction handler uses its knowledge of common mistakes to diagnose our problem, and comes up with an accurate description. There is probably some truth in this point of view; however, in terms of our current understanding, it is explaining *obscuris per obscuros*, since we have no idea how a contradiction handler could work.

A related difficult problem is in object discrimination. It often happens that a vision system originally reports a single object, but, on coming closer, finds that there are two objects. For example, one might first see a single wall, and then see that it is broken, and therefore, in MERCATOR terms, there are two walls. Again, this is probably a problem for a contradiction handler. Alternatively, a subtler theory of objects might be invoked in which the two descriptions were complementary rather than contradictory. (See section 8.4.8.)

* Drew McDermott has recently suggested that such cases be handled by giving an approximation to the convex hull which is accurate to within a grain-size, and then giving bounds on the dimensions of the concavities of the object. (Personal communication)

A good vision module should be able to provide information which is in some ways better than that assumed by MERCATOR. For one thing, it will probably be fairly consistent in dividing boundaries into edges. Though MERCATOR allows it, it will not represent a square object as an octagon. (See figure 8-2.) Understanding an actual vision module will make it possible to predict such regularities and use them to make the matcher more efficient and effective.

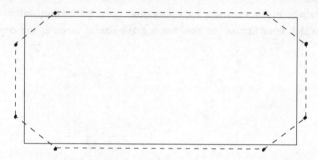

Figure 8-2: An Improbable Approximation

A general vision system will presumably also be directable; one will be able to tell it to look for objects of particular types or to try to get some particular detail or measurement accurately. If the system is well directed, the maps it produces should be regular and complete in a way which will make assimilation easy. (See section 8.4.4.)

The MERCATOR program is unnecessarily pessimistic in treating each new scene from scratch. A reasonable vision system could track things as the robot moves, keeping its eye on a given object, or (equivalently from the point of view of MERCATOR), matching low level features. In this way it could find correspondences, even before doing object identification, let alone any of the MERCATOR operations.

Possibly, this information could be input to MERCATOR as correspondences which the matcher knows to be true. But there may be more involved. There may be information calculable in this way which is not expressible in terms of the correspondences we have defined. The stepwise process move, look, assimilate, move, look, assimilate, ... may be replaced by a system in which vision triggers a call to the MERCATOR assimilator when a new object or a new object part appears.

8.4. Extensions

There are many possible extensions of MERCATOR that would increase its range, effectiveness, and/or efficiency as a spatial reasoner. One of the most important measures of the success of MERCATOR is the ease with which such extensions can be made. In this section I will review some of these in increasing order of difficulty and discuss what the extension would involve. I omit minor implementation bugs and algorithm improvements discussed in chapters 2 through 5.

8.4.1. Other Types of Retrieval

A cognitive map is useful for many other tasks than the three which we have programmed. The most often studied is the navigation problem: plan to get from one place to another, and carry out the plan.

A solution to this problem requires a solution to the absence problem. The problem solver must know that the presence of free space implies the absence of walls and vice versa. However, we do not require a complete absence representation. One approach, applicable in the *plenum* situation, would be to have certain clumps marked with a "traversible" property and have it understood that there are no barriers in the interior of traversible clumps. Then by using strings of overlapping traversible clumps, it will be possible to describe free paths: a free path is one which at all points lies within a traversible clump. Having defined the problem in this way, it will be possible to plan local paths by considering the robot as moving from one free space polygon to another, and finding a path in the connected polygons. (See figure 8-3.)

More extensive paths can be found using GPS-like strategies such as those developed in [McDermott and Davis, 84], in which first a conduit is found which goes most of the way, then, recursively, paths are found from the start and destination to the parts of the conduit nearest to each. The "piano movers" problem (planning a path for a large object) could be solved by combining these techniques with local solutions to the piano movers problems, such as discussed in [Brooks, 82], [Lozano-Perez, 81], [Schwartz and Sharir, 81], [Wallace, 84]. The latter depends on having generalized cones of free space which would be fairly easy to generate from the polygons of free space objects.

In the *vacuum* situation, where free space is not explicitly represented, and it is assumed that all solid objects in the area of interest are explicitly represented, the problem is much harder. The open passages must be calculated from the edges which separate the solid objects. The calculation would be difficult and easily complicated by the presence of "bogus" edges connecting distant objects.

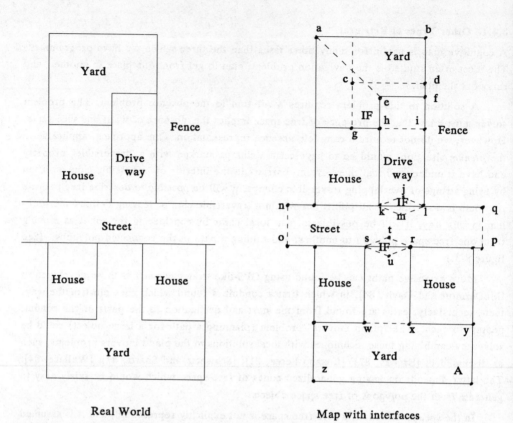

Real World	Map with interfaces

A free-space path from a to A would traverse the following polygons: $a-e-f-b$ in the yard overlaps $c-g-i-d$ in the first interface overlaps $e-k-f-d$ in the driveway overlaps $j-k-m-l$ in the second interface overlaps $n-o-p-q$ in the street overlaps $s-u-r-t$ in the third interface overlaps $s-w-x-r$ in the yard borders $v-z-A-y-x-w$ in the yard.

Figure 8-3: Finding a Path through Free Space

8.4.2. General rules

General rules, based on physical inference, teleological inference, default assumptions, or other sources, are potentially valuable in assimilation. They may place constraints on fuzzy quantities, fill in unseen parts of objects, or add constraints useful for the matcher and the merger. If it is known that tables are usually rectangular, then this constrains the lengths of the opposite sides of a table to be equal, and their orientations to be anti-parallel. Moreover, if two adjacent sides of the table are seen, the other two sides can be filled in. Another example: suppose that the rule is known that an object's shadow is not far from the object. Applying this rule, if MERCATOR knows of a car, and then sees a corresponding shadow, then the matcher should prefer to place the shadow near the car, and, if it succeeds, the merger should create connecting edges between them.

The difficulty of applying these rules depends on where in the assimilation process they can be applied and on the complexity of the rule. The rule about tables can often be applied to the scene description before the assimilation algorithm begins; such an application involves nothing more than adding more sides and tightening fuzz ranges appropriately. (See figure 8-4.) It can be applied with equal ease after the merger has finished. Sometimes, however, this information constrains only the matcher; such cases are difficult. In figure 8-5, for example, the match Table-K < = > Table-S is inconsistent with the table being rectangular; but it would seem to be almost impossible to discover this until the merger is nearly complete.

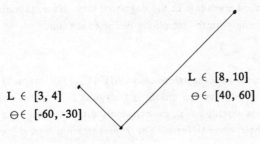

L ∈ [8, 10]
Θ∈ [40, 60]

L ∈ [3, 4]
Θ∈ [-60, -30]

Perceived Table

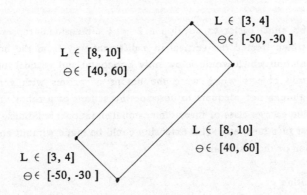

L ∈ [3, 4]
Θ∈ [-50, -30]

L ∈ [8, 10]
Θ∈ [40, 60]

L ∈ [8, 10]
Θ∈ [40, 60]

L ∈ [3, 4]
Θ∈ [-50, -30]

Table filled in by rectangularity

Note the constricted orientation fuzz on a-b.

Figure 8-4: Applying Default Knowledge

The rule about the car and the shadow could be likewise be accommodated outside the assimilator proper. We would first apply the rule to the scene description by itself, and use it to infer a car (or a large, shadow-casting object) near the shadow. We would therefore create a car clump, and attach it by connecting edges to the shadow. Once this is done, the matcher can run as usual. It will get extra brownie points for matching the inferred car with the known car, and it will take the connecting edges into account in doing the joint consistency check. Everything will work out fine. Alternatively, we may have applied the rule to the

169

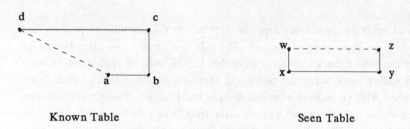

Known Table   Seen Table

Figure 8-5: Applying Default Knowledge in the Matcher

known car, and have placed a shadow in the cognitive map. Note, though, that the success of this example depends strongly on the simplicity of the constraint.

8.4.3. Three dimensions

The most obvious and most general extension of MERCATOR maps to three dimensions is to represent object boundaries as the union of polygons in 3-space, and object interiors as unions of polyhedra. This would, I feel, be extremely difficult. Only the retrieval algorithms could stay similar to their current form. The representation would have to become much more sophisticated. The matching and merging algorithms would have to be entirely different. In particular, Theorem 4-2 has no three dimensional analogue. Matching three-dimensional surfaces is very different and much harder than matching two-dimensional curves.

It would be much easier to develop a 2 + 1 dimensional representation; that is, a representation which treated the vertical in a different way from the horizontal. I have in mind a representation which would allow only horizontal and vertical lines and surfaces. It could handle only objects which were the unions of prisms with vertical axes. Such a representation, though not adequate to describe the actions of a robot's manipulator, would suffice to describe a large class of three dimensional situations: buildings, floors within buildings, stairs, most furniture, etc. This extension could be made without enormous revision of the representation or the assimilator.

8.4.4. Investigation

Given a query which the robot cannot answer from the cognitive map, devise a plan which will get him the answer. The logical form of this problem is quite different from ordinary retrieval problems, because, in principle, it is a problem of reasoning about action and knowledge. ([Moore, 80] discusses the difficulties of such problems.) In many cases, though, it can be treated as simply another retrieval problem like route planning, and it would involve a simple set of heuristics like "Go towards the objects which are mentioned in the query and look around."

A much more difficult task is to have investigations which are spawned by other cognitive tasks and interact with them. For example, it would often be useful for the matcher to be able to say, "Take another look at the scene and check out certain facts." If looking is a relatively cheap task, this may be an easy way of saving the matcher a lot of computation, or of resolving ambiguities. This problem relies on a directable vision system as discussed above.

8.4.5. Indescribable States of Knowledge

The MERCATOR representation is not expressive in all the right ways. There are many prominent shape or location features which cannot be expressed. If these features are all that is known about the scene, the scene cannot be described. If the scene is also known in great geometric detail, it can be described, but these important features will be only implicit in the representation, and difficult to recover from it. Some of these features are known as a result of applying general rules or being told; some are actual visual features.

One such feature is the assertion of relative lengths or orientations of two edges. This problem actually has a reasonably straightforward solution outlined in section 8.5.3. There are many other kinds of information, however, which we do not know how to represent or how to use. The following is a representative sample:

- Quantifiers are not allowed. You cannot say that a comb has many teeth, that a wall has many windows, or that a tree has many branches, each with many leaves

- Implicit boundaries are not represented. You cannot say that a comb is basically rectangular, or that the upper part of a tree is hemispherical; such pseudo-boundaries have no existence in the MERCATOR ontology.

- There is no way in MERCATOR to assert that two objects are exactly adjacent across a curved boundary; for example, that a river is adjacent to its two banks. There is no way to assert that two object are adjacent to within an inch without shape descriptions accurate to within an inch.

- There is no way to assert that two objects do not overlap.

- There is no way to assert that two objects are separated by a given distance, without specifying which are the closest parts of those objects.

- Disjunctions cannot be expressed. You cannot say that the painting is on one of the walls.

These problems have different scopes. (1) and (2) are the most difficult and most important. They arise naturally in scene descriptions. One would like the vision module to be able to report a description like that in figure 8-6. Moreover, they encode information which would be difficult to retrieve from a detailed MERCATOR representation. The coarse description in figure 8-6 expresses facts which the detailed description obscures or suppresses.

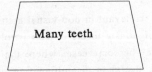

Crude, global comb description   Fine, local comb description

Figure 8-6: Representing the Shape of a Comb

Two solutions spring to mind; neither is adequate, at least in simple form. The first is that the coarse description of the comb is simply a description at a high grain-size. The problem is that it would have to be a *very* high grain-size. In fact, the grain-size would be the *length* of the teeth of the comb, not their width; and, at this grain-size, the shape description basically says nothing at all. Modifying the definition of grain-size to get around this leads to trouble. (See section 2.4.)

The second solution is that this is a problem for the vision module. The vision module should simply "smooth out" the teeth of the comb, and report the outer hull. This is all right, as long as one can be sure that the vision module will always do that. However, should the vision module ever report one of the teeth, either because the robot is too close, or because part of the comb is occluded, and it looks like the tooth boundary forms the true boundary, then MERCATOR will be in trouble.

(3) is similar in arising naturally in scene descriptions. However, (3) does not have the same retrieval problems. Adjacency information can be easily retrieved from any map accurate enough to express it.

(4), (5), and (6) are only problems when the disambiguating information is lacking, which will almost never be the case in visual input. Usually, if one can see the distance between two objects, one sees the two closest parts; and likewise for the other properties. Therefore, these are not a problem for a visual assimilation program. However, this is the kind of information which is provided by general rules or by other sources of geographic knowledge. (See sections 8.4.2 and 8.4.6.)

8.4.6. Other Types of Assimilation

Visual input, though the most important source of geographic knowledge, is by no means the only source. Indeed, other modes have been rather more studied within the AI literature. Assimilation from natural language texts has been studied in [Waltz, 81], [Boggess, 79], and [McDermott, 74]. Assimilation from arbitrary inference has been studied in [McDermott and Davis, 84]. Assimilation from route instructions and executions has been studied in [Kuipers, 78] and [Riesbeck, 80]. These alternative theories have been studied in Chapter 6. Here we consider how easily these tasks can be performed by the MERCATOR system.

Scene descriptions differ from geographic information from other sources in being much more complex, complete, and structured. A scene description shows a number of objects, and gives a lot of information about how they are related. A quantum of spatial information from other sources — a sentence of text, a single inference from general rules, etc. — typically relates only a few (two or three) objects in a crude way.

Most of the existing matcher and merger are therefore irrelevant in non-visual assimilation. In many cases, the input information will refer unambiguously to the objects involved. In such cases, the matcher is wholly superfluous. There may be some cases where the first step of the matcher, the call to the object retriever, will be useful in disambiguating reference. For example, if the protagonist of a story is in Chicago and the story asserts that he goes to sit by "the lake", then the object retriever can show that the only possible lake is Lake Michigan.* However, the remainder of the matcher will almost always be superfluous.

---

* I am not, of course, claiming that the spatial information is *sufficient* to make this conclusion.

The bulk of the matcher is a comparison of the relative positions in the cognitive map with those in the new information. In non-visual assimilation, since the relative position information will be so scanty, matching reduces to verifying whether it could be true; in general, a simple call to the appropriate retriever function.

Similar remarks apply to the merger. The merger handles four types of information: new objects, improved measurements, more precise shape descriptions, and more complete shape descriptions. Non-visual information will often present new objects, but this assimilation is trivial. More rarely, it will give improved measurements. These assimilations are easy individually, but difficult taken together, because, in general, they will not necessarily relate objects which are close together. (See below). Improved shape descriptions are rare in non-visual information, and it is very rare for them to be in forms assimilable to MERCATOR. Partial shape descriptions would be almost unknown.

On the other hand, non-visual assimilation raises a large class of new problems not handled well by MERCATOR. Firstly, much of the information it provides cannot be expressed in MERCATOR terms. This we have considered in section 8.4.5. Secondly, even the expressible information is not well structured. It does not follow any of the normalcy conditions of section 2.8. The information may relate objects which are widely separated. The object hierarchy may not be properly presented.

8.4.7. Absence information

The major gap in the MERCATOR representation, as we have often remarked, is the lack of universal quantifiers. You cannot be sure, from a MECATOR map, that there are no rhinoceroses in your office; you cannot be sure that you have seen all the tables in your office; you cannot even be sure that there is not another table largely overlapping the known table but shifted one inch to the right. (See Figure 8-7.)

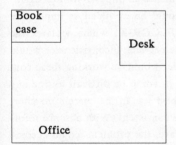
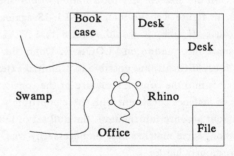

MERCATOR map of office   What office could really look like

Figure 8-7: Lack of Absence Information

For special cases, it is often possible to improvise an *ad hoc* solution. For example, section 8.4.1 presents two ways in which the program can use an assumption that all obstacles are represented. The problem is to find a general representation for this kind of information, to use this information to constrain matching, and to combine this information properly

173

in the merger.

A partial solution might be to mark a clump as *complete* with respect to certain kinds of objects, if one knows that all such objects which are actually inside the object are represented in the map as inside the clump. Thus, my office might be complete with respect to wild animals and desks.

To some extent, explicit completeness markings can be replaced by heuristics such as those of [Collins et. al., 75]. From my thorough knowledge of other objects in my room, I can infer that, had there been a rhinoceros there, I would remember it too. As far as MERCATOR goes, this kind of inference works in exactly the same way as an explicit marking, as long as this information is easily retrievable for inference.

We may wish also to mark clumps as complete with respect to overlapping other clumps of certain types. That is, all objects of the specified type which in fact overlap the given clump are marked as overlapping it. This would enable us to state a number of physical rules. For example, the assertion that all solid clumps are complete with respect to overlap of other solid clumps would enforce the rule that no two objects can overlap. To do this would of course require explicit representation of overlapping between clumps.

A harder problem is the representation of absences in the interstices between objects. Suppose our map shows a sidewalk and a street with adjacent regions at a grain-size of 6 inches. (There is actually a curb between them.) We wish to assert that there are no obstacles — fences or the like — between them. This is not a completeness property of either the street or the sidewalk. One solution to this problem is to use an overlapping blank object, as suggested in section 8.4.1; but this involves difficult technical problems, besides its obvious clumsiness. A better solution might involve a good solution to the adjacency problem discussed above in section 8.4.5.

In the matcher this information would rule out certain matches as impossible. For example, in figure 8-8 the match WALL-1S against WALL-1K could be excluded as impossible because, if true, it would require that WALL-2S overlap FLOOR-K, which violates the absence information on FLOOR-K. Doing the geometry to detect such inconsistencies would be fairly difficult, but possible to a limited extent. Much harder would be working these constraints into the control structure of the consistency checker. It would be difficult to find any set of matches consistent with these constraints, let alone the best set. In the current matcher, without absence information, the null set of matches is always consistent. With absence information, some matches may be necessarily true. In the worst case, the problem would become enormously harder.

On the other hand, absence information will sometimes make things easier for the matcher, by providing effective pruning. It could be used to cure the most irritating aspect of running MERCATOR, the enormous labor spent assimilating completely redundant information. In the current version, no matter how many times or how recently the robot has explored a particular area, when he sees it again he has to go through the whole assimilation process: creating correspondences, running the consistency checker, and merging. Absence information, properly applied, could short circuit this whole process, since the robot will know that there can't be anything new here.

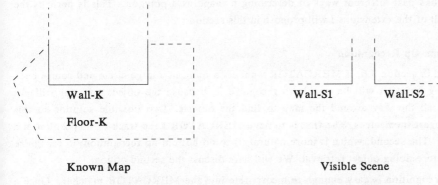

| Known Map | Visible Scene |

Figure 8-8: Match Excluded by Absence Information

The merger has its own problems with this kind of data. Consider: how do you determine that a room is devoid of rhinoceroses? Clearly, by putting together visible pieces of a room, each devoid of rhinoceroses. When you merge two regions representing part of the office, and each is marked as lacking rhinoceroses, then their join likewise lacks rhinoceroses. But consider the following case. You get three partial views of the room, A, B, and C, in order. A is complete with respect to rhinoceroses, desks, and ghosts. B is complete with respect to rhinoceroses and ghosts. C is complete with respect to rhinoceroses and desks. Combining these, the merger can derive that the join of A, B, and C is complete for rhinoceroses; the join of A and B is complete for ghosts; and the join of A and C is complete for desks. In the worst case, the merger would have to keep track of 7 subregions of the room, each of which was complete for something else. The problem grows exponentially with the number of views taken of the room.

8.4.8. Richer object ontology

The MERCATOR program takes a rather boxy view of the world. MERCATOR's world is a collection of well-defined things, each with a well defined border. The actual world is not so simple. The cognitive map must keep track of attributes of space which are not well-defined things: patches of color, ground elevation, city neighborhoods.

Moreover, even where borders exist, their association with an object may be tenuous. How was it decided, for example, that the pond was not part of the field in figure 2-1? Can we be sure that the next time the vision module looks out, it will not decide to classify the field as containing the pond?* Answering this question in the affirmative, or making adequate provision for the negative answer, would require a good theory of object discrimination.

Solving these problems would involve major extensions to the underlying ontology as well as to the representation and the algorithms. The very language of retrieval queries would have to change once we were no longer talking about discrete objects. The matcher would have to be built to look past different ways of describing a scene in terms of objects,

---

* I thank Dr. Carlo Sequin for pointing this out to me.

175

as it now looks past different ways of describing a shape as a polygon. This is perhaps the most difficult of the extensions I will propose in this section.

8.4.9. Bottom Up Recognition

As discussed in section 3.6, if MERCATOR wanders around in a large circle and comes back to its starting point, it will be unable to recognize it, because the object retriever will not know to go all the way around the map to find the objects. Two possible solution to this problem suggest themselves. The first is to have MERCATOR keep track of its position in a global sense. The second, which is more natural, is to do bottom up recognition; to recognize the place before doing object retrieval. We will here discuss the second option.

Such recognition is easy enough to incorporate into the MERCATOR matcher. Once a place has been recognized, we use retrieve all the objects around it, and consider them as potential matches, in exactly the same way as we now retrieve the objects around the robot. If the object is seen in the distance, then we retrieve the objects that we expect to see between ourselves and it.

The problem is to do the recognition. We can distinguish three cases.

1) The object is unique in the world. We run across the Statue of Liberty, the Eiffel Tower, or the Grand Canyon. In this case, recognition is equivalent to identification by the vision module.

2) The object is known to be unique in the area. The Union Trust Bank in New Haven can be confused with other buildings elsewhere, but not other buildings in New Haven. Therefore, if one is sure that he hasn't left New Haven, and he sees something looking like the Union Trust, it must be the Union Trust.

This information is clearly a kind of completeness statement (see section 8.4.7.) The inference is easy enough; the problem is to set up indices so that it can be found quickly. Possibly, one could use a discrimination tree, where object descriptions which are unique to a large area are indexed under that area. In processing a new view, we would then look under all the containing large areas for objects unique to that area, and match description comparable to something in the scene. As with all completeness information, it is a problem to ensure that the areas considered remain well structured.

3) The layout of objects is known to be unique in the area. New York is full of box-like tall buildings, but there is only one pair which is close together, the same size, and much taller than any of the surrounding buildings.

This is similar to (2), but harder, since the descriptive language for relative positions is so complicated. One possibility here is to try to match the World Trade Center whenever two tall box-like buildings are seen.

8.4.10. Error correction

Error correction is a necessary part of any algorithm for assimilation into a data base. If the input contradicts the data base, something must be done. The lack of such error correction is probably the most important deficiency in MERCATOR. It seems unlikely that MERCATOR can be made robust without somehow solving this problem.

Intuitively, visual assimilation should be a particularly easy domain for error correction. Seeing is believing; the input is presumably right and the cognitive map must just be changed to correspond to it. The problem, of course, is what in the cognitive map to change. The subtlety of this problem may be measured by noting that, by most measures of simplicity, the simplest operation to restore consistency to the map — and one which is *always* successful — is to assume that robot's estimate of his own position is grossly mistaken, and that he is actually in *terra incognita*, seeing entirely new objects. However simple, this is rarely correct.

Another subtlety is that, in the current semantics, the input never does contradict the cognitive map. One may be simply seeing a whole new bunch of objects previously ignored. Thus, the error corrector will never be invoked. Two approaches suggest themselves. The first is to defer working on error correction until the problem of absence information is solved. Given absence information, there can be contradictions between input and map; you may see a wall where you know there is no wall. The other is to have the matcher look for near matches, and when it finds a near match which does not quite work, make it get suspicious and call the error corrector. I feel that, though the latter approach would be very difficult to work out, it will ultimately be necessary, even in a system with absence information.

In general, error correction depends on knowing where errors are introduced into the system, and how such an introduced error relates to the perceived contradiction. Since MERCATOR is largely deductive, there are only a few possible entry points for mistakes. Firstly, the vision system may produce an invalid map. We described in section 8.3 how a vision system might well miss a deep, thin hole in a wall, for example. A vision system might also misinterpret an object or mismeasure a quantity. Secondly, the matcher might have propose a mismatch. Thirdly, there might have been a computation error due to round-off in the merger. Lastly, there might have been a mismeasure of the robot's motion.

In general, computation errors should be rare and easy to correct; all that is involved is changing some parameter. The difficulty of correcting vision mistakes varies with the degree to which vision mistakes can be characterized and the nature of the mistake. Misinterpreting a seen object as a similar object — seeing a cat and thinking it a rabbit — should be easy to detect and correct, given a forgiving matcher. Mistakes of shape, like missing small holes, are more difficult, but, if it is known that vision makes these mistakes, should be possible. Mismatches will be much more difficult to correct. A mismatch can distort the world in very weird ways; it tends to cause other mismatches. By the time the contradiction is detected, a large part of the map will be distorted.

The only general AI framework for error correction is the Truth Maintenance System of [Doyle, 79] and [McAllester, 80], which relies on dependency directed backtracking. This is not applicable to MERCATOR because of the extreme waste in keeping every original premise and inference in memory, and, more importantly, because the strong interaction between the input facts in calculation means that almost every fact in the current cognitive map depends indirectly on almost every other fact input through vision and every assumption made by the matcher.

8.4.11. World change and object motion

The static world of MERCATOR is an idealization. In the real world, objects move, they change, they are created and destroyed. A cognitive map should be able to accommodate motion.

Of course, this is a back door entrance to temporal reasoning, a domain at least as hard as spatial reasoning. Here, I will merely give examples of some of the particular problems encountered in introducing motion and change into a cognitive map.

- Continuous Motion. Describe the motion of a car. Infer that, unless it turns, it will crash into the wall in less than a minute. Infer that a plane which flies from Washington to Toronto must at some point have passed over the Canadian border. Some work has been done on this problem; see [DeKleer, 75], [Forbus, 79], [Davis, 84].

- Continuous Shape Deformation. Describe the winding of a string into a ball, or the unrolling of a roll of toilet paper.

- Histories. Maintain a data base which records the present and past positions of objects without having a separate MERCATOR map for each instant. (This is, of course, a form of the frame problem [McCarthy and Hayes, 69].) In particular, do this in the presence of continuously moving objects.

- Prediction. Given a MERCATOR map of an area which was valid at some previous time, use persistence rules ([McDermott, 82]) or other means to predict what the area looks like now. In particular, predict which completeness assertions are still true. (See section 8.4.7.)

- Recognition of a Changed Scene. Identify a particular place, despite the changes. Distinguish between changes and errors in the cognitive map. (The confusion between error correction and temporal updating, endemic to AI temporal reasoning, is particularly difficult in recognition problems)

8.5. Technical Improvements

Besides the major omissions discussed above, there are a number of non-trivial technical problems in MERCATOR which materially degrade its behavior. I here discuss three such problems, and propose solutions to two.

8.5.1. Vertex d-trees

As discussed in section 3.3, the clump hierarchy fails to provide efficient retrieval in any of four cases: if the downward branching factor in the hierarchy is large, if the upward branching factor is not close to 1, if there are many regions with very many vertices, or if clumps have peculiar shapes. One way around this is to create a separate hierarchy, a discrimination tree of vertices.

This discrimination tree is just an abstraction of the clump hierarchy. From the point of view of the path-finding algorithm, the following properties of clumps are important.

1. A clump contains a set of vertices. A son of a clump in the hierarchy contains a subset of the clump's vertices. The vertices inside a clump form a coherent group in space.

2. Any two clumps have a common ancestor in the hierarchy, which can be easily found.

3. A clump has a small number of a distinguished *boundary* vertices, which are well distributed through the vertices contained in the clump.

4. The boundary vertices of a clump are connected by edges.

5. The boundary vertices of all the immediate sons of a clump are connected by edges to each other and to the clump.

Since these are the only properties of clumps used by the path-finder, the path-finder can use any structure with these properties. A vertex d-tree is a hierarchy of nodes which have the above clump properties. Each node represents an area in space which contains a number of vertices. (See Figure 8-9.)

The problem is to maintain the above properties. Forming nodes of coherent vertices is not too difficult, especially if the map satisfies the topological closeness property. The quick time to find a common ancestor is maintained by keeping the node hierarchy a tree, or nearly a tree. The tricky part is choosing the boundary vertices to satisfy the last three properties. One way to make this easy might be to follow the clump hierarchy as long as possible, and modify it when it gets into trouble.

8.5.2. Region characterization

In calculations involving a clump with many regions, both the retriever and assimilator begin by choosing a single region of the set to use an approximation, and the criterion they employ for this choice is very crude. They characterize the region on the basis of a single measure, its grain-size. This is acceptable only if each region has a roughly constant grain-size for its various edges. The merger tries to arrange the regions so that this is true. However, if some parts of the object are known much more than others, then a region which shows the known parts in great detail is not correctly differentiated from one which shows them only very crudely. (See figure 8-10.)

A related but more difficult problem occurs when the robot knows some part of an object in detail, but does not know where that part fits into the object as a whole. In a situation like this, the options are either to construct an incomplete region which represents the detailed part of the object and other complete regions for the object as a whole, or to link this detailed description to a extremely coarse description. (See figure 8-11.) The first option is ineffective because it is always better to use a complete region than an incomplete one. The second leaves the region marked as extremely inaccurate, while the information to be recorded is very accurate.

Which normalcy conditions should be abandoned and how the algorithms can use regions of widely varying accuracy are very difficult problems. The nature of these problems together with the difficulties of finding good heuristics in the merger for choosing or putting together good regions, suggests to me that the region construct is inadequate for the tasks it is being asked to perform. It is far from clear what modifications would be improvements.

179

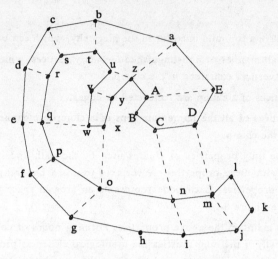

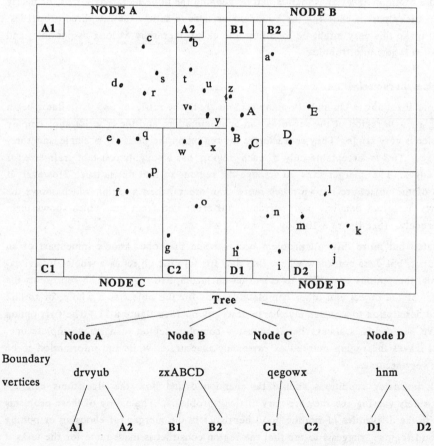

Figure 8-9: Vertex Discrimination Tree

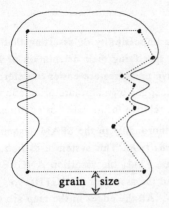 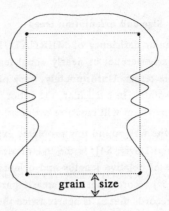

The overall grain-size of the first is no less than that of the second,
even though the first carries more information.

Figure 8-10: Regions Poorly Characterized

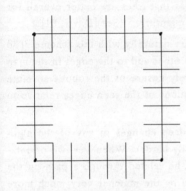

Coarse approximation

(Grainsize shown by hatches)

Fine detail in unknown position

The only merge which preserves the detail is this shape above, where the grain-size of
the dotted line is equal to the diameter of the object.

Figure 8-11: Where a Small Part of a Region is Precisely Known

8.5.3. Size and orientation trees

One major deficiency of MERCATOR maps is the impossibility of asserting that two lines are nearly parallel or nearly equal lengths without specifying their orientation or lengths in absolute terms. Unfortunately, very often the relative measures are easier to determine than the absolute. In particular, the robot must always keep his own absolute orientation, because a vision system will measure every other orientation relative to the robot orientation.

One way round this problem, explored fairly thoroughly in the SPAM system [McDermott and Davis, 84], is the use of *size and orientation trees*. This system uses fuzz ranges to record the relative lengths and orientations of edges. Thus, the assertion ANGLE(e_1, e_2) ∈ $[-5°, 5°]$ records that e_1 is nearly parallel to e_2, and the assertion LENGTH(e_1, e_2) ∈ $[1.95, 2.05]$ records that e_1 is nearly twice the length of e_2. All the edges in the map are connected by length assertions, so that any two lengths are ultimately comparable; likewise, all edges are connected by orientation assertions. A technical design decision has to be made whether the length and orientation assertions are restricted to form a trees over the edges or are allowed to form a general graph. Trees are easier to manipulate and search; graphs provide more flexible representation. Our experience in SPAM was that trees are better overall for size and orientation, which are effectively one dimensional quantities. (See [Davis, 81].)

The problem with robot orientation can be handled very naturally with this scheme. The robot's current and previous orientation are related to each other and to the edges in the map through the orientation tree. In this way, we can be entirely unsure of the robot's absolute orientation, and nonetheless be able to express the orientations of the seen edges relative to the robot.

Adding size and orientation trees does not require deep changes in any of the algorithms. It does, however, make the calculations substantially harder. Whenever two orientations or two lengths have to be computed with, they must be related through a path on the appropriate tree. It makes the process of fuzz constriction by the matcher very much more powerful and necessary (see section 4.11). For example, in figure 8-12, if the robot's direction is completely unknown, then it will find that edge A-B can match P-Q, because they might be parallel, and that edge B-C can match Q-R, because *they* might be parallel. However using tentative fuzz constriction, it will find that, if A-B matches P-Q, then the position of the robot in the second scene is perpendicular to his position in the first, in which case B-C cannot match Q-R. In this way, it can rule out the invalid match.

The problems of the sketcher would either go away or be very much transmuted if size and orientation trees were added to MERCATOR maps. Presumably, many of the dependencies now deduced through X-Y boxes would be directly expressed within these trees. On the other hand, it would be impossible to create meaningful X-Y boxes, since there would be so many other types of dependencies to consider. The following algorithm would seem appropriate:

One subtle problem with this algorithm is that defining the cost of a tree or of a link becomes difficult when scales have fuzzy relations. (See [Davis, 81]). However, this can probably be surmounted.

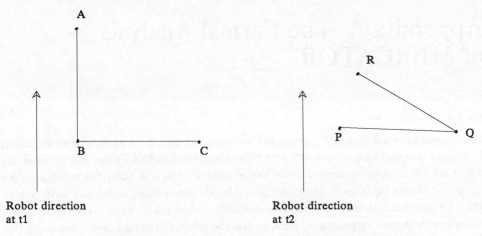

Robot direction
at t1

Robot direction
at t2

Figure 8-12: Matching Without Absolute Orientations

Find the minimum cost tree.

Choose random edge parameters consistent with the scale and orientation trees.

Place an arbitrary vertex at the origin.

Calculate the other vertex positions by propagating out along tree edges.

Algorithm 8-1: Sketching with scale and orientation trees

8.6. Conclusions

These extensions and improvements can be divided into four classes:

- New Problem Types. This includes new types of retrieval and assimilation, error correction, and investigation.

- Geometric issues. This includes three dimensions, indescribable states, vertex d-trees, regions, and size and orientation trees.

- Logical issues. This includes absence information, object ontology, and change and motion.

- Models of vision.

I find two encouraging features in this enumeration of unsolved problems. Firstly, the problems are reasonably independent, despite some interaction. It would make sense to work on almost any of the above problems independently of any of the others. Secondly, many problems which are not on this list turn out to be special cases of problems which are, often in subtle ways. I have in mind, for example, the reduction of the redundant assimilation problem to the absence information problem, or the incorporation of the disoriented robot problem into the general scheme of an orientation tree, whose primary function is to say that edges are parallel.

A geometric reasoner with all the above features would be an extremely powerful theory. MERCATOR is a first step on a long road. The above discussion suggests at least that MERCATOR is a useful framework in which to pose difficult problems.

183

Appendix A The Formal Analysis of MERCATOR

A.1 Introduction

This appendix collects results more formally mathematical than those in the rest of the thesis. It contains a restatement of the MERCATOR representation and of the objectives of the MERCATOR program in formal terms and a number of results regarding complete algorithms for certain subtasks in MERCATOR. The various sections are largely independent. They are connected in that they are all essentially mathematical. They are discussed here, rather than with their respective subjects, so that the non-mathematical reader can easily skip it.

None of this material is critical to an understanding of MERCATOR; only the material on PCO's was essential to its developement. Nonetheless, I feel that it should be included, for several reasons. The chapter as a whole serves to connect MERCATOR to mainstream mathematics. Formalizing the problem and representations (sections A.2 to A.4) gives a new perspective, and suggests new generalizations, extensions, and analogies. Sections A.6 and A.7 present original results and algorithms of intrinsic mathematical and computational interest. Finally, in studying heuristic algorithms, it is important to know why the problem is difficult. This can be done directly, as in section A.5, which shows that computations on fuzz are necessarily difficult; or by studying special cases where the problem is easy, as is done in section A.6. This appendix is both a re-examination of MERCATOR and an exploration of the problem space around MERCATOR.

A.2 Formal Semantics

In this section we restate the definition of the formal semantics given in section 2.2 with more rigor. In this way, we come as close as possible to removing any ambiguity.

We repeat the definition of the MERCATOR microworld. An *object* O is a subset of R^2 homeomorphic to a disk with finitely many holes. Equivalently, O is closed and connected and its boundary, denoted BOUNDARY (O), consists of a finite number of disjoint simple closed curves: one exterior curve, and a number (possibly zero) interior curves. (For example, figure A-1 cannot be the shape of an object, since the boundary is a figure eight.) With each of these curves, we associate a direction which is *counterclockwise around the object* O. For the exterior curve, this direction will be counterclockwise in the absolute sense; for the interior curves, it will be clockwise in the absolute sense.

A *property* is a function from objects to arbitrary sets. Typical properties are "color" with image set { red, blue, white ... }; "style" with image set { Gothic, Georgian, Bauhaus ... }; "is-a" with image set { robot, building, wall, ...}. The world is a set of objects and a set of properties.

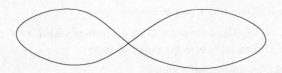

Figure A-1: An Impossible Object

Now we define the elements of the map. I assume the existence of a set of *unstructured entities*, whose only interesting predicate is inequality from all other members of the set, and from all other elements of a MERCATOR map.

Definition A.1: A *vertex* is an unstructured entity.

Definition A.2: An *edge* E is a four-tuple consisting of

1. HEAD (E), a vertex
2. TAIL (E), a vertex
3. LENGTH (E), a real interval
4. ROT (E), a closed arc in the unit circle.

Definition A.3: A *joint* J is a six-tuple consisting of

1. TAIL (J), a vertex
2. HEAD (J), a vertex
3. EDGE (J), an edge
4. PAR-LEN (J), a real interval
5. PERP-LEN (J), a real interval
6. ROT (J), a closed arc in the unit circle

such that either HEAD(J) = TAIL(EDGE(J)) or HEAD(J) = HEAD(EDGE(J)).

Definition A.4: A *polygon* P is a pair consisting of

1. VERTICES (P), a non-empty sequence of vertices.
2. EDGES (P), a set of edges

If VERTICES (P) contains only one element, then EDGES (P) is null.

If VERTICES (P) contains two elements U and V then EDGES (P) contains a single edge E, and either U = HEAD(E) and V = TAIL(E) or V = HEAD(E) and U = TAIL(E).

If VERTICES (P) contains $m>1$ elements, numbered $<V_1 \cdots V_m>$ in order, then EDGES (P) contains m elements. Moreover the elements of EDGES (P) may be ordered $E_1, E_2 \cdots E_m$ so that for each i, either $V_i = \text{HEAD}(E_i)$ and $V_{(i+1) \bmod m} = \text{TAIL}(E_i)$ or $V_{(i+1) \bmod m} = \text{HEAD}(E_i)$ and $V_i = \text{TAIL}(E_i)$.

185

Definition A.5: A *clump* C is a pair consisting of

1. DESCRIPTION (C), a function D on properties such that if property P is in the domain of D then D(P) is in the range of P.

2. IDENT (C), an unstructured entity.

(In other words, a clump is a thing which has values for certain properties. If clump C corresponds to object O, then DESCRIPTION (C) (P) is supposed to be P(O). The above is the way to say that in mathematical rigor.)

Definition A.6: A *clump − containment* is an ordered pair of clumps; <container, containee>.

Recall from section 2.7 that a *corner* corresponds to a traversal of a vertex in going around the boundary of a region.

Definition A.7: A *corner* CC is a triple consisting of

1. CLUMP (CC), a clump

2. VERTEX (CC), a vertex

3. TYPE (CC), a boolean

TYPE (CC) is T if the vertex is real vertex of the region, and NIL if it is a knowledge vertex.

Definition A.8: A *bound* B is a six-tuple consisting of

1. CLUMP (B), a clump

2. TAIL (B), a corner

3. HEAD (B), a corner

4. EDGE (B), an edge

5. TYPE (B), a boolean value

6. GRAIN-SIZE (B), a real number

such that either both TAIL (EDGE (B)) = VERTEX (TAIL (B))
and HEAD (EDGE (B)) = VERTEX (HEAD (B));
or both HEAD (EDGE (B)) = VERTEX (TAIL (B))
and TAIL (EDGE (B)) = VERTEX (HEAD (B)).

TYPE (B) is T if B is a real bound of its region, and NIL if B is a knowledge bound.

Definition A.9: A *region* REG is five-tuple consisting of

1. CLUMP (REG), a clump

2. GRAPH (REG), a non-empty set of polygons

3. GRAIN-SIZE (REG), a real number

4. CORNERS (REG), a set of corners, such that if C ∈ CORNERS(REG), then CLUMP(C) = CLUMP(REG).

5. BOUNDS(REG), a set of bounds, such that if B ∈ BOUNDS(REG), then CLUMP(B) = CLUMP(REG).

Moreover, the bounds and corners must satisfy the following:

1. For each B ∈ BOUNDS(REG), TAIL(B) ∈ CORNERS(REG) and HEAD(B) ∈ CORNERS(REG).

2. For each C ∈ CORNERS(REG), there exist unique bounds B and D ∈ BOUNDS(REG), such that C = TAIL(B) = HEAD (D).

These conditions ensure that the region is bounded all the way around.

Definition A.10: A *partial cyclic ordering* PCO is a triple consisting of

1. A clump, CLUMP (PCO)

2. A set of corners CORNERS (PCO) such that for all C ∈ CORNERS (PCO), CLUMP (C) = CLUMP (PCO).

3. A three-place relation CC (PCO) over CORNERS (PCO) satisfying the following:

   a. If $<u,v,w>$ ∈ CC(PCO) then not $<u,w,v>$ ∈ CC(PCO);

   b. If $<u,v,w>$ ∈ CC(PCO) then $<v,w,u>$ ∈ CC(PCO) and

      $<w,u,v>$ ∈ CC(PCO)

   c. If $<u,v,w>$ ∈ CC(PCO) and $<u,w,x>$ ∈ CC(PCO)

      then $<u,v,x>$ ∈ CC(PCO).

(See section A.7.)

Now putting together all the pieces and checking for closure:

Definition A.11: A *MERCATOR map* is a set of PCO's, regions, bounds, corners, clumps, clump-containments, polygons, joints, edges, and vertices, such that

1. Every appropriate field of every element in the map is an element of the map.

2. For every bound B in the map, there exists a region REG such that B ∈ BOUNDS (REG).

3. For every corner C in the map, there exists a region REG such that C ∈ CORNERS (REG).

Now we define three types of functions to connect maps to the real world.

Definition A.12: A *coordinate* function is a function from vertices to points in R^2.

Given a coordinate function from vertices to points, we extend it to be a function from edges, polygons, or unions thereof onto point sets in the obvious way.

Definition A.13: A *realizing* function is a function from clumps to objects.

Definition A.14: A *covering* function is a continuous, one-to-one function from R^2 to R^2.

Finally, the truth condition.

Definition A.15: A MERCATOR map is *valid* for a world iff there exists a coordinate function COOR, a realizing function REAL, a covering function $COVER_b$ for each real bound b, and a covering function $COVER_{R,\epsilon}$ for each region R and each real number ϵ, such that

1. The fuzzy measurements of edges contain their measurements under COOR.

    Formally, for every edge EE:

    a. DIST (COOR(TAIL(EE)), COOR(HEAD(EE))) $\in$ LENGTH(EE) and

    b. DIR (COOR(TAIL(EE)), COOR(HEAD(EE))) $\in$ ROT(EE)

2. The fuzzy measurements of joints contain their measurements under COOR.

    Formally, for a joint JJ, let t = COOR(TAIL(JJ)), h = COOR(HEAD(JJ)), m = the projection of t onto COOR(EDGE(JJ)). Then

    a. DIST (t, m) $\in$ PERP-LEN (JJ)

    b. DIST (m, h) $\in$ PAR-LEN (JJ)

    c. DIR (m, h) $\in$ ROT (JJ)

3. For each polygon P, if VERTICES(P) = $< V_1 \cdots V_k >$ then the points $<$ COOR(V_1) $\cdots$ COOR(V_k) $>$ form the vertices of a counter-clockwise non-self-intersecting polygon.

4. Clump properties are true of the objects.

    Formally, for each clump CL, if property P is in the domain of CL then (DESCRIPT (CL)) (P) = P (REAL (CL)).

5. The containment statements statements are true.

    Formally, for each clump containment CC, REAL (CONTAINER (CC)) $\supset$ REAL (CONTENT (CC))

6. The interior of the region lies on top of the object.

    Formally, for each region R, there exists a real number δ such that, for all $\epsilon < \delta$,

    a. $COVER_{R,\epsilon}$ (BALLOON (COOR (GRAPH (R))), ϵ)) $\subset$ REAL (CLUMP (R))

    b. For all $x \in$ BALLOON (COOR (GRAPH (R)), ϵ),

        DIST $(x, COVER_{R,\epsilon}(x))$ $<$ GRAIN-SIZE (R)

    (BALLOON is defined in section 2.7 as a function on (powerset of R^2) $\times$ R such that $x \in$ BALLOON (S, ϵ) iff $\exists$ $y \in$ S $|$ DIST (x, y) $<$ ϵ. The need for this convoluted definition for use with one-dimensional representations is discussed there.)

7. Bounds lie within the grain-size of the object boundary, and go forwards around the boundary.

Formally, let B be an arbitrary bound, and let O = REAL (CLUMP (REG (B))), the object whose boundary B describes. Then $COVER_B$ has the following properties.

a. For $x \in$ COOR (B), $COVER_B(x) \in$ BOUNDARY (O)

b. For $x \in$ COOR (B), DIST $(x, COVER_B(x))$ < GRAIN-SIZE (B)

c. Let $f : [0,1] \Rightarrow$ COOR (B) be the standard parametrization,

   $f(t) = (1-t) \cdot$ COOR (TAIL (B)) + $t \cdot$ COOR (HEAD (B)).

   That is, f goes uniformly from COOR (TAIL (B)) to COOR (HEAD (B)). As t goes from 0 to 1, $COVER_B(f(t))$ must go counterclockwise around O. That is, going around BOUNDARY (O) in the direction shown by B, O is always on the left.

8. Boundaries do not break at real vertices.

Formally, for each region R, for each corner $C \in$ CORNERS (R) such that TYPE (C) = T, let V = VERTEX (C). By the definition of regions, there exist bounds B and D such that C = HEAD (B) = TAIL (D). Then $COVER_B$ (COOR (V)) = $COVER_D$ (COOR (V))

9. The PCO's are true.

Formally, for any partial cyclic ordering PCO, let corners U, V, W $\in$ CORNERS (PCO) so that <U, V, W> $\in$ CC (PCO) . Then there exist bounds B, C, and D such that U is the head or tail of B, V is the head or tail of C, and W is the head or tail of D, and such that the points $COVER_B(U)$, $COVER_C(V)$, $COVER_D(W)$ fall on one of the closed curves constituting BOUNDARY (O), in order counterclockwise around (O).

The functions REAL, COOR, $COVER_R$, and $COVER_b$ are *valid* if they satisfy these conditions.

A MERCATOR map thus presents a set of constraints on the real world. Any world which satisfies a MERCATOR map M is called a *model* of M. The statements which can be legitimately inferred from M are precisely those which are true in all its models. A world together with the functions REAL, COOR, and the covering functions is called a *construed model* of M.

Though there is only one true world, there can be many valid construals of a map in that world. For example, if the map specificies only that there is a building and a street nearby, then there are many real instances that will satisfy it. Even if the referent of the clumps is fixed, there are almost always ways of modifying COVER and COOR slightly so as create a new correspondence.

There are certain allowed transformations of a model that leave it a model. These correspond to world properties left unspecified by the MERCATOR map. In particular, the following are allowed:

1. Translation. If W is a model of M, than adding vector $\vec{x}$ to each object in W leaves it still a model of M.

2. Addition of properties. If W is a model of M, then extending the domain of any of the properties in W to include some more objects, and assigning any value to the properties on the new domain members will leave it a model.

3. Addition of objects. Adding more objects to W which are not in the range of REAL leave W still a model.

A.3 More semantics for the assimilator

A number of additional formal definitions must be given for our analysis of the matcher and merger.

The correspondences used in the matcher are defined in terms of two particular construals of two maps. Given two MERCATOR maps M and N, a world which is a model of both maps, and construals for each map:

1. Given two clumps $C \in M$ and $D \in N$, then cl-match(C,D) iff $REAL_M(C) = REAL_N(D)$

2. Given two bounds $p \in M$ and $q \in N$, then bound-match(p, q) iff
    there exists a line segment $s \subset COOR_M(p)$
    such that LENGTH $(s) \geq 1/2 \cdot$ LENGTH $(COOR_M(p)$
    and such that $COVER_p(s) \subset COVER_q(COOR_N(q))$.

3. Given an edge $e \in M$ and a vertex $v \in N$, then a joint connecting the two is true iff the measurements of the joints are satisfied in the sense defined above (Definition A.15 (2)) under the functions $COOR_M$ on e and $COOR_N$ on v.

A.4 Statement of Problems

With this context, we can state the various problems of MERCATOR in formal terms.

Retrieving relative position: as in section 3.5

Given two subsets P and Q of R^2, define $P - Q \equiv$ the set of values of $p - q$ for $p \in P$ and $q \in Q$.

Given a MERCATOR map M, two clumps C and D, and a function f from point sets to reals, find the set of values attained by f(REAL(C)-REAL(D)) varying over all models of M.

Object retrieval:

Given a MERCATOR map M, a clump C, a distance d, and a minimum size s, find all the clumps A in M such that in some model W of M, the distance from REAL(A) to REAL(C) is less than d, and the diameter of REAL(A) is larger than s.

Sketching:

Given a MERCATOR map M, and a set of vertices VVS $\subset$ M, find the values of COOR(VVS) in some valid construal of M.

190

Assimilation:

Given two MERCATOR maps M and N, and a small set of correspondences (in MERCATOR, the statement that the same robot is in the cognitive map as in the scene description) find the "simplest" map P such that P implies M, N and the correspondences. Equivalently, any model of P can serve as a model of M and N; P must capture all the information in both M and N. We leave the sense of "simplest" unformalized.

Matching:

Given two MERCATOR maps M and N and a small set of correspondences, find the "best" set of correspondences of M and N, containing the given correspondences, which are simultaneously true in some fixed world which is a model for both M and N and in some fixed, valid construals of M and N using that world.

Merging:

Find the "simplest" MERCATOR map which is equivalent to two given MERCATOR maps and a set of correspondences.

Retrieval can be performed completely deductively. For example, given a MERCATOR map containing two objects A and B, it will usually be possible to find some provable upper bounds on the distance from A to B. It will, in fact, be possible to prove optimal bounds on the distance; that is, prove for some LO and HI that (1) there is no model in which DIST (A, B) is not in [LO, HI] and (2) that there exist models in which DIST (A, B) comes arbitrarily close to LO or to HI.

Matching may be thought of as deductive at a meta-level. The matcher "proves" that its correspondences are consistent (or even that they are the best set of correspondences.) Merging is deductive (ideally) at the object level; the resultant map is implied by the matcher and the correspondences.

Needless to say, the actual algorithms are not actually deductive. The retriever typically gives ranges which may be too large, owing to the fact that it considers only some of the constraints involved, or they may be too small, owing to limitations of Monte Carlo methods. Thus, there is no logical statement which is necessarily true about the results of the retriever. However, it is important to understand what kinds of inference the MERCATOR map supports and the MERCATOR algorithms are trying to approximate.

The assimilator as a whole cannot be deductive; there is no way in the MERCATOR system to prove that two clumps represent the same object. How is this possible, when the assimilator is simply the composition of the matcher with the merger? The answer is that we make a logical jump in going from the output of the matcher to the input of the merger. The matcher has shown that the correspondences are *consistent* with the maps; the merger must assume that they are *true*. Interestingly, this jump, which is the most interesting action taken by the program from a logical point of view, is a computational no-op.

The assimilator may be thought of as *abductive* or *explanatory*. To the extent that information is not lost in assimilation, the output map implies both of the input maps. The truth of the correspondences explains the similarities between the maps. The coincidence that (1) you see a tree and (2) you know that a tree ought to be there is explained by the hypothesis that the tree you know about is the tree you see.

The most difficult logical issue faced in the assimilator is when to use a strong possible explanatory hypothesis and when to use a weak one. For example, to assume that as many clumps match as possible or that perceived bounds overlap to the greatest extent possible is a strong hypothesis. On the other hand, to use fuzz ranges on joints which are as large as possible is a weak hypothesis. If we want to be cautious, why match at all? Why not merely add the new clumps into the map? Conversely, if we are interested in the simplest possible map which explains the input, why not look for a solution where as many vertices as possible coincided, by picking joint measurements of 0.0? The output map would still explain the input, and it would be simpler than the one we are producing. Of course, we would run the risk of picking mismatching vertices, but, as is, we run the risk of mismatching clumps.

The justification for the difference is that clumps represent something physically real, while vertices do not. That is, in MERCATOR's outlook, objects are likely to be seen again and again, but vertices are arbitrary interpolation points, which we have no reason to think will reappear. In a different view of the vision system, perhaps more realistic, which acknowledged that in many cases vertices are picked somewhat systematically and reproducably, there would be advantage to matching such vertices. In other words, identifying vertices has no explanatory power; it creates a coincidence, rather than explaining one.

Edge matches are harder, particularly edge matches of incomplete clumps. In order to maximize explanatory power, we should match as much of the two boundaries as possible. However, there are a number of tradeoffs to consider. Overlap conflicts with ignorance: if we demand absolute maximal overlap, this constrains relative positions very strongly, perhaps unrealistically so. Extent of overlap conflicts with quality of overlap: the edges often fit better in matches with less overlap. Finally, maximal overlaps conflict with each other: if there are two sets of edge matches to consider, it may be geometrically inconsistent to assign them both the maximal overlap. (See figure A-2.) We have no principles to resolve any of these conflicts. The solution we have implemented, to leave each individual edge match as weak as possible and to maximize the total score of the edge matches, has no logical interpretation whatever, but it fits nicely into the structure of the matcher. It is not surprising, though, that in many cases it is inadequate (see section 4.11.)

A.5 The complexity of fuzz

Two particular geometric problems, involving fuzzy quantities and grain-sizes respectively, are basic in dealing with MERCATOR maps. They are discussed in this section and the next.

Much of the difficulty in computing with MERCATOR maps arises at the geometric level, involving only the graph of vertices and edges with fuzzy measurements. (We will treat joints as pairs of edges in this section.) These are the major constraints on the function COOR.

All the basic retrieval problems have analogues in this restricted setting. Relative position of clumps is analogous to relative position of vertices: What are the range of values that a given quantity (such as the distance between two points) can attain under some consistent value of COOR? Object retrieval becomes vertex retrieval: Enumerate all the vertices which

To assume that $a - b$ is identical to $x - y$ seems unwarranted.

Conflict of maximality with ignorance.

With large enough grain-sizes it is possible that $x - y$ matches $a - b$ and $y - z$ matches $b - c$, but it seems more likely that $x - y$ matches $b - c$.

Conflict of maximality with quality of edge match.

The following are possible:
1) $a - b$ fully overlaps $w - x$ and $c - d$ is disjoint from $x - y$.
2) $c - d$ fully overlaps $x - y$ and $a - b$ is disjoint from $w - x$.
3) Both pairs partially overlap.
Which is the best match?

Figure A-2: Conflicts with "Maximal Overlap" Rule

are within a given distance of a center vertex for some value of COOR? Sketching is unchanged: Find valid values for COOR. One more question is taken for granted in MER-CATOR, but is actually fundamental: consistency. Is there any valid value of COOR?

It turns out that all these questions are computationally equivalent. An algorithm which solves one in all cases can be used as a subroutine to solve any of the others. Clearly, each of the others involves a consistency check; if the graph is inconsistent, then each of the other questions should return failure. (In fact, we can build a consistency checker out of a retriever which operates only on consistent graphs and returns arbitrary answers for an inconsistent graph.) We sketch how to reduce quantity retrieval to consistency; the other reductions are similar.

Suppose we wish to retrieve the distance from vertex p to q, subject to a given graph G. We can test the question "Is it consistent with G that DIST $(p, q) \geq 2.0$" by augmenting G with an edge from p to q whose length is between 2.0 and infinity, and whose orientation is unspecified. (See figure A-3.) We then call the consistency checker. If the answer is "No", the upper bound of DIST (p, q) must be less than 2.0; if "Yes", the upper bound must be greater than two. Similarly, by using intervals starting at zero, we can limit the lower bound. By using binary search, we can get arbitrarily good accuracy on lower and upper bounds in time logarithmic in the desired accuracy.

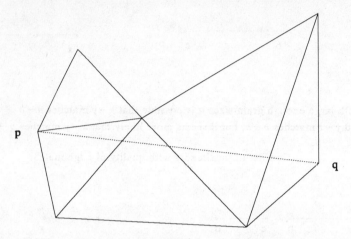

Graph G in solid lines. To test whether DIST (p, q) can be greater than 2.0, add the dotted edge with bounds "$L \in [2, \infty]$, $\theta \in [0, 2\pi]$" and test for consistency.

Figure A-3: Converting Quantity Valuation to Consistency Check

Let C be the time required to check the consistency of G plus extra edge. The quantity retriever thus requires time O (C · log(accuracy)). The object retriever requires time C+O(#vertices). The sketcher requires time O(C · log(accuracy) · #vertices).

These additional factors are largely irrelevant, however, since the consistency problem is intractable. In fact, even the special case where there are no distance fuzzes and all angles vary from 0 to 2π the "position-location" or "linkage" problem, is NP-hard. [Yemini, 79] proves this by a reduction of the partition problem.

This intractability proof is perhaps less discouraging than it appears. It relies on "flips", cases where the local constraints have two, widely separated solutions. (See figure A-4.) Such disjunctive uncertainties are presumably rare in MERCATOR maps, and should be handled by other means (not available in MERCATOR) when they do occur. (See section 8.4.5.) Conceivably, we could pose conditions on MERCATOR maps which will rule out such discrete uncertainties and which would thereby simplify the consistency problem. At this time, I have no idea how to define this objective rigorously, let alone how to find such conditions.

The consistency problem is easy to describe algebraically. Each fuzzy constraint is an inequality in the coordinates of the endpoints of the edge. The constraint LENGTH(edge($a - b$)) $\in [l,h]$ is equivalent to the inequalities $l^2 \leq (a_x - b_x)^2 + (a_y - b_y)^2 \leq h^2$. The constraint ROT(edge($a - b$)) $\in [l,h]$ is equivalent to the inequalities $(b_x - a_x) \cdot arctan(l) \leq b_y - a_y \leq (b_x - a_x) \cdot arctan(h)$ (if l and h are in the first or fourth quadrants.

194

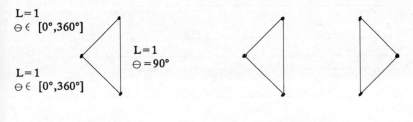

L=1
$\ominus \in [0°, 360°]$

L=1
$\ominus = 90°$

L=1
$\ominus \in [0°, 360°]$

Constraints   Solutions

There are two solutions to the constraints.

Figure A-4: A Disjunctive Flip

Otherwise, some signs are reversed.) The constraints thus form a system of linear and quadratic inequalities. We may apply the results of [Tarski, 51] to conclude that, in the worst
case, problems in fuzzy quantities can be solved in time doubly exponential in the number of
vertices.*

The same analysis applies to the joint consistency checker. Finding the consistency of a
set of fuzzy joints is equivalent in difficulty to finding the consistency of a set of fuzzy edges;
that is, at least NP-hard, and not worse than doubly exponential. The prospects for finding a
structure which would reduce this complexity to tractable levels are much dimmer for the
joints produced by the matcher than for MERCATOR edges.

A.6 Boundary Descriptions

The other basic geometric problem relates to the approximation of a curve by a sequence of
edges with grain-sizes. The problems here are the matching and the merging problems — can
two such approximations describe the same curve and, given two approximations, find a single approximation which incorporates the information in each.

Clearly, these problems are basic to the matcher and the merger. There is also a more
subtle connection to the retriever functions. A map might have a clump with two regions
whose boundaries combined in such a way that the two together gave much tighter constraints
on the curve than either did singly. (See figure A-5.) In such a case, a complete retriever
function would have to interpolate the true curve between the two region boundaries. The
MERCATOR retriever algorithm assumes that regions are structured so that this is not
necessary. (This is the *well ordered regions* condition of section 2.8.)

Analyzing these problems requires some further definitions. A *chain* C in region R is
defined as a pair consisting of

1. a sequence of bounds $<b_1 \cdots b_k> \subset$ BOUNDS (R)

2. a sequence of corners $<c_1 \cdots c_{k+1}> \subset$ CORNERS (R)

---

* It has been suggested to me that the results of [Collins, 75], improving those of Tarski, give a solution which is exponential in the number of vertices. Unfortunately, I am not competent to read Collins
enough to judge whether this would follow from his theory.

The two edges come from different regions, but describe the same boundary.

The "submarines" show the area within the grain-size of each.

The actual curve must lie in the narrow overlap of the two submarines.

Figure A-5: Two Mutually Constraining Regions

such that

For $i = 1, \cdots k$, TYPE $(b_i) - T$

For $i = 2, \cdots k$, TYPE $(c_i) = T$

For $i = 1, \cdots k$, TAIL $(b_i) = c_i$

For $i = 1, \cdots k$, HEAD $(b_i) = c_{i+1}$

C is said to be a *open chain* if $c_1 \neq c_{k+1}$ For simplicity, we will consider only open chains henceforth. Closed chains can be handled in a similar way, but with more complex details.

We can reformulate the definition of the validity of a boundary representation given in definition A.15, items 8 and 9, in terms of chains. If the map is valid, then for each chain C in region R, there exists a covering function $COVER_C$ such that

$COVER_C$ (COOR (C)) ⊂ BOUNDARY (REAL (CLUMP (R)))

$\forall b \in C \ \forall x \in COOR(b) \quad DIST(x, COVER_C(b)) <$ GRAIN-SIZE(b).

The curve $COVER_C$ (COOR (C)) is said to *satisfy* the chain C.

Single chains are unproblematic. A single chain C is always internally consistent, and COOR (C) itself is always a satisfying curve. The grain-size around a bound defines a submarine shaped region for the satisfying curves. Note that it is not sufficient that the curve remain within the union of these regions. It must go from one end of each submarine to the other in sequence with only limited backtracking. The curve must approach each corner within the smaller of the grain-sizes of the adjoining bounds, its tight grain-size. This defines a circle around the corner through which the curve must pass. (See figure A-6.)

196

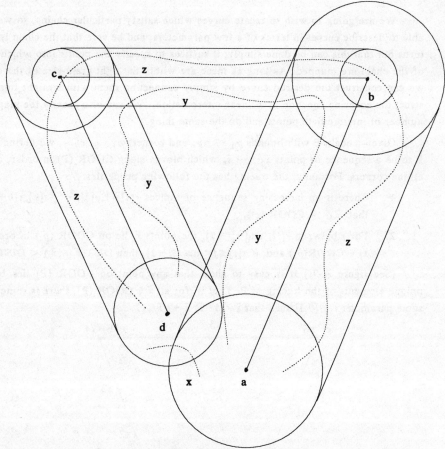

$a - b - c - d$ is a chain. The grain-size area is shown around the edges. Curve x does not satisfy the chain, because it does not go through the chain in sequence. Curve y does not satisfy the chain, because it does not come within the tight grain-size of b or c. Curve z does satisfy the chain.

Figure A-6: Region and Curve

We are going to wish to create curves which satisfy particular chains, so we wish to be able to describe curves in terms of a few parameters, and be sure that the chain is satisfied. It turns out that this can be done simply; it suffices to specify the points into which the corners of the chain are mapped. As long as these are within the tight grain-size of the corner, then we can construct the desired curve by simply connecting them with straight lines, and construct the covering function as a linear interpolation. We can also specify the mapping of any number of intermediate points and do the same thing.

Given a chain P with bounds $p_1 \cdots p_k$ and corners $c_1 \cdots c_{k+1}$, we define a *tracing* of P to be a sequence of points $\bar{x}_1 \cdots \bar{x}_n$ which moves along COOR (P) in order, and includes all the corners. Formally, the tracing has the following properties:

1. There is an increasing sequence of indices $s[1]=1, s[2], \cdots s[k], s[k+1]=n$, such that $\bar{x}_{s[i]} = $ COOR (c_i).

2. For j between $s[i]$, and $s[i+1]$, the points $\bar{x}_j$ lie on COOR (p_i) in order. That is, $\bar{x}_j \in $ COOR(p_i) and, if $s[i] \leq j < m \leq s[i+1]$, then DIST$(\bar{x}_{s[i]}, \bar{x}_j) < $ DIST$(\bar{x}_{s[i]}, \bar{x}_m)$.

(See figure A-7.) It is easy to show that any point on COOR (P) lies between two unique elements of the tracing of P. That is, for all $\bar{x} \in $ COOR (P), there is some index j and some parameter $t \in [0,1]$ such that $\bar{x} = (1-t) \cdot \bar{x}_j + t \cdot \bar{x}_{j+1}$.

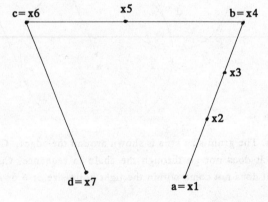

$(x_1 \cdots x_7)$ is a tracing of $a - b - c - d$.

Figure A-7: A Tracing

Theorem A.1 shows that, given a series of points in space which stay within grain-size of a tracing of a chain, then, connecting these points with straight lines gives a curve which stays within grain-size.

Theorem A.1:

Given

1. a chain P, with corners $c_1 \cdots c_{k+1}$ and bounds $p_1 \cdots p_k$;

2. a coordinate function COOR;

3. a series of increasing indices, $s[1] \cdots s[k+1]$;

4. a tracing of P, $\overline{x}_1 \cdots \overline{x}_n$ such that $\overline{x}_{s[i]} = COOR(c_i)$

5. a sequence of points $\overline{w}_1 \cdots \overline{w}_n$ such that, for all j, if $s[i] < j < s[i+1]$ then $DIST(\overline{x}_j, \overline{w}_j) < GRAIN\text{-}SIZE(p_i)$.

Define a curve C by connecting the w_i in order by straight lines. Define the covering function $COVER_P$ by a linear interpolation. That is, if $\overline{x} = (1-t)\overline{x}_j + t\overline{x}_{j+1}$ then $COVER_P(\overline{x}) = (1-t) \cdot w_j + t \cdot w_{j+1}$.

Then C satisfies P under $COVER_P$ (See figure A-8.)

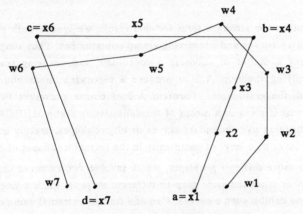

Figure A-8: Linear Interpolation

Proof: The continuity and well-definedness of $COVER_P$ is immediate. All that has to be proven is that it does not move points further than their grain-size. Let $\overline{x} = (1-t) \cdot \overline{x}_j + t \cdot \overline{x}_{j+1}$, where $s[i] \leq j < s[i+1]$, so that $\overline{x} \in COOR(p_i)$.

Then $DIST(\overline{x}, COVER_P(\overline{x})) = LENGTH(COVER_P(\overline{x}) - \overline{x})$

$= LENGTH([(1-t) \cdot \overline{w}_j + t \cdot \overline{w}_{j+1}] - [(1-t) \cdot \overline{x}_j + t \cdot \overline{x}_{j+1}])$

$= LENGTH((1-t) \cdot (\overline{w}_j - \overline{x}_j) + t \cdot (\overline{w}_{j+1} - \overline{x}_{j+1}))$

$\leq (1-t) \cdot LENGTH(\overline{w}_j - \overline{x}_j) + t \cdot LENGTH(\overline{w}_{j+1} - \overline{x}_{j+1})$

$< (1-t) \cdot GRAIN\text{-}SIZE(p_i) + t \cdot GRAIN\text{-}SIZE(p_i)$

$= GRAIN\text{-}SIZE(p_i)$.

The only problem is that we don't know that the resultant curve doesn't cross itself or even lie on top of itself. This problem is beyond the scope of this chapter. I have hopes that the basic results of this section can be modified to produce curves that do not cross themselves, but I have no proof of it. In what follows, I will ignore this problem, so all these results must be read as subject to the proviso that the curve does not cross itself.

It follows directly from theorem A.1 that a curve which satisfies a number of chains can be turned into a sequence of straight lines joined at the images of the corners and still satisfy the chains.

Theorem A.2: Given a curve CURVE which satisfies a number of chains $P_1 \cdots P_m$, under the coordinate function COOR and covering functions $COVER_1 \cdots COVER_n$, define the sequence $w_1 \cdots w_n$ to be the images of the corners of the respective P's under the respective covering functions in sequence as they occur along CURVE. Then the curve consisting of edges connecting the w_i in sequence likewise satisfies all the chains $P_1 \cdots P_m$.

Proof: Apply theorem A.1 to each chain in sequence.

This leads to another interesting result:

Theorem A.3: If a MERCATOR map has a model, then it has a model in which all the object bounds are piecewise linear; and in which the total number of vertices is no greater than the sum over all the regions in the map of the number of boundary vertices in the region.

"Theorem" is rather too strong a term for this result; we ignore both preventing self-intersection on boundary curves and preserving clump containment. Thus simplified, proving theorem A.3 is simply a matter of choosing a coordinate and covering functions for the model, and then applying theorem A.2 to produce a piecewise linear boundary for each object, obedient to all the grain-sizes. Theorem A.2 of course preserves PCO's. Theorem A.3 is important because it gives us a means of formally stating that a MERCATOR map has a model without quantifying over boundary curves or object shapes, merely quantifying over vertex position. This saves us a level of complexity in the formal treatment of MERCATOR.

We now turn to more difficult problems, which involve two or more chains of a time. Given two chains, either from the same map or different maps, is there a single curve which satisfies both? Can one exhibit such a curve? Can one find an extremal value of such curves? Can one find a single chain which is equivalent to the two chains; i.e., which is satisfied by exactly those curves which satisfy both chains?

Since we are using open curves, we will assume, for most of this exposition, that we are looking for the exact same curve to satisfy each; i.e. that the starting and ending points of each correspond. This is merely a technical device to simplify the exposition; it does not affect the major issues.

In the matching algorithm, we characterized the relation between chains in terms of edge matches. For our theoretical analysis, we find that a more useful construct is the *cmatch*. This is defined where everything has been fixed: the two chains P and Q, fixed values of COOR, a curve which satisfies both P and Q, and covering functions from P and Q to the curve. (If P and Q are from different maps, we combine the different COOR functions into a single function.) Then for each corner c in P, we define cmatch (c) as follows:

Definition A.16:

1. If there exists a corner $d \in Q$ such that

$$COVER_P (COOR (c)) = COVER_Q(COOR(d))$$

then cmatch(c) = d.

2. Else, there must exist a bound b in Q such that

$$COVER_P (COOR (c)) \in COVER_Q (COOR (b)).$$

Then cmatch(c) = b.

(See figure A-9.) Cmatch is defined on corners in Q analogously.

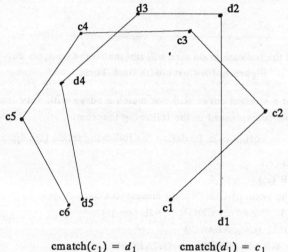

$$cmatch(c_1) = d_1 \qquad cmatch(d_1) = c_1$$
$$cmatch(c_2) = d_1 - d_2 \qquad cmatch(d_2) = c_3$$
$$cmatch(c_3) = d_2 \qquad cmatch(d_3) = c_3 - c_4$$
$$cmatch(c_4) = d_3 - d_4 \qquad cmatch(d_4) = c_4 - c_5$$
$$cmatch(c_5) = d_4 - d_5 \qquad cmatch(d_5) = c_6$$
$$cmatch(c_6) = d_5$$

Figure A-9: A C-Match

A number of facts are evident. Firstly, this definition gives a unique value of cmatch for every corner.

Secondly, if we define an ordering on all the corners and bounds of P in the natural way — $c_i < b_i$, $b_i < c_{i+1}$ — and likewise for Q, then cmatch respects that ordering, in the following sense:

1. If corners c and d are both in P or both in Q and $c < d$ then cmatch(c) $\leq$ cmatch(d).

2. If c is a corner in P and d is a corner in Q and cmatch(c) $< d$, then $c <$ cmatch(d)

    From this it follows that, if c and d are corners and cmatch(c)=d then cmatch(d)=c.

Thirdly, we have the following: for any corner c in P,

$$\text{DIST (COOR } (c), \text{ COOR (cmatch } (c)))$$
$$\leq \text{DIST (COOR } (c), COVER_P \text{ (COOR } (c)))$$
$$+ \text{DIST } (COVER_P \text{ (COOR } (c)), \text{ COOR (cmatch } (c)))$$
$$< \text{GRAIN-SIZE } (c) + \text{GRAIN-SIZE (cmatch } (c)).$$

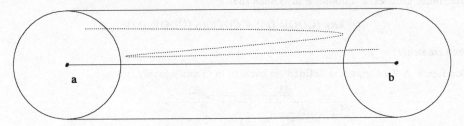

Edge $a - b$ at the indicate grain-size will not match the squiggly curve.

Figure A-10: Curve with Back Turns

Finally we note that a straight curve will not match a curve with very long back turns. (See figure A-10) This can be expressed in the following theorem:

Theorem A.4: For any corner c_i in P, define the following terms (see figure A-11):

Let $cm_i = \text{cmatch } (c_i)$.
Let $CC_i = \text{COOR } (c_i)$.
Let $NEARC_i$ be the point of $\text{COOR}(cm_i)$ closest to CC_i.
Let $DPAR_i = \text{DIST } (NEARC_i, \text{ COOR (TAIL } (cm_i)))$.
Let $DPERP_i = \text{DIST } (CC_i, NEARC_i)$
Let $MAXDIST_i = \text{GRAIN-SIZE}(c_i) + \text{GRAIN-SIZE}(cm_i)$.
Let $PARSHIFT_i = \sqrt{(MAXDIST_i^2 - DPERP_i^2)}$.

(Note by the third result above, $MAXDIST_i$ is always greater than $DPERP_i$, so the square root can always be taken.)

Let c_i and c_j be two corners in Q such that $j > i$ and $\text{cmatch}(c_i) = \text{cmatch}(c_j)$. Then

$$DPAR_j - DPAR_i > - (PARSHIFT_i + PARSHIFT_j)$$

We will call this the *sequential line* condition.

Proof: For $\bar{x}$ on $\text{COOR}(cm_i)$, let $QVAL(\bar{x}) = \text{DIST}(\bar{x}, \text{COOR(TAIL}(cm_i)))$. For each corner c_i, there exists a point $\bar{x}_i$ on $\text{COOR}(cm_i)$ such that $COVER_Q(\bar{x}_i) = COVER_P(cc_i)$ By a simple geometric argument, $QVAL(\bar{x}_i) \in [DPAR_i - PARSHIFT_i, DPAR_i + PARSHIFT_i]$. (See figure A-11.)

Moreover, if $j > i$, then $QVAL(\bar{x}_j) > QVAL(\bar{x}_i)$. This follows from the fact that $COVER_i$ and $COVER_j$ are one-one and continuous. Therefore, it cannot be the case that the interval for $\bar{x}_i$ is strictly greater than that for $\bar{x}_j$. Therefore $DPAR_i - PARSHIFT_i < DPAR_j + PARSHIFT_j$, which is equivalent to our condition above. □

202

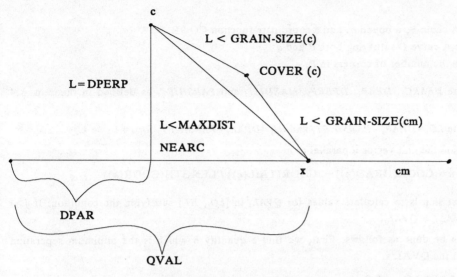

Figure A-11: Proof of Theorem 2.4

The above four conditions are not only necessary but also sufficient for a c-match.

Theorem A.5: Let P and Q be chains of region R, COOR be a coordinate function, and m be a function from the corners of each to the corners and bounds of the other satisfying the following:

1. m respects the order of P and Q, in the sense defined above.

2. For all corners $c \in P \cup Q$,
    $DIST(COOR(c), COOR(m(c))) \leq GRAIN\text{-}SIZE(c) + GRAIN\text{-}SIZE(m(c))$

3. The sequential line condition is satisfied.

Then there exists a curve C and covering functions $COVER_P$ and $COVER_Q$ from COOR (P) and COOR (Q) to C for which $cmatch(c) = m(c)$.

Proof: The proof is constructive. We present algorithm A.2 which calculates points w_i; then we apply theorem A.1 to construct the curve by interpolation. We will indicate the proof of the correctness of the algorithm in the course of its development. We begin our presentation with a subroutine (algorithm A.1) which calculates an interpolating curve between a chain and a single bound. This relies only on conditions 2 and 3 above, particularly the latter.

Input: A chain P, a bound q, and a coordinate function COOR.

Output: A curve C satisfying both P and q

Let k be the number of corners in P.

Calculate $NEARC_i$, $DPAR_i$, $DPERP_i$, $MAXDIST_i$ and $PARSHIFT_i$ as defined in theorem A.4 for $i = 1 \cdots k$.

Calculate $LO_i = DPAR_i - PARSHIFT_i$ and $HI_i = DPAR_i + PARSHIFT_i$ for $i = 1 \cdots k$.

Calculuate the unit vector $\hat{u}$ parallel to q:

$$\hat{u} = \text{COOR(HEAD}(q)) - \text{COOR(TAIL}(q)) \, / \, \text{LENGTH(COOR}(q))$$

The next step is to calculate values for $QVAL_i$ in $[LO_i, HI_i]$ satisfying the condition: If $j > i$ then $QVAL_j > QVAL_i$.

This can be done as follows. First, we find a quantity δ which is the minimum separation between the QVAL's:

LAST-LO := 0.0;

SMALL-SEP := ∞;

For $i := 1$ to k do

  LAST-LO := max (LAST-LO, LO_i);

  SMALL-SEP := min (SMALL-SEP, $HI_i -$ LAST-LO)

endloop;

$\delta :=$ SMALL-SEP $/\, k + 1$.

After the ith iteration, LAST-LO is the maximum value of LO_m for $m \leq i$. SMALL-SEP is the minimum value of $HI_n - LO_m$ for $m \leq n \leq i$. Note that this loop gives a linear time test for the sequential line condition; the condition is true if SMALL-SEP > 0.0 at the end.

Having found δ, we can now find the QVAL's

$QVAL_0 := 0.0$;

For $i := 1$ to k do $QVAL_i := \text{MAX}(QVAL_{i-1}, LO_i) + \delta$;

It is easy to show that this gives increasing values for $QVAL_i$ which fall within the correct bounds.

Having found the QVAL's, the rest is easy. Set $\bar{x}_i$ to be the point corresponding to $QVAL_i$: $\bar{x}_i = QVAL_i \cdot \hat{u}$. Next, find a point w_i which is within GRAIN-SIZE(c_i) of CC_i, and within GRAIN-SIZE(q) of $\bar{x}_i$. One such point is

$$[\text{GRAIN-SIZE}(q_i) \cdot CC_i + \text{GRAIN-SIZE}(c_i) \cdot \bar{x}_i] \, / \, MAXDIST_i.$$

(See figure A-13.)

Finally, use theorem A.1 to construct the curve and covering functions.

Algorithm A.1: Interpolating between a Bound and a Chain

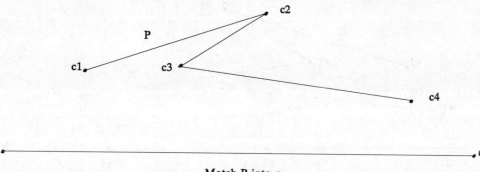

Match P into q.

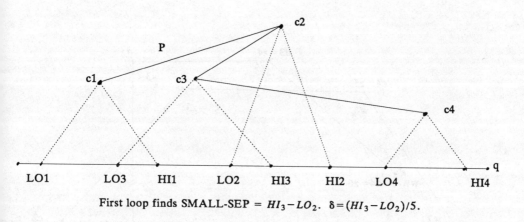

First loop finds SMALL-SEP $= HI_3 - LO_2$. $\delta = (HI_3 - LO_2)/5$.

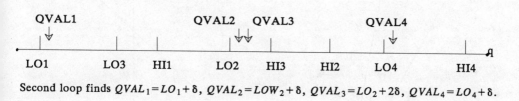

Second loop finds $QVAL_1 = LO_1 + \delta$, $QVAL_2 = LOW_2 + \delta$, $QVAL_3 = LO_2 + 2\delta$, $QVAL_4 = LO_4 + \delta$.

Figure A-12: Calculating QVAL's

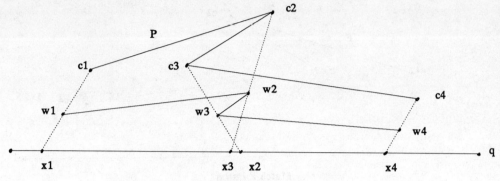

Place w_i between x_i and CC_i within grain-size of each.

Connect the w_i in order.

Figure A-13: Curve Points

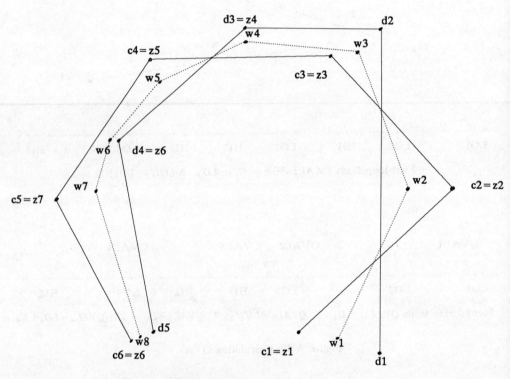

Order the corners $z_1, z_2, \cdots$

Use Algorithm A-1 to find the points w_i.

Draw the curve by linear interpolation.

Figure A-14: Proof of Theorem A.5

206

Input: Chains P and Q, a matching m relating P and Q, and a coordinate function COOR.

Output: A curve C satisfying both P and Q.

We begin by using m to define a single order on most of the corners of P and Q; to be precise, all the corners of P and Q, except that, where m matches two corners into each other, one is left out as redundant. Let P have corners $b_1, b_2, \cdots$ and let Q have corners $c_1, c_2, \cdots$. We define the ordering $z_1, z_2, \cdots$ as follows:

$$z_1 = b_1$$

If $z_i = b_j$ then
    if there exists any corner c_k
        such that $m(c_k) = $ bound (b_j, b_{j+1})
    then z_{i+1} is the first such c_k
    else $z_{i+1} = b_{j+1}$.

If $z_i = c_j$ then
    if there exists any corner b_k
        such that $m(b_k) = $ bound (c_j, c_{j+1})
    then z_{i+1} is the first such b_k
    else $z_{i+1} = c_{j+1}$.

All of the corners of P and Q are placed in the z ordering except for corners which are matched into corners, of which only one in each pair is placed. Also, the corners appear in the same order in the z ordering as in the P and Q orderings. These follow easily from the fact that m preserve ordering.

We next partition the ordering z_i into sequences on which m is constant. For each such subsequence $z_i \ldots z_j$, if m maps these onto a bound q, we use algorithm A-1 to find points w_i interpolating between the z's and q. In the case of unit subsequences z_i that are mapped onto corners, we define w_i to be some point within the proper grain-sizes of $COOR(z_i)$ and $COOR(m(z_i))$; for example,

$$\frac{GRAIN - SIZE(m(z_i)) \cdot COOR(z_i) + GRAIN - SIZE(z_i) \cdot COOR(m(z_i))}{GRAIN - SIZE(z_i) + GRAIN - SIZE(m(z_i))}$$

Again, we use theorem A.1 to define the curve and the covering functions.

Algorithm A.2: Interpolating between Two Curves

We thus have necessary and sufficient conditions that a proposed cmatch can actually describe a real correspondence of two chains. Moreover, the conditions can be checked, and an interpolating curve constructed, in linear time.

The next problem is to find the satisfying curve if the coordinates are given but the cmatches are not. It is easier to think about this problem in terms of finding the correct ordering z_i, rather than finding cmatches. The naive algorithm for doing this would be to begin by proposing the first possible z_1, then the first possible z_2, and so on, and backtracking when stuck. This would require exponential time in the worst case. Fortunately, it is possible to improve on this. We use a variant of the algorithm for recognition of a string by a non-deterministic finite automaton [Aho, Hopcroft, and Ullman, p. 327] We will only sketch the algorithm. The algorithm loops through the z_i. At each step, it keeps all the possible values of z_i and cmatch(z_i) in parallel. Together with each of these, it keeps the minimum possible value of LAST-LO for that particular pair. Using all these, it finds all the possible states for z_{i+1}. The algorithm require time cubic in the size of the chains.

This seems to be the most difficult form of the chain satisfaction problem for which we can find quick, clean algorithms. There are two natural generalizations of this problem. The first is to find a satisfying curve when the length and orientation of each line is given, but the coordinates are not, so the correct translation relating the two chains must be found. The second is to find a curve satisfying three or more chains, given coordinates and some equivalent of cmatches. Neither of these seems to be tractable.

In the first problem, we must do a two-dimensional search for the correct relating translation. Two-dimensional searches are usually fairly tractable, if testing with one value gives some information as to where to look for a better value. Otherwise, the problem is much harder. There is no obvious way to extract this information from our algorithm.

The second problem is difficult because it cannot be factored into pairwise matches. Given a corner and two matching bounds, it does not suffice to match the corner against each bound separately; the matching points interact strongly. There does not seem to be any analogue to algorithm A-1.

The matching algorithm which we have implemented handles a generalization of the first problem, where we know constraints on the coordinates, but no exact values. There we decided to use edge matches rather than cmatches. For one thing, edge matches are much easier to prune than cmatches. There are simple criteria which allow most pair of edges to be excluded from matching. There are no such criteria for cmatches. For another thing, edge matches are ambiguous in the right way, while cmatches are ambiguous in the wrong way. For example, in figure A-15, examples A1 and A2 have the same edge matches, but different cmatches. Examples B1 and B2 have different edge matches but the same cmatches. Clearly, the former are more alike than the latter. One can transform A1 into A2 without losing the match. This cannot be done with the B1 and B2.

On the other hand, in the case where the coordinates *are* known, cmatches are more useful than edge matches. I have found no simple set of necessary and sufficient conditions for edge matches, that serves the way theorem A.5 does for cmatches.

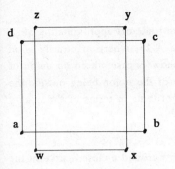 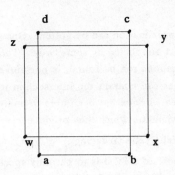

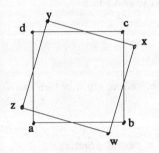 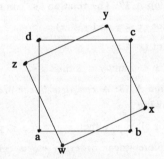

A1 has the same edge-matches as A2, but different cmatches.

B1 has the same cmatches as B2, but different edge-matches.

Figure A-15: Ambiguous Cmatch and Edge-match

Given that cmatches are definitely the wrong data structure for MERCATOR, the reader may wonder why I have bothered with this exposition of algorithms for cmatches at all. There could be cases where coordinates are known well enough to make the algorithm worthwhile. Or there could be ways in which ideas from this algorithm could be used in the actual matcher. More importantly, in devising heuristic algorithms, it is important to know why the problem is difficult. One clue to this is looking at special cases where the problem is easy.

Finally, I should say something about the merging problem: given two chains, find the strongest single chain which is implied by them. If we are given the coordinates to start with, we can describe the problem geometrically, as finding a single chain of submarines which contains the intersection of two chains of submarines. Clearly the intersection of two submarines is not a submarine, nor even the union of submarines. There is no best union of submarines; figure A-16 shows a case where, by taking more and more submarines a better and better approximation can be gotten. One must therefore try to trade off approximation quality against simplicity in some way. The situation in figure A-16, where arbitrarily good approximations can be found, is not universal. Figure A-17 shows a case where no union of submarines can contain the intersection without at least 36% of the union being outside the target area. I have not been able to analyze any merging algorithms in terms of the quality of approximation which they produce.

A.7 Partial Cyclic Orderings

The purpose of a PCO is to partially specify the order of points around a closed curve in the same way that a partial ordering of the usual kind (abbreviated p.o.) partially specifies the order of points on a line. That is, a PCO is to a full cyclic ordering (FCO) as a p.o. is to a linear ordering. We therefore would naturally define a PCO analogously to a p.o. Of course, a PCO, like an FCO is basically a three-place relation "counter-clockwise" (cc), while a p.o. is a binary relation.

The standard definition of a partial ordering is as follows:

Definition A.17: The relation "$<$" on set S is a p.o. iff for x, y, and z in S

A1. Not ($x < y$ and $y < x$)

A2. Not ($x < x$)

A3. If $x < y$ and $y < z$ then $x < z$

Definition A.18: A *complete linear ordering* may then be defined as a p.o. which satisfies the following

B1. For all x, y, either $x = y$ or $x < y$ or $y < x$

A complete linear ordering $<_c$ is called an extension of a partial ordering $<$ if $<_c$ includes $<$; that is, for all x and y, if $x<y$ then $x<_cy$. It is easily shown that any partial ordering can be extended to a complete linear ordering.

We can modify definition A.17 to a definition of PCO's, following [Megiddo, 76]:

Definition A.19: A *PCO* on a set S is a relation cc (counter-clockwise) satisfying the following axioms: for all w x, y and z in S

C1. Not (cc (x, y, z) and cc (x, z, y))

C2. Not cc (x, x, y)

C3. If cc (x, y, z) then cc (y, z, x) and cc (z, x, y) (Invariance under rotation.)

C4. If cc (w, x, y) and cc (w, y, z) then cc (w, x, z). (Transitivity).

Definition A.20: A *full cyclic ordering (FCO)* is a local PCO satisfying the following additional axiom:

D1. For all x, y, z, one of the following is true: $x = y$, $x = z$, $y = z$, cc (x, y, z) or cc (x, z, y)

Definition A.21: An FCO oo is an *extension* of a PCO cc if oo includes cc; that is, for all x, y, and z, cc (x, y, z) implies oo (x, y, z).

210

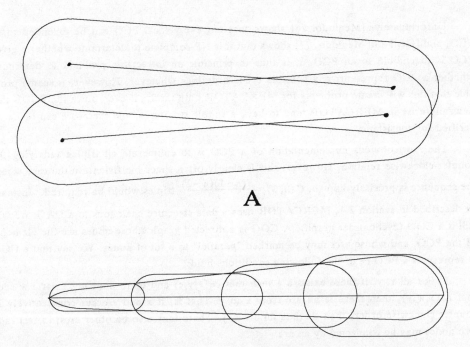

The intersection of the two submarines in A is the wedge shaped region. By using more and more submarines, a better and better approximation can be built up.

Figure A-16: An Intersection of Submarines

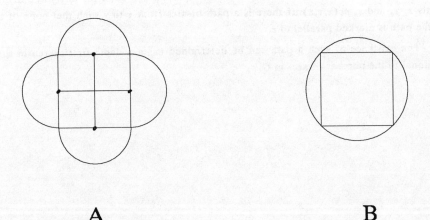

A   B

The intersection of the two submarines in A is a square. The best chain of submarines to approximate the square is the single circle.

Figure A-17: A Worse Intersection of Submarines

Unfortunately, [Mcgiddo, 76] shows that not every local PCO can be extended to an FCO, and [Galil and Megiddo, 77] shows that it is NP-complete to determine whether a given PCO is extendible to an FCO. It is thus in principle an intractable problem to determine whether a PCO represents any possible cyclic orderings whatever. However, it seems probable that this will create problems for MERCATOR only rarely, if ever, since the PCO's that naturally arise in MERCATOR tend to have a simple structures, and therefore can be easily verified for consistency.

The most obvious implementation of a PCO is to enumerate all triples satisfying the counter-clockwise relation. However, this is clearly often space inefficient; in the case where the sequence is precisely known, $C(n, 3) = \dfrac{n(n-1)(n-2)}{6}$ triples would be required. Instead, as described in section 2.1, MERCATOR uses a data structure analogous to a DAG; we will call it a COG (cyclic order graph). A COG is a directed graph whose nodes are the elements of the PCO, and whose arcs may be marked "parallel" to a set of nodes. We say that a COG G represents a PCO cc of the following conditions hold:

1. For all x, y, if there exists a z such that $cc(x,y,z)$ and there does not exist a w such that $cc(x,w,y)$, then there is an arc from x to y. That is, if x and y occur consecutively in counter-clockwise order, then there is an arc $x \rightarrow y$. There may also be other arcs; in fact, any two nodes may be connected by an arc.

2. If there is an arc $x \rightarrow y$ and it is not specified in the PCO that $cc(x,y,z)$, then z is marked parallel to the arc $x \rightarrow y$.

The following theorem allows us to go from COG's to PCO's.

Theorem A.6: Let the COG G represent the PCO cc. Then for any three distinct elements x, y, and z, $cc(x,y,z)$ iff there is a path of arcs from x to y such that none of the arcs on the path is marked parallel to z.

The existence of such a path can be determined using a depth-first search in time proportional to the number of arcs in G.

---

* The original version of this thesis had some speculations as to general classes of PCO's which could easily be shown to be extendible to FCO's. These speculations have been shown to be false.

Bibliography

[Aho, Hopcroft, and Ullman, 74]
> Alfred V. Aho, John E. Hopcroft, and Jeffrey D. Ullman.
> *The Design and Analysis of Computer Algorithms.*
> Addison-Wesley, Reading, Mass., 1974.

[Alefeld and Herzberger, 83]
> G. Alefeld and J. Herzberger.
> *Introduction to Interval Computations.*
> Academic Press, 1983.

[Ballard, 81]
> Dana H. Ballard.
> "Strip Trees, A Hierarchical Representation for Curves."
> *Communications of the ACM,* Vol. 24, No. 5, 1981, pages 310 - 321.

[Ballard and Brown, 82]
> Dana H. Ballard and Christopher M. Brown.
> *Computer Vision.*
> Prentice Hall, Englewood Cliffs, N.J., 1982.

[Boggess, 79]
> Lois C. Boggess.
> "Computational Interpretation of English Spatial Prepositions."
> Tech. Rep. T-75, U. of Illinois Coordinated Science Lab, 1979.

[Brady, 81]
> Michael Brady, ed.
> *Special Issue on Vision.*
> *Artificial Intelligence,* Vol. 17, Nos. 1-3, 1981.

[Brooks, 81]
> Rodney A. Brooks.
> "Symbolic Reasoning among 3-D models and 2-D images."
> *Artificial Intelligence,* Vol. 17, Nos. 1-3, 1981, pages 285 - 348.

[Charniak, Riesbeck, and McDermott, 80]
> Eugene Charniak, Chris Riesbeck, and Drew V. McDermott.
> *Artificial Intelligence Programming.*
> Lawrence Erlbaum Associates, Hillsdale, N.J., 1980.

[Cheng and Gallistel, 83]

Ken Cheng and C.R. Gallistel.
"Testing the Geometric Power of an Animal's Spatial Representation."
in H.L. Roitblat, T.G. Bever, and H.S. Terrace (eds.), *Animal Cognition,*
Lawrence Erlbaum Associates, Hillsdale, N.J., 1983.

[Collins et. al., 67]

Allan Collins, Eleanor Warnock, Nelleke Aiello, and Mark L. Miller.
"Reasoning from Incomplete Knowledge."
in D. Bobrow and A. Collins (eds.) *Representation and Understanding: Studies in Cognitive Science.*
Academic Press, New York, 1975.

[Collins, 75]

G.E. Collins.
"Quantifier Elimination for Real Closed Fields by Cylindrical Algebraic Decomposition."
in *Second GI Conference on Automata Theory and Formal Languages,*
Lecture Notes in Computer Science, vol. 33, Springer Verlag, New York, 1975.
Cited in [Schwartz and Sharir, 82].

[Davis, 81]

Ernest Davis.
"Organizing Spatial Knowledge."
Tech. Rep. 193, Yale University Computer Science Dept., 1981.

[Davis, 84a]

Ernest Davis.
"Representing and Acquiring Geographic Knowledge."
Tech. Rep. 292, Yale University Computer Science Dept., 1984

[Davis, 84b]

Ernest Davis.
"Shape and Function of Solid Objects: Some Examples."
Tech. Rep. 147, NYU Computer Science Dept., 1984

[Davis, 85]

Ernest Davis.
"Constraint Propagation on Real-Valued Quantities."
Tech. Rep. 189, New York University Computer Science Dept., 1985.

[Davis, 86]

Ernest Davis.
"Conflicting Requirements in Reasoning about Solid Objects."
Unpublished MS, 1986

214

[de Kleer, 75]   Johann de Kleer.
                   "Qualitative and Quantitative Knowledge in Classical Mechanics."
                   Tech. Rep. 352, MIT AI Lab, 1975.

[Downs and Stea, 73]
                   Roger M. Downs and David Stea.
                   Cognitive Maps and Spatial Behavior: Process and Products.
                   Aldine Publishing Co., 1973.

[Doyle, 79]   Jon Doyle.
                   "A Truth Maintenance System."
                   Artificial Intelligence, Vol. 12, No. 3, 1979, pp. 231 - 272.

[Dyer, 83]   Michael G. Dyer.
                   In-Depth Understanding: A Computer Model of Integrated Processing for Narrative Comprehension.
                   MIT Press, Cambridge, Mass., 1983.

[Forbus, 81]   Kenneth D. Forbus.
                   "A Study of Qualitative and Quantitative Knowledge in Reasoning about Motion."
                   Tech. Rep. 615, MIT AI Lab, 1981.

[Freeman, 74]   H. Freeman.
                   "Computer Processing of Line-Drawing Images."
                   Computing Surveys, Vol. 6, No. 1, 1974, pp. 57-97.

[Galil and Megiddo, 77]
                   Z. Galil and N. Megiddo.
                   "Cyclic ordering is NP-complete."
                   Theoretical Computer Science, Vol. 5, 1977, pp. 179 - 182.

[Hart and Moore, 73]
                   Roger A. Hart and Gary T. Moore.
                   "The Development of Spatial Cognition: A Review."
                   in Roger M. Downs and David Stea (eds.) *Image and Environment.*
                   Aldine Publishing Company, 1973

[Hayes, 77]   Patrick Hayes.
                   "In Defence of Logic."
                   Proc. IJCAI 5, 1977, pp 559 - 565.

[Hayes, 79]   Patrick Hayes.
                    "Naive Physics 1: Ontology for Liquids."
                    Working Paper, University of Essex, 1978.
                    reprinted in J. Hobbs and R. Moore (eds.), *Formal Theories of the Commonsense World*, ABLEX, 1985.

[Hintzman et. al., 81]
                    Douglas L. Hintzman, Carla S. O'Dell, and David R. Arndt.
                    "Orientation in Cognitive Maps."
                    Cognitive Psychology, Vol. 13, No. 2, 1981, pp. 149 - 206.

[Hollerbach, 75]   John M. Hollerbach.
                    "Hierarchical shape description of objects by selection and modification of prototypes."
                    Tech. Rep 346, M.I.T. AI Lab, 1975.

[Kolodner, 80]   Janet Kolodner.
                    "Retrieval and Organizational Strategies in Conceptual Memory: A Computer Model."
                    Tech. Rep. 180, Yale University Computer Science Dept., 1980.

[Kosslyn and Schwartz, 77]
                    Stephen Kosslyn and Steven Schwartz.
                    "A simulation of visual imagery."
                    Cognitive Science, Vol. 1, No. 3, 1977.

[Kuipers, 77]   Benjamin Kuipers.
                    "Representing Knowledge of Large Scale Space."
                    Tech. Rep. 418, M.I.T. AI Lab, 1977.

[Kuipers, 78]   Benjamin Kuipers.
                    "Modelling Spatial Knowledge."
                    Cognitive Science, Vol. 2 No. 2, 1978.

[Lavin, 77]   Mark A. Lavin.
                    "Computer Analysis of Scenes from a Moving Viewing Point."
                    Ph.D. Thesis, M.I.T. Computer Science Dept., 1977.
                    Available on microfiche.

216

[Lieblich and Arbib, 82]
        Israel Lieblich and Michael A. Arbib.
        "Multiple Representations of Space Underlying Behavior."
        The Behavioral and Brain Sciences,
        Vol. 5, No. 4, 1982, pp. 627 - 659.

[Lynch, 60]   Kevin Lynch.
        The Image of the City.
        M.I.T. Press, Cambridge, Mass., 1960.

[Marr, 82]   David Marr.
        Vision.
        W.H. Freeman, San Francisco, 1982.

[Marr and Nishihara, 76]
        David Marr and H. Keith Nishihara.
        "Representation and Recognition of the Spatial Organization of Three-dimensional Shapes."
        Tech. Rep. 377, M.I.T. AI Lab, 1976.

[McAllester, 80] David A. McAllester.
        "An Outlook on Truth Maintenance."
        Tech. Rep. 551, M.I.T. AI Lab, 1980

[McCarthy and Hayes, 69]
        John McCarthy and Patrick Hayes.
        "Some Philosophical Problems from the Standpoint of Artificial Intelligence."
        in B. Meltzer and D. Michie (eds.), *Machine Intelligence 4,* Edinburgh University Press, 1969.

[McDermott, 74] Drew V. McDermott.
        "Assimilation of New Information by a Natural Language Understanding Program."
        Tech. Rep. 291, M.I.T. AI Lab, 1974.

[McDermott, 78] Drew V. McDermott.
        "Tarskian Semantics, or, No Notation without Denotation!"
        Cognitive Science, Vol. 2, No. 3, 1978.

[McDermott, 80] Drew V. McDermott.
        "Spatial Inferences with Ground, Metric Formulas on Simple Objects."
        Tech. Rep. 173, Yale University Computer Science Dept., 1980.

[McDermott, 81] Drew V. McDermott.
"Finding Objects with Given Spatial Properties."
Tech. Rep. 195, Yale University Computer Science Dept., 1980.

[McDermott, 82] Drew V. McDermott.
"A Temporal Logic for Reasoning about Plans and Processes."
Cognitive Science, Vol. 6, 1982, pp. 101 - 155.

[McDermott, 83] Drew V. McDermott.
"NISP Reference Manual."
Tech. Rep. 274, Yale University Computer Science Dept., 1980.

[McDermott and Davis, 84]
Drew V. McDermott and Ernest Davis.
"Planning and Executing Routes through Uncertain Territory."
Artifical Intelligence, Vol. 22, 1984, pp. 107 - 156.

[Meehan, 79]   James R. Meehan.
The New UCI Lisp Manual.
Lawrence Erlbaum Associates, Hillsdale, N.J., 1979.

[Meggido, 76]   Nimrod Meggido.
"Partial and Complete Cyclic Orders."
Bulletin of the American Mathematical Society, Vol. 82 No. 2, 1979, pp. 274 - 276.

[Montanari, 70] U. Montanari.
"A note on minimal length polygon approximations."
Communications of the ACM, Vol. 13, 1970, pp. 41 - 47.

[Moore, 80]   Robert Moore.
Reasoning about Knowledge and Action.
Tech. Rep. 191, SRI AI Center, 1980

[Moravec, 81]   Hans P. Moravec.
"Rover Visual Obstacle Avoidance."
Proc. IJCAI 7 1981, pp. 785 - 790.

[Piaget and Inhelder, 67]
Jean Piaget and Barbel Inhelder.
The Child's Conception of Space,
Basic Books, New York, 1967.

218

[Popper, 59] Karl R. Popper.
The Logic of Scientific Discovery.
Basic Books, New York, 1959.

[Requicha, 80] A.A.G. Requicha.
"Representations for Rigid Solids: Theory, Methods, and Systems."
ACM Computing Surveys, Vol. 12, No. 4, 1980

[Requicha, 83] A.A.G. Requicha.
"Towards a Theory of Geometric Tolerancing."
The International Journal of Robotics Research, Vol. 2, No. 4, 1983
pp. 45 - 60

[Riesbeck, 80] Christopher K. Riesbeck.
"'You Can't Miss It!': Judging the Clarity of Directions."
Cognitive Science, Vol. 4 No. 3, 1980, pp. 285 - 303.

[Rosenberg and Rowat, 81]
Richard Rosenberg and Peter Rowat.
"Spatial Problems for a Simulated Robot."
Proc. IJCAI 7, 1981, pp. 758 - 765.

[Rowat, 79] Peter F. Rowat.
"Representing Spatial Experience and Solving Spatial Problems in a
Simulated Robot Environment."
Tech. Rep. 79-14, University of British Columbia Computer Science
Dept., 1979

[Schwartz and Sharir, 82]
Jacob T. Schwartz and Micha Sharir.
"On the 'Piano Movers' Problem: II. General Techniques for
Computing Topological Properties of Real Algebraic Manifolds."
Tech. Rep. 41, New York University Computer Science Dept., 1982

[Shostak, 77] R.E. Shostak.
"On the sup-inf method for proving Presburger formulas."
Journal of the ACM, Vol. 24, 1977, pp. 529 - 543.

[Tarski, 51] A. Tarski.
A Decision Method for Elementary Algebra and Geometry.
University of California Press, 1951.

[Thompson, 77]   Alan M. Thompson.
"The navigation system of the JPL robot."
Proc. IJCAI 5, 1977, pp. 749 - 758

[Thorndyke and Stasz, 80]
Perry W. Thorndyke and Cathleen Stasz.
"Knowledge Acquisition from Maps."
Cognitive Psychology vol. 12 no. 1, 1980, pp. 137 - 175.

[Tolman, 32]   E.C. Tolman.
Purposive Behavior in Animals and Men.
Century Publishing, 1932.

[Tversky, 81]   Barbara Tversky.
"Distortion in Memory for Maps."
Cognitive Psychology, Vol. 13 No. 3., 1981, pp. 407 - 433.

[Waltz, 75]   David Waltz.
"Understanding Line Drawings of Scenes with Shadows."
in Patrick Winston, ed., *The Psychology of Computer Vision*,
McGraw Hill, New York, 1975.

[Waltz, 81]   David L. Waltz.
"Towards a Detailed Model of Processing for Language Describing
the Physical World."
Proc. IJCAI 7, 1981, pp. 1 - 6.

[Yemini, 79]   Yechiam Yemini.
"Some Theoretical Aspects of Position-Location Problems."
Proc. 20th Symp. on the Foundations of Computer Science, 1979, pp.
1 - 7

Index

grain-size, 21, 25-31, 33-34, 141, 189, 196-198
-- of a vertex, 33-34, 196-198

Hart, R., 141
Hayes, P., 23, 139, 144
Herzberger, J., 143
HIGH function, 32
Hintzman, D., 142
Hollerbach, J., 164
Hopcroft, J., 54, 208

Inhelder, B., 142
interval arithmetic, 143
interval range : see fuzzy measurement
investigation, 9, 170-171

joint, 19-20, 33, 73, 85, 91-95, 185, 190
-- consistency, 88, 91-95
-- checker, 91-95

knowledge base, 9, 99, 163-164
Kolodner, J., 164
Kosslyn, S., 142
Kuipers, B., 132-133, 172

Lavin, M., 133-136
Lieblich, I., 2, 142
link, 42
LOW function, 32
Lynch, K., 142

Marr, D., 143, 164
matcher, 11, 69-98, 191-192
-- , algorithm of, 73-76
-- , inadequacies of, 95-98
McAllester, D., 177
McCarthy, J., 139
McDermott, D.V., 13, 23, 68, 99, 129-132, 145
                163, 167, 172, 178, 182
measurements, preserving, 115-116
Meehan, J., 145
Meggido, N., 210
MERCATOR, 9-12
-- , implementation of, 145-161

-- , running times for, 160
-- , scope of, 12-13
MERCATOR map, 10, 16-23, 187
-- , validity of, 26-27, 188-189
-- , semantics of, 23-27, 184-190
merger, 11, 99-128, 191
-- , algorithm of, 118
Montanari, U., 139, 164
Monte Carlo methods, 44-48, 57-58
Moore, R., 170
Moravec, H., 136
motion assimilator, 12, 148
motion simulator, 12, 148

natural language, 172
navigation, 167-168
Nishihara, H.K., 163
normalcy conditions, 36-40, 104-105

object, 24, 184
ontology, extended, 176
orientation tree, 182

partial cyclic ordering (PCO), 22-23, 187, 210-21
-- , splicing of, 108-109, 119
path, 42
-- , cost of, 48, 50
path finding, 48-52
patience principle, 14, 99-100
Piaget, J., 142
plenum condition, 40, 105, 117, 167
polygon, 17, 185
-- , merging of, 111-114, 120-128
polygon fitting condition, 38, 104
Popper, K., 142
properties of objects, 21-22, 24, 184
psychology, cognitive, 2, 141-142

query, 10, 41

REAL (realizing) function, 24, 187
recognition, bottom-up, 176
redundancy in maps, 105
region, 17, 21, 179, 186-187